The Psychology of Happiness

DATE DUE

14.75

A 12790

The Psychology

of

·HAPPINESS·

Michael Argyle

ROUTLEDGE. LONDON & NEW YORK

First published in 1987 by
Methuen & Co. Ltd

Reprinted 1989
by Routledge
11 New Fetter Lane
London EC4P 4EE

Simultaneously published
in the USA and Canada
by Routledge – a division of
Routledge, Chapman and Hall, Inc.
29 West 35th Street
New York, NY 10001

Photoset by Rowland Phototypesetting Ltd
Bury St Edmunds, Suffolk
Printed in Great Britain by
Richard Clay Ltd, Bungay, Suffolk

British Library Cataloguing in
Publication Data

Argyle, Michael
    Psychology of happiness.
    1. Happiness
    I. Title
    152.4   BF575.H27

    ISBN 0-415-04522-3

·CONTENTS·

·FIGURES·

·TABLES·

ACKNOWLEDGEMENTS

The author and publishers gratefully acknowledge the following for permission to reproduce copyright material:

Plenum Publishing for Figures 1.1 and 1.2 from Andrews and Withey (eds) (1976), *Social Indicators of Well-being*

Basic Books, Inc. for Table 1.2 and Figures 8.1 and 8.3 from *The Quality of American Life* by Angus Campbell, Philip E. Converse, and William L. Rodgers. Copyright © 1976 by Russell Sage Foundation. Reprinted by permission of Basic Books, Inc., Publishers

Oxford University Press for Table 1.3 from *The General Health Questionnaire* D. Goldberg (1972) 'The Detection of Psychiatric Illness by Questionnaire'

CBS College Publishing for quotes in Chapter 1 from *Mood and Personality* by Alden E. Wessman and David F. Ricks, © 1966 by Holt, Rinehart & Winston, Inc.

The Eugenics Society for Figure 2.2 from C. Walker (1977) 'Marital satisfaction and family life cycle' in R. Chester and J. Peel (eds) *Equalities and Inequalities in Family Life*

The Observer for Figure 3.1 from K. Whitehorn (1984) 'Whistle while you work'

US Government Printing Office for Figure 3.2 from R. D. Caplan *et al.* (1975) *Job Demands and Worker Health*

The Sunday Times for Table 3.3 from C. Cooper (24 February, 1985). Work carried out by Professor Cary L. Cooper, University of Manchester Institute of Science and Technology, England.

Cambridge University Press for Table 3.5 from M. H. Banks and P. R. Jackson (1982) 'Unemployment and risk of minor psychiatric disorder in young people' *Psychological Medicine*, 12, 789–98

The Controller of Her Majesty's Stationery Office for the following Crown copyright material: Tables 3.6, 4.5, 4.6, 4.7, 9.6 and Figures 4.1 and 4.2 from *Social Trends* (1982–4), Tables 4.3, 4.4 and 4.8 and Figures 4.3 and 4.4 from Birch (1979) *Population Trends*, and Figures 10.2(a) and 10.2(b) from D. Black (1980) *Inequalities in Health*

Praeger Publishers for Table 4.2 from *How Americans Use Time* by J. P. Robinson. Copyright © 1977 Praeger Publishers, Inc. Reprinted by permission of Praeger Publishers.

John Wiley & Sons Ltd for Table 4.9 from B. Kabanoff (1982) *Journal of Occupational Behaviour*, 3, 233–45

Longman Group Ltd for quotes in Chapter 5 from R. Cochrane, *The Social Creation of Mental Illness*

Tavistock Publications for Figure 5.1 from G. W. Brown and T. Harris (1978) *Social Origins of Depression*

Norman M. Bradburn for Table 5.2 from N. M. Bradburn (1969) *The Structure of Psychological Well-Being*

Ed Diener, Robert Emmons and Jeff Horwitz, Department of Psychology, University of Illinois for Table 5.3 from 'Happiness of the very wealthy' (1985)

Academic Press Inc. for Figure 5.2 by R. A. Easterlin, 'Does economic growth improve the human lot?' in P. A. David and M. Abramovitz (eds) *Nations and Households in Economic Growth*

Penguin Books Ltd for quotes in Chapter 6 from M. Argyle, *The Psychology of Interpersonal Behaviour*, Pelican Books, 1967, fourth edition 1983, © Michael Argyle, 1983

American Psychological Association for Figure 7.1 from J. A. Russell (1980) 'A circumplex model of affect', *Journal of Personality and Social Psychology*, 39, 1161–178.

D. Reidel for Figure 8.2 from A. C. Michaelos 'Satisfaction and Happiness' in *Social Indicators Research*, Volume 8, No. 4

Journal of Gerontology for Figure 9.1 from P. M. Lewinsohn and D. J. MacPhillamy (1974) 'The relationship between age and engagement in pleasant activities', *29*, 290–4 and Figure 9.3 from E. Spreitzer and E. E. Snyder (1974) 'Correlates of life satisfaction among the aged', *29*, 452–8

American Journal of Epidemiology for Figure 10.1 from L. F. Berkman and S. L. Syme (1979) 'Social networks, host resistance, and mortality' 109, 186–204.

Population Studies for Figure 10.3 from M. H. Preston (1975)

Pergamon Press for Table 10.4 from S. M. Sales and J. House (1971) 'Job dissatisfaction as a possible risk factor in coronary heart disease'. *Journal of Chronic Diseases*, 23, 862–73

New Zealand Psychology Society for Figure 11.1 from S. Lichter, K. Maye and R. Kamman (1980) 'Increasing happiness through cognitive training', *New Zealand Psychologist*, *9*, 57–64

The author and publisher have made every effort to obtain permission to reproduce copyright material throughout this book. If any proper acknowledgement has not been made, or permission not received, we would invite any copyright holder to inform us of this oversight.

·PREFACE·

I became interested in this topic while working on social relationships, and writing *The Anatomy of Relationships* (1985, with Monika Henderson). Here was clearly a major source of human happiness. Reading the literature suggested two other important sources – work and leisure – so I have given these three some priority in this book. The next most important is probably personality: there are happy people just as there are depressed ones, but research on them is at an early stage. Some other possible sources – wealth and class, for example – proved to be relatively unimportant, which is theoretically very interesting.

Indeed the whole field is extraordinarily interesting, so I have tried to put it all together – and have greatly enjoyed doing so. There are very few books on this subject, but there is a lot of research, reported in numerous journal articles. I am particularly indebted to the writings of the late Angus Campbell and others at the Survey Research Center, University of Michigan, and to Ed Diener, Mihalyi Csikszentmihalyi, Peter Lewinsohn; and in this country to Michael Apter, and to Peter Warr and Paul Jackson and others at the Social and Applied Research Unit, Sheffield University, and in Germany to Fritz Strack and Norbert Schwarz.

Charles Antaki read the whole manuscript and made many useful suggestions. Mary Ann Kernan of Methuen has been a most valuable source of guidance.

At Oxford I am grateful to many collaborators in research, and those who have read chapters, especially to David D. Clarke, David M. Clark, Peter Collett, Jill Crossland, Adrian Furnham, Monika Henderson, Sonia Livingstone, Kathy Parkes, and Edmund Rolls. And, for about the twentieth time, I am indebted to Ann McKendry for her superb work, now on the word processor, and to the librarians of the Radcliffe Science Library and the PPE Reading Room, New Bodleian.

Eights Week,
May, 1985

Michael Argyle
Department of Experimental
Psychology, Oxford

1
HOW HAPPY ARE PEOPLE?

What is the highest of all goods achievable by action? . . . both the general run of man and people of superior refinement say that it is happiness . . . but with regard to what happiness is they differ.   (Aristotle, *Nicomachean Ethics*, Book 1, Chapter 4)

We hold these truths to be self-evident – that all men are created equal; that they are endowed by their Creator with certain unalienable rights; that among these are life, liberty, and the pursuit of happiness.   (*Declaration of Independence*)

WHAT IS HAPPINESS?

Most work on emotions in psychology has been concerned with anxiety, depression and other negative states. We now know that making people happy and stopping them from being miserable are rather different operations. This book is primarily concerned with the causes and explanation of positive happiness, and how our understanding of it can be used to make people, including ourselves, happy. It is possible that some, though not all, of the techniques that have been found to be successful in relieving depression might also increase the happiness of people who are not depressed.

The empirical evidence that has been accumulated points to the existence of a single, measurable dimension of happiness. Some measures emphasize its emotional side – feeling in a good mood – others emphasize the cognitive, reflective side – reporting satisfaction with life. People may describe happiness in terms of contentment, satisfaction, peace of mind, feeling fulfilled, or in terms of enjoyment, pleasure and having fun; research on the components of well-being and happiness produces two partly independent dimensions that correspond to these two emphases.

A number of large-scale studies have found a clear general factor of overall *satisfaction*: this can be subdivided into satisfaction with specific areas, for example work, marriage, health, the respondent's own competence or self-fulfilment. Measures of well-being have also assessed the more emotional side of happiness: feelings of *elation* and other positive emotions, usually by asking people to describe their typical mood over the last few weeks, or to say how much of the time they have been feeling happy. The third important dimension that has been measured is that of *psychological distress*, with its inverse links with satisfaction. Measures are based on judgements of unhappiness, depression and anxiety. The final component that we shall consider is *health* – closely correlated with the others, and as we shall see, both a cause and an effect of them.

Our faith in the validity of subjective measures of happiness or satisfaction is increased by the findings that will be presented in this book. Happiness, along with health and mental health, is increased by the presence of certain social relationships and depressed by losing these and by other stressful life events. These findings are remarkably consistent and they make a lot of sense. So we shall rely to a large extent on subjective reports of how people feel: if people say they are happy then they *are* happy. If people say they are depressed then they *are* depressed.

Subjective reports do not, however, always agree either with ratings made by other people or with objective measures. We shall regard such findings as problems to be explained, accepting that if people say they are dissatisfied then they are, whether we think they ought to be or not.

Another problem is that people may have different conceptions of what 'very satisfied', for example, would entail. It is possible to ask directly about such comparison levels. Reported satisfaction can be predicted by how far present conditions fall short of aspirations or of what people feel they are entitled to, or what other people are thought to have.

The ladder method, described in Figure 1.1 below, is an attempt to get subjects to report satisfaction in terms of anchoring points at top and bottom. It is interesting that this scale shows quite small differences between countries which have very large differences of material prosperity, housing and health. However if someone says they are very satisfied with, say, their mud hut on stilts, then we must assume that they *are*.

There does seem to be a tendency to exaggerate reported happiness. We shall see that while most people claim to be satisfied or very satisfied, not so many admit to being depressed or anxious, or to being in poor health. Similarly most married couples claim to be very happily married, though nearly half of them will later get divorced. The tendency to exaggerate reported well-being could be due to a common tendency to give socially desirable answers to interviewers, yet there is little correlation between measures of subjective well-being and lie scales or with social desirability scales (Diener, 1984). This may be a problem that particularly affects single-item measures of general satisfaction.

Finally, some of these judgements seem to be affected by passing moods to a surprising degree. The explanation is probably that emotions make it easier to recall memories that are congruent with the same emotion (Bower, 1981), and these memories are then used as information in the assessment of satisfaction. This effect is less for satisfaction with specific questions, or if attention is drawn to the weather or other sources of influence, and it is greater for negative influences, e.g. rainy days rather than sunny days. Nevertheless, this is clearly a potential source of error, in measuring judgements of satisfaction with life as a whole. Although reports of well-being change to some extent with mood, they are in fact relatively stable aspects of persons, with a long-term reliability of .55 to .70 (Diener, 1984).

There are, then, problems with measuring happiness, but these can to some extent be avoided by the skilful design of measuring methods, for example by asking rather specific questions. And we shall keep them in mind when considering the interpretation of empirical findings.

HAPPINESS AND UNHAPPINESS

In 1969 Bradburn announced an important discovery; that happiness is not the opposite of unhappiness. He found this in a study in which people were asked, 'During the past few weeks did you ever feel . . .', e.g.

	%
– pleased about having accomplished something?	80
– that things were going your way?	68
and:	
– so restless that you couldn't sit long in a chair?	43.7
– bored?	35

(Bradburn, 1969)

The key finding was that these two dimensions were almost totally independent of each other. This has been confirmed by later studies using similar methods.

It is not possible to feel happy and unhappy at the same time. Kammann and Flett (1983) in New Zealand constructed scales for positive and negative affect which ask subjects to report the frequency of these feelings. The positive and negative scales are negatively related (r = −.58). The same has been found for similar scales (Warr, Barter and Brownbridge, 1983; Diener, 1984).

However, while the *frequencies* of positive and negative emotions are inversely related, the *intensities*, i.e. the strength with which emotions are felt, are positively related. People who feel intense happiness also often experience intense unhappiness (Diener, Sandvik and Larson, 1985). Further evidence that there is some independence of positive and negative feelings comes from the rather different factors that predict them, some of which are given in Table 1.1.

The partial independence of positive and negative affect has also been found in the field of marital satisfaction. Partners can have strong positive feelings (related to frequency of intercourse, for example) as well as negative ones (related to the frequency of rows, for example) (Argyle and Henderson, 1985). It is still possible to combine positive and negative affect in a single measure, and a lot of the research to be reported has done this.

Table 1.1   Sources of positive and negative feelings

positive	*negative*
extraversion	neuroticism
education	low social status
employment	women
social participation	poor health
positive life events	low self-esteem
satisfying leisure	stressful life events

Sources Bradburn, 1969; Warr, Barter and Brownbridge, 1983; Headey, Holmstrom and Wearing, 1984.

THE SATISFACTION DIMENSION

A number of recent studies have isolated a dimension of general well-being. This is somewhat different from happiness as a positive emotional state and distress as a negative one. It can be defined as a thoughtful appraisal of quality of life as a whole, a judgement of satisfaction with life. It emerges as the common ground both of many other measures of satisfaction – work, marriage, health – and of different rating scales, like *enjoyable –miserable*. Finally it is the common ground of many different ways of putting the question, with graphical and verbal scales, for example (Andrews and Withey, 1976).

A problem is that these judgements of satisfaction tend to be relative: people compare their present state with different periods in their past life, or with what they know or imagine about others' lives. Some measures ask people to anchor a ladder by making the top and bottom points on the scale, for example 'the best life I could expect to have', and 'the worst life I could expect to have' (Cantril, 1965). The results of two American national surveys in 1973 averaged, using a 9-point ladder, are shown in Figure 1.1.

Another way of putting the question is as follows, with the percentages of people at each point:

How satisfied are your with your life as a whole these days?

COMPLETELY DISSATISFIED			NEUTRAL			COMPLETELY SATISFIED
1	2	3	4	5	6	7
0.9%	2.1%	3.7%	11.3%	20.7%	39.6%	21.7%

(Campbell, Converse and Rodgers, 1976)

Figure 1.1 The satisfaction ladder

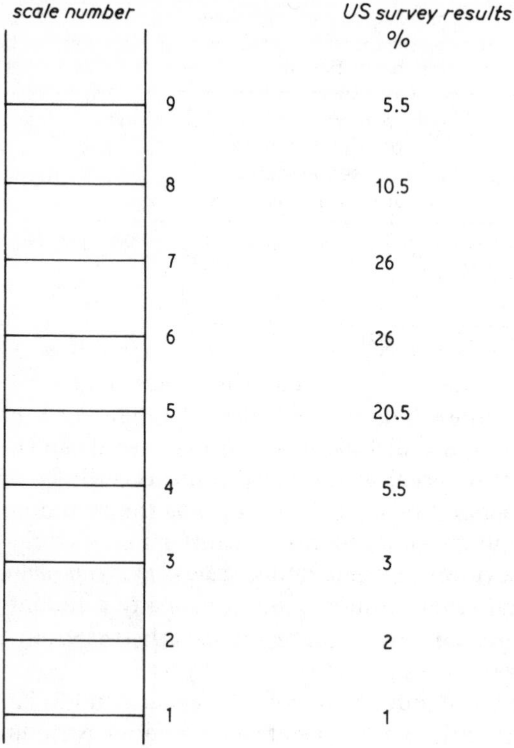

scale number	US survey results %
9	5.5
8	10.5
7	26
6	26
5	20.5
4	5.5
3	3
2	2
1	1

Source   Andrews and Withey, 1976.

Most of the population cluster around point 6 on this scale. It can be seen from these studies that self-reported satisfaction is skewed towards the upper end, with a typical score of 6 on a 7-point scale. Rather few admit to being below the mid-point.

We have discussed satisfaction with life as a whole: it is also possible to assess satisfaction with different areas or domains of life. One way of obtaining an overall satisfaction score is to combine satisfaction in a number of particular domains. Which domains are most important? There are two ways of finding out. One is to ask people which areas are most important. The other is to correlate satisfaction in each domain with overall satisfaction. Table 1.2 reports some of the findings of an American national sample survey of 2164 people in the summer of 1971. The numbers

Table 1.2   Sources of satisfaction in everyday life

	mean importance rating	regression coefficient
family life	1.46	.41
marriage	1.44	.36
financial situation	2.94	.33
housing	2.10	.30
job	2.19	.27
friendship	2.08	.26
health	1.37	.22
leisure activities	2.79	.21

Source   Campbell, Converse and Rodgers, 1976.

in the second column of the table are correlations: a figure of 1.0 represents a perfect relationship, 0 stands for no relationship at all, intermediate values show relationships of different strengths.

We shall return to these domains later in the book and discuss them in more detail. While satisfaction with work or marriage or religion *can* be assessed from a single question, there are much more elaborate scales for each of these domains, and it is possible to obtain a number of sub-scores for different aspects of job satisfaction for example.

Average satisfaction varies, for instance between countries. It is greatest for marriage, followed by family life, in both Britain and the USA, but job satisfaction is higher in Britain. For some individuals work satisfaction is the best predictor, the most important part, of overall life satisfaction. For others, work is less important than family life, or leisure, or housing, or other aspects of life. For some, religious outlook and experience are very important. This has to be remembered when comparing the satisfaction of men and women, the old and the young. It is a particular problem in comparing well-being in different countries.

Satisfaction with health, which will be discussed in more detail later, is an important aspect of overall satisfaction: the average correlation in a number of studies was .32.

Satisfaction with the self is another domain. Two aspects of it have been found to correlate strongly with overall life satisfaction – self-esteem and feelings of 'internal control', the belief that one can control what happens. These are discussed under Personality in Chapter 6.

POSITIVE HAPPINESS

We turn now to the emotional side of happiness, that is to positive feelings of elation or joy. How can we measure these? Emotions fluctuate a great deal. It is necessary to obtain a sample, or an average over time, for each individual. Another problem with emotions is that they have a number of different dimensions. One of these, perhaps the most important, is 'elation–depression'. It can be measured by a single scale, on which subjects are asked to estimate their average level over the past day, or over a longer period.

How elated or depressed, happy or unhappy, did you feel today?

10 Complete elation. Rapturous joy and soaring ecstasy.
 9 Very elated and in very high spirits. Tremendous delight and buoyancy.
 8 Elated and in high spirits.
 7 Feeling very good and cheerful.
 6 Feeling pretty good, 'OK'.
 5 Feeling a bit low. Just so-so.
 4 Spirits low and somewhat 'blue'.
 3 Depressed and feeling very low. Definitely 'blue'.
 2 Tremendously depressed. Feeling terrible, miserable 'just awful'.
 1 Utter depression and gloom. Completely down. All is black and leaden.

(Wessman and Ricks, 1966)

The average scores on this scale for American students were 6.0 for males, 6.14 for females, but there was quite a lot of daily variation: plus and minus nearly half a scale point each day.

In a British study respondents were asked how much of the time they felt 'very pleased with things yesterday':

	%
all of the time	25
most of the time	34
about half the time	10

some of the time	11
just a little of the time	4
not at all	13

(Warr and Payne, 1982)

It is not clear whether this is a measure of mood or satisfaction or a combination of the two, (see p. 2).

We reported the results for the Bradburn positive affect scale earlier (p. 4). This showed rather high levels of positive experiences for 'the past few weeks'.

Finally, people can simply be asked to rate their feelings about life. The following measure uses facial expressions, a non-verbal index of emotion, instead of verbal labels. Subjects were asked to select the face which best expressed their feelings (Figure 1.2).

There is more than one type of positive affect, and more than one kind of pleasant event. As well as a happy–sad dimension there is also an arousal–sleep dimension. In addition there is recent evidence for a third dimension of depth, such as experiences due to music, religion, scientific discovery or natural scenery.

Figure 1.2 Faces and feelings

here are some faces expressing various feelings. Which face comes closest to expressing how you feel about your life as a whole?

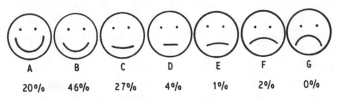

A	B	C	D	E	F	G
20%	46%	27%	4%	1%	2%	0%

Source Andrews and Withey, 1976.

NEGATIVE AFFECT, AND DISTRESS

We now turn to unhappiness, depression and other negative emotional states. There is more than one kind of negative emotion. Depressed, gloomy, the opposite of happy, is the central type, tired and bored are the combination of negative emotion and sleep, and afraid, angry and tense are the combination of negative emotion and high arousal (see Figure 7.1). The study of emotion from facial expressions produces very similar types of negative emotion – sadness, fear, anger, disgust/contempt (Ekman, 1982), and perhaps shame (Izard, 1977).

We shall treat depression as the main negative state, but we will also be concerned with the anxiety–fear–tense group of emotions. Some surveys have used combinations of these negative states. In a British study, respondents were asked if they had experienced 'unpleasant emotional strain yesterday':

	%	
all of the time	4	
most of the time	5	
about half the time	4	
some of the time	7	
just a little of the time	13	
not at all	65	(Warr and Payne, 1982)

We earlier gave the results of Bradburn's study (p. 4) in which people reported periods of boredom, depression, etc., over the past few weeks.

Psychological distress consists of negative emotions and related conditions: depression, anxiety and worry; minor physical symptoms like headaches, sleeplessness and exhaustion; feelings of personal inadequacy, or of impending nervous breakdown. There is extensive evidence that such feelings are found in the same individuals, and that this forms a 'general factor' of personality. Both Eysenck's famous 'neuroticism' dimension (Eysenck, 1976) and Goldberg's equally famous General Health Questionnaire (Goldberg, 1972) find these traits to be linked. There are different kinds of patients, some mainly anxious, others depressed, but within the general population it is surprising how often these symptoms occur together. It has been found that they go together more for people who are 'field dependent', that is, much influenced by the immediate environment; this group includes a greater proportion of female and working-class people, i.e. most mental patients. There is more differentiation of symptoms for males and middle-class individuals (Parkes, 1980).

Probably the most valid measure of psychological distress is an examination by a psychiatrist. There is a lengthy standard form used in Britain known as the Present State Examination (PSE), and a shorter version for community studies (Wing, 1976). A number of questionnaire measures have been found to agree well with the PSE, and to be easy to administer. The General Health Questionnaire (GHQ) appears to be a particularly satisfactory measure. It is valid; it agrees well with other measures, and it discriminates between patients and others. It has been widely used in British research. It comes in several versions, with 60, 30 or 12 items. The short version is given in Table 1.3. If you want to work out your score, give yourself 0 for the first category of response, and 1, 2 or 3 for the others. Add them up. I shall be referring to a number of surveys using this scale, to show the effects of social class, unemployment and other variables on mental health. Do people tell the truth when they are asked these questions? If they are patients at a clinic they probably do, as it is in their interest to do so. If they are being selected for a job they may conceal their psychiatric symptoms, and if they are part of a social survey they may do the same, particularly in reporting anxiety or depression as opposed to bodily symptoms. The scale excludes items which were reported by over 10 per cent of normals, such as 'Having a lot of worry over money' (19 per cent of normals), and 'Feeling easily upset over things' (15 per cent), so it is focused on the more severely distressed end of the scale.

American surveys have often used another scale, which includes a number of physiological symptoms such as heart beat

Table 1.3   The General Health Questionnaire (GHQ) (12-item version)

Have you recently
* 1 been able to concentrate on whatever you're doing?
2 lost much sleep over worry?
* 3 felt that you are playing a useful part in things?
* 4 felt capable of making decisions about things?
5 felt constantly under strain?
6 felt you couldn't overcome your difficulties?
* 7 been able to enjoy your normal day-to-day activities?
* 8 been able to face up to your problems?
9 being feeling unhappy and depressed?
10 been losing confidence in yourself?
11 been thinking of yourself as a worthless person?
*12 been feeling reasonably happy all things considered?

*These items are scored in reverse; 0 means agree strongly.

Source   Goldberg, 1978.

and pains in the head (Langner, 1962). In the USA, the average score for males is 2.4 of these symptoms, while females average 4.0. A difficulty with this scale, which presumably also applies to other such measures, is that it is affected by 'yea-saying' errors: people who tend to agree with suggestions get higher scores. Those who have had less education and members of some racial minority groups tend to be yea-sayers, which partly explains their higher scores on this scale.

Then there are those who are in the care of psychiatrists. Of the mentally disturbed patients seen by GPs in Britain, only about 5 per cent are referred to a psychiatrist or mental hospital; the others are given medication, or no treatment at all. Of those reporting mental symptoms 11 per cent take medicine prescribed by a doctor, and 19 per cent take unprescribed medicine (Dunnell and Cartwright, 1972).

A recent survey found that about 50 per cent of adults had one or more mental symptoms each, mainly forms of anxiety and depression, while the General Household Surveys found that about one person in three reported psychiatric symptoms. Most of these people did not go to see the doctor about it: 71 per cent did nothing, 12 per cent talked to friends or relations, and 17 per cent saw a doctor. This is no doubt partly because they thought the symptom too slight to bother about, partly through ignorance of what psychiatry could do for them (*General Household Surveys*; Hannay, 1979).

About 14–17 per cent of the population who see a GP in the course of a year are diagnosed as having a psychiatric problem. We conclude that half of the population report severe headaches, sleeplessness, exhaustion, anxiety, depression or other symptoms of mental ill-health, while about one-sixth of the population are diagnosed by their doctors as having some degree of mental disturbance. Most people do nothing about it. If they see their doctor they are given either no treatment or some kind of tranquillizer.

Mental ill-health is often associated with bodily ill-health. We have seen that mental disturbance often manifests itself in bodily states, and these can lead to various forms of illness recognized to be primarily induced by stress. Do the mentally ill die sooner? This is a complicated issue; there is evidence on both sides. However, the effect of mental health on mortality is probably quite a small one, if the effects of age, social class and marital status are held constant. On the other hand mentally ill people die from different causes. They are less likely to die of cancer, but more likely to die from heart attacks, strokes, cirrhosis of the liver, suicides and (in the USA) murder (Singer *et al.*, 1976).

CONCLUSIONS

Happiness can be understood as a reflection on satisfaction with life, or as the frequency and intensity of positive emotions. Happiness is not entirely the opposite of unhappiness.

We need to consider three aspects of happiness: (1) satisfaction, and different domains of satisfaction, (2) joy and (3) distress, including anxiety and depression. In Chapter 10 we shall consider a fourth component, health, which has some correlation with each of the other three.

There are a number of measurement problems, but these can mostly be overcome by appropriate research methods.

2

SOCIAL RELATIONSHIPS

THE EFFECT OF RELATIONSHIPS ON HAPPINESS AND SATISFACTION

Many studies have shown the effects of social interaction and social networks on happiness, but we shall focus on studies that demonstrate the separate effects of each kind of relationship.

There are several ways of comparing the benefits of different relationships. The prediction of life satisfaction from different domains gave the regression coefficients shown below from the *Quality of American Life* study; these show the strength of the independent effect of each relationship separately.

family life	.41
marriage	.36
friendships	.26
community	.25
organizations	.12

(Campbell, Converse and Rodgers, 1976)

In our own study, with a smaller British sample, of the estimated satisfaction from different relationships we obtained the results shown in Figure 2.1. The scores are the ratings on 1–5 scales of satisfaction for each relationship, averaged across the scales correlating most highly with each factor. We found *three* dimensions of satisfaction: material, tangible help; emotional support; and shared interests. It can be seen that the spouse is by far the greatest source of satisfaction, close relatives and friends next, and work-mates and neighbours last. Our second dimension, emotional support, includes degree of trust and disclosure, use of other as a confidant. Another aspect of relationships which has been found to be important is amount of concern for the other (Brim, 1974; Crandall, 1984). We shall now see exactly how each relationship contributes to happiness, relief of distress, and health (see also Argyle and Henderson, 1985).

Figure 2.1   Sources of satisfaction in different relationships

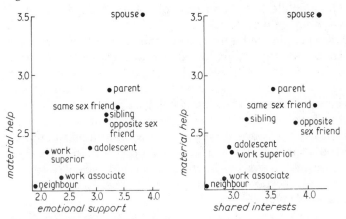

Source   Argyle and Furnham, 1983.

Love and marriage

The clearest example of a relationship producing happiness is surely falling in love. This is the most intense of all relationships, and creates the most positive affect (as well as some negative affect). Falling in love is one of the most highly rated positive life events. The phenomenon is familiar, though not fully understood. Sexual intimacy and arousal are central features, whether or not pre-marital intercourse occurs. In addition to bodily intimacy there is also a great deal of self-disclosure and mutual care and concern. Many pleasant hours are spent simply enjoying each other's company. There is probably a biological origin, through the need to bond couples together long enough for the production and care of children. There are considerable cultural variations; for example arranged marriages are common and apparently successful in much of the world. While passionate love continues into marriage, it is eventually replaced by a quieter 'companionate' love.

As is well-known, and as research confirms, the path of love is often not smooth. There can be a lot of conflict between lovers. As two people come to know each other better, and to share more of their lives, there is more to disagree about. If they are to advance to a closer relationship they need to face up to the sources of disagreement and try to work through them (Braiker and Kelley, 1979). Meanwhile here is an example of the independence of positive and negative affect.

Married people are happier, on average, than those who are unmarried, divorced or widowed. An average of US national surveys in 1957 and 1976 is given in Table 2.1. A meta-analysis of fifty-eight American studies found that the overall correlation between subjective well-being and being married rather than not was .14; the effect was greater for men than for women, was much greater for younger people, and was stronger in studies carried out at an earlier date (Haring-Hidore et al., 1985). This has been confirmed in surveys in which other variables, like education, income, occupation and age, have been held constant (Glenn and Weaver, 1978).

There is evidence that unmarried men are less happy than

Table 2.1 Happiness of the married, single and divorced

	percentage 'very happy'	
	men	women
married	35.0	41.5
single	18.5	25.5
divorced	18.5	15.5

Source   Veroff et al., 1981.

unmarried women, which suggests that men get more out of marriage than women. This is partly because women in general report greater satisfaction than men, but men appear to gain more satisfaction from marriage than women. Wives provide more social support, act as better confidants, to husbands than vice versa (Vanfossen, 1981). Women are also more likely to use their female friends or relatives for such support.

What about people who are living together? It has been found that these couples are happier than single people, though not as happy as the married. They have more sex than married people of the same age and are more satisfied with sex, though less satisfied with love. There are a number of other alternatives to marriage which in some cases can work very well, at any rate in the provision of companionship and social support.

The benefits of marriage also depend on the *quality* of marriage. There are many ways of measuring this, the simplest being to ask, 'How happily married are you?'. As we showed earlier, marital satisfaction is highly correlated with overall satisfaction or happiness.

Why does marriage provide so much satisfaction? A number of studies have compared behaviour in happy and disturbed marriages. Happy marriages tend to have more pleasing verbal acts and fewer negative ones, especially criticisms. In disturbed marriages it is common for a negative act from one partner to be reciprocated by a negative act from the other; husbands dislike this more than wives, who may want some response to their negative feelings (Levenson and Gottman, 1985). There are also more pleasing non-verbal acts, e.g. a kiss, a present, helpful behaviour, and fewer negative ones; a more enjoyable sex life; a lot of time spent together; agreement over finances; and a problem-solving approach to matters to be decided.

Obviously being rewarded by one another is very important; each partner provides certain rewards, and some, like sex and companionship, are simultaneously rewarding to both. Joint activities mean that the other is instrumental to satisfaction. Couples talk a lot; this has the effect of building up a shared cognitive world, where each one's view of the world is supported by the other. In a study of 131 student couples it was found that the introspective individuals engaged in more self-disclosure, which in turn led to greater satisfaction – because it helped them to understand themselves. Those who were good at seeing others' points of view were also satisfied – because they were better at resolving conflicts (Franzoi, Davis and Young, 1985).

Marriage is the source of a lot of conflict. However it is perfectly possible to enjoy a great deal of satisfaction at the same time – another example of positive and negative affect being independent. A couple may have some very happy and rewarding times, as well as a lot of rows (Argyle and Furnham, 1983). Overall satisfaction with marriage depends on both together. In one study a good prediction of marital satisfaction was achieved from frequency of intercourse minus number of rows. Total satisfaction depends on the balance of the two (Howard and Dawes, 1976).

Friends

As many studies have shown, people who have more friends, or who spend more time with their friends, tend to be happier; the correlations are consistent, but small (Larson, 1978). Friendship is an independent source of happiness, less important than marriage or family life, but on average more important than work or leisure (though for some people, middle-aged men, for example, this is not true). Friendship is most important for young people, from adolescence to marriage, when it is the main relationship, and becomes important again in old age, after retirement and bereavement have removed other social attachments. In between these two periods family and work take up a lot more time than friendship. There is a very interesting sex difference here: women form closer friendships than men, and engage in more intimate conversation and more self-disclosure. Men are more likely to engage in joint activities, like playing games. Their talk is about sport, work and other non-intimate topics.

We can learn a lot about friendship by seeing what friends do together. In a recent Oxford study we found that the activities characteristically shared with friends were eating, drinking, talking, and joint leisure like dancing and going to the pub or for walks. The combination of talk with eating or drinking seems to be highly characteristic of meetings between friends (Argyle and Furnham, 1982).

Perhaps the first thing that friends provide is an immediate elevation of mood, whether in the form of fun in children and young people, or a quieter kind of satisfaction among older ones. Research on 'positive social events' and on sources of joy shows that making new friends and seeing old ones are at the top of the list (p. 129). We shall discuss *why* other people produce positive emotions in Chapter 8.

Why do people need friends? For the three reasons shown in Figure 2.1: (1) material help and information, though they provide less than family or workmates; (2) social support, in the form of advice, sympathy, acting as confidants, or simply sharing a way of looking at the world (for some married women, friends are more important than husbands here); and (3) shared interests, joint activities, playing games together (this is often what brings friends together in the first place, and may provide the occasions for their meetings).

The social skills involved in gaining and keeping friends include rewardingness, repaying debts and favours, and the expression of affection. Our research on the rules of friendships has drawn attention to another important area, the handling of third-party relationships. Friends come not one at a time, but in whole networks, and it is important to handle the network skilfully (Argyle and Henderson, 1984). Friendships can lapse if people are jealous of other relationships, fail to keep confidences, or fail to stand up for each other in their absence.

Being a parent

The effects of children on happiness are a little surprising. University of Michigan surveys found that, compared with childless couples, parents worried more, had more marital problems, and felt less adequate as spouses. Figure 2.2 shows a number of British and American studies of marital satisfaction at different points in the family cycle. The vertical variable is marital satisfaction. It can be seen that marital satisfaction is depressed when there are children in the home, especially adolescent children. Young children depress marital happiness, especially when there is a pre-school child (3–5), when there are boys, and when there is an infant (0–2) as well as a pre-school child (Abbott and Brody, 1985).

However there is also a positive side to having children. A

Figure 2.2 Marital satisfaction and the family life cycle

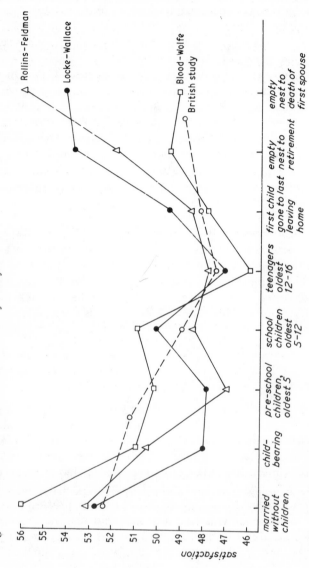

Source Walker, 1977.

study by Hoffman and Manis (1982) in which people expressed their views about the value of children found that the main values of children were thought to be as in the following table. Most people think that children make their own marriages closer (Veroff, Douran and Kulka, 1981), despite the evidence to the contrary. After the age of fifty, if there are no children under eighteen, there is no difference in happiness between those who do and do not have children (Glenn and McLanahan, 1981).

	parents %	non- parents %
providing love and companionship	63	58
stimulation and fun, pleasure from watching them grow up	58	38
self-fulfilment	34	33
feeling more adult and mature	21.5	10.5

Source Hoffman and Manis, 1982.

Children are a very interesting problem from our point of view, and one that illustrates the independence of positive and negative affect. They obviously do provide great positive satisfaction, and of kinds unique to this relationship, such as self-fulfilment and feeling mature. They also incur considerable costs: sheer exhaustion when they are young, emotional costs during adolescence.

Relatives

Many of the strongest social ties outside the home are to kin, particularly to siblings, parents and adult children. Many working-class people live near enough to some of their relatives to see them daily or weekly. This was first found in Bethnal Green, London (Young and Wilmott, 1973), but a similar pattern is found elsewhere (Argyle and Henderson, 1985). Many relatives live in the same part of the country, and keep in touch by telephone, regular visits, and family gatherings, such as at Christmas. Often relatives do not do very much when they meet, apart from having a meal and keeping up with the family news. They just enjoy being together.

One of the most interesting things about kin is that they are prepared, if necessary, to provide major help, like looking after children, lending or giving money, help with jobs and over trouble with the authorities. These relationships are virtually permanent: frequency of contact and level of help carry on unchanged decade after decade. On the other hand there is much less joint leisure of the kind enjoyed with friends, and often there are quite different attitudes, values and ways of life. The explanation for these powerful bonds may be that during the long intimacy of early family life some kind of conditioning or imprinting takes place. It has been found that favourite cousins in later life are those who were childhood playmates (Adams, 1968). The closeness of kin is maintained in later life by shared reminiscences of times when the children were young (Ross and Milgram, 1982). Another possibility is the 'selfish gene' hypothesis, that people are concerned about the welfare of their genes, and hence for those who share them.

Siblings are one of the greatest sources of satisfaction here, but it is a complex relationship. There can be strong feelings of closeness and shared identity, but also a lot of rivalry from childhood onwards, especially over achievement and success (Ross and Milgram, 1982). And sometimes siblings 'deidentify' with one another, especially by modelling themselves on different parents (Schachter, 1982). Women are more involved with kin than men, especially with the female–female links, like mother–daughter, and between sisters.

What then is the origin of happiness derived from kin? Instrumental help – much greater than that provided by friends – and very strong, long-lasting attachments result in a life-long concern and pleasure in each other's company.

Work relationships

These will be discussed fully in Chapter 3, so only the main points will be mentioned here. We shall deal with the two main work relationships: with work-mates or colleagues, and between supervisors and subordinates. Job satisfaction is one of the main domains of overall satisfaction, and satisfaction with work relationships is one of the main components of job satisfaction.

Work-mates

Job satisfaction is greater for those who are popular, who belong to small and cohesive work groups and have opportunities for social interaction at work. The satisfactions are primarily instrumental, for example through help and advice with the work or the satisfaction of co-operating over a joint task. There is a sex difference here: men derive greater instrumental satisfactions, while women emphasize co-operation. These differences show themselves even in childhood: pairs of boys enjoy taking part in serious games, where girls prefer to make friends (Shaver and Buhrmeister, 1983). At the workplace there is also a great deal of talk, gossip, games and jokes, during coffee and lunch breaks, and during the work itself. There is a lot of sheer fun and enjoyment of the company of others. While most co-workers are only seen at work, a proportion become friends and are seen outside work as well.

Supervisors and subordinates

Job satisfaction also depends on relationships in the hierarchy. Subordinates are happier under certain styles of supervision, notably 'consideration' and the encouragement of participation in decisions. Supervisors are a greater source of instrumental satisfaction than work-mates, because they can do more to increase the material rewards of work. They are also a greater source of conflict, through their demands for more work and their greater power. Again there is a sex difference: men are happier in hierarchical roles than are women, who prefer equality within small groups.

The rewards of work relationships, it seems, are partly instrumental, partly from co-operation over tasks, and partly from fun over and above the work.

Neighbours

This is a minor domain of satisfaction, but one that makes a contribution which is independent of other sources. The level of satisfaction from neighbours is modest, as Figure 2.1 showed. The main source of satisfaction is a high level of minor mutual help (gardening, lending things, watering plants and so on). There is a high frequency of casual chat over the garden fence or its equivalent, and from time to time there may be co-operation over serious matters of local concern (such as proposed new housing or roads). Neighbours are important to families, especially for those members who are at home most of the time; there is mutual help with children and shopping. They are even more important for the elderly, for whom neighbours may be their main social contacts. These are the overall findings, but there are local variations, and some groups of neighbours, for example a homogeneous group of families living close together, may form a closer relationship (Festinger, Schachter and Back, 1950).

There are often neighbourhood contacts with members of local organizations, like churches, clubs, and groups for various leisure activities. These will be discussed in Chapter 4.

HOW DO RELATIONSHIPS PRODUCE HAPPINESS?

We will look first at the sources of positive affect. The greatest joy comes from the most intense relationships: from being in love, and between parents and young children. Friends have a lot of fun, from joint leisure, or from eating and drinking, as do work-mates during the intervals from work. Some theories trace positive emotion to the early positive social signals between mother and infant which cause them both joy; this then generalizes to other relationships (p. 131f).

One of the main sources of satisfaction is the *quality* of relationships, the amount of affection, intimacy, acting as confidant, providing reassurance of self-worth, which can generally be called 'social support'. This is particularly important in marriage and between friends, especially female friends. It is not known whether these benefits are due to the innate power of smiles and gazes to activate the pleasure centres, or to the benefits for self-esteem, the need to be loved, a need for companionship, or some other process. Other sources of satisfaction include material help, information and advice, which may come from spouse, kin, friends, work superiors or others. Another source of satisfaction is doing things together, playing games, working together, sharing domestic life together. It seems likely that it is the regularity and predictability of contact between, for example, spouses, kin and close friends, which makes these relationships particularly satisfying. It is possible to rely on the rewards obtained for the indefinite future.

Do good social relationships lead to happiness, or vice versa? Experiments have found that increases in social contacts lead to increases in happiness (Reich and Zautra, 1981), while loss of relationships produces unhappiness. Extraverts are happier than introverts, but it is the level of social contact that is mainly responsible (p. 115f).

DISTRESS AND MENTAL DISORDER

How do relationships contribute to the relief or avoidance of distress in its various forms – negative affect, depression, anxiety, loneliness, mental illness and suicide? Many studies, for example using inventories of stressful life events, have found that distress is caused by stress. This effect is, however, greatly reduced or minimized if there are supportive relationships. This is known as 'buffering' and has been likened to the effect of sun-tan oil: it only operates when there is some stress to be coped with (Cohen and McKay, 1984). Some studies have found main effects of relationships as well, for instance that mental health is improved in the absence of stress – though perhaps there is always *some* stress. There is also a main effect of social support, for example from the degree of integration in a large community (Cohen and Wills, 1985).

It has recently been found that minor, repeated daily 'hassles', involving for example money, noisy neighbours, transport difficulties or adolescent children, are more predictive of distress than the major life events of earlier studies – bereavement, loss of job, trouble with police, etc. (Kanner *et al.*, 1981).

Many studies have examined the effects of social support in general, summating the effects of family, friends and others, and have found that the strength of relationships has a greater effect than the sheer presence of relationships, e.g. being married (Wilcox, 1981). The greatest effects, in some studies the only effects, are produced by spouse or others in the immediate household (e.g. Eaton, 1978). However all relationships have a positive effect in reducing the effects of stress: depression is least in women who are married *and* have a job *and* have children (Kandel, Davies and Raveis, 1985). The effect is greater if the other person acts as a confidant, and if this is reciprocated (Surtees, 1980). The effects are greater at higher levels of stress: mental disorder results from the combination of high stress and low social support.

We shall look at investigations that have tried to separate out the effects of particular relationships (see Reis, 1984). A problem is that of 'reverse causation': perhaps people lack friends because they are depressed, rather than vice versa? Being emotionally disturbed can lead to disruption of relationships, or negative perceptions of relationships. Research on this issue concludes that both directions of causation operate, but that there is an effect of social support, shown for example by the prediction of psychological distress from social support over an interval of a year (Holahan and Moos, 1981). Intervention studies similarly have shown the benefits for mental health of support from health professionals or other support groups (Kessler, Price and Wortman, 1985). Studies of coping show the same: if people are asked questions like 'What do you do when you are feeling depressed?', one of the main things they do is to see spouse, family or friends (Veroff *et al.*, 1981). Evidently this works.

Marriage

Married people are less likely to suffer from mental disorder than those who have never married, or who are separated, divorced or widowed. The ratios from single to married are shown in Table 2.2; for example men who have never married are 3.13 times as likely to suffer mental disorder than married men. The table

Table 2.2 Ratios of single/married for mental disorder

	never married	*divorced*	*widowed*
men	3.13	5.09	2.53
women	1.74	2.80	1.43

Source Gove, 1972.

shows averages from a number of studies, some of mental hospital inmates, others of out-patients seeing psychiatrists, in the USA. It can be seen that men benefit more from marriage than women do. The separated, divorced and widowed have of course *lost* something, and their level of distress is particularly high for 1 to 3 years after the loss. This is rated as the most stressful kind of life event. Some of the never married may have remained single because of mental disturbance, but all three single states are distressed to a similar degree, including those who were once married. The single either live alone, or with others, such as parents, who provide less social support and more conflict than would a spouse (Hughes and Gove, 1981). However the health and mental health of the single are better if they share accommodation with others, and if they are sexually co-habiting the benefits are nearly as great as for marriage (Freedman, 1978).

There is no doubt that marriage and its equivalents are the most important sources of social support for buffering distress. And they are effective at all levels of stress, where other relationships are only effective at high levels (Warheit, 1979).

It is not just being married, but the quality of the relationship that counts. In a famous study in South London (Brown and Harris, 1978) it was found that women who had experienced a lot of stressful life events were less likely to be depressed if they had a spouse who acted as confidant – 'someone to whom you can talk about yourself and your problems' (Table 2.3). This is a very good illustration of how social support buffers stress.

Table 2.2 shows that 41 per cent of women who had experienced stressful life events and who did not have a supportive husband became depressed, compared with only 10 per cent of

Table 2.3 Depression, stress and social support
(% depressed)

	support		
	high	*mid*	*low*
% women who had stressful life event	10	26	41
% women with no such events	1	3	4

Source Brown and Harris, 1978.

those who did. We shall discuss later the various 'vulnerability' factors that put people at risk in relation to stressful events. However the presence of close social support is one of the main protective factors.

We do not really know whether having a confidant or having an affectionate (or sexual) relationship is most important. Another investigation found that while quality of relationship with husband was important, tangible help was not, in buffering depression during pregnancy (Paykel *et al.*, 1980).

Friends

Although friends clearly provide less social support than spouses for most people, a number of studies show that close friendships can help to buffer stress and avert mental disorder (Reis, 1984). Neurotic patients are particularly short of friends and social contacts outside the family; they have far fewer friends than other people, and if they do have more than one friend these tend not to be part of a network (Henderson and Duncan-Jones, 1981). Friends are often the closest attachments, not only for the single, but also for wives, especially working-class wives, whose husbands are often not very good confidants (Vanfossen, 1981). O'Connor and Brown (1984) have recently found that working-class female psychiatric patients were less likely than others to have a close, confiding relationship outside the home.

Perhaps the greatest benefit provided by friends is in averting distress due to loneliness. There is a high correlation between loneliness and depression (Peplau and Perlman, 1982). Lonely people also experience anxiety, boredom and loss of self-esteem. About 14 per cent of the adult population feel lonely once a month or more, 8 per cent once a week or more (MORI, 1983). It is particularly common among the young, especially girls, and the old. There are two ways of being lonely. If people lack a network of friends they feel anxious and depressed, if they lack a close relationship they are likely to feel depressed (Russell *et al.*, 1984). While lonely people typically have fewer friends, some do have friends but still feel lonely. Why do they feel lonely? It is necessary to have a *dense* network (Stokes, 1985). It has recently been discovered that lonely people do not have sufficiently intimate conversations with their friends, do not make enough self-disclosure. Talking for hours about sport is not enough (Williams and Solano, 1983). Conversations with females do more to relieve loneliness, for members of both sexes, because these conversations are found to be pleasanter, more intimate, to involve more self-disclosure, and to be in general more 'meaning-ful' than those with men (Wheeler, Reis and Nezlek, 1983). Lonely people lack social skills in other ways too: they take less interest in other people, for example asking fewer questions, are less rewarding, and like and trust others less, and fail to send positive non-verbal signals via facial expression or tone of voice (Argyle and Henderson, 1985). They are less extraverted, and more neurotic (Stokes, 1985).

Relationships at work

Work can be stressful in a number of ways – long hours, repetitive machine-paced work, time-pressure, noise and heat, responsi-bility for others, conflict with others. An American study of a random sample of 636 men found that social support from co-workers was the most effective, followed by that from super-visors, family and friends, in reducing the effects of stress on depression, irritation and somatic complaints, though not on anxiety (LaRocco, House and French, 1980). Other investigations also found that people at work provide the best buffers against work stress, especially work-mates and supervisors (Cohen and McKay, 1984). We found that interaction with intimate co-workers, people who become friends, was most important for coping with work stress (Henderson and Argyle, 1985). Super-visors have the power to solve problems; indeed, if they are helpful, fewer stresses occur (Kobasa and Puccetti, 1983). Work-mates can provide collective support against supervisors or others.

People at work are also one of the main *sources* of stress. Work-mates can be in competition for promotion or other benefits or do not pull their weight, while supervisors may put on pressure for more work, or give arbitrary orders without con-sultation, for example.

Simply being at work rather than not appears to be good for mental health. Women who have jobs tend to have better mental health than those who do not (Nathanson, 1980). And as we shall see in the next chapter, the unemployed are more distressed than those who are at work (p. 55).

How do relationships relieve distress?

It is not clear to what extent distress is relieved by material help or money; not greatly in a number of American studies. However, distress in divorced women *is* affected by a drop in income, and is greater the more children there are (Gerstel, Riessman and Rosenfield, 1985). And distress is not relieved by the quantity of social interaction, but rather by its quality. The crucial factor in the relief of distress is the provision of social support, which has been defined as 'the perception that one feels cared for, esteemed, or otherwise closely involved with other people' (Reis, 1984), though it has also been defined as the availability of 'someone whom you can talk to about yourself and your problems' (Brown and Harris, 1978). We do not know whether having a confidant or an affectionate relationship is the more important. One study separated the effects of different aspects of social support, and found that depression was buffered most by availability of a confidant, and by self-esteem (partly based on positive reactions from others) (Cohen and Hoberman, 1982). A statistical analysis of social support at work found that increasing self-esteem and feeling of mastery was the key process (Pearlin *et al.*, 1981). Both social interaction and self-esteem have been proposed as key factors (Thoits, 1982), and the process may be different for men and women. The effects of stress on mental health are reduced more for women by affectional bonds, and for men more by social integration (Henderson *et al.*, 1980). A study of depression found that an intimate confiding relationship reduced the effects of daily parental, housework and economic stresses, while social integration had little effect, though was suggested that it may help more serious life-events (Kessler and Essex, 1982).

Those who have a concern for other people and concerns that go beyond the self have fewer stressful experiences, and stress has less effect on anxiety, depression and hostility; they make more active attempts to cope with their problems (Crandall, 1984).

There are several ways in which these kinds of social support can relieve distress. (1) There may be an immediate effect on the self-system, increasing self-esteem and self-confidence. (2) There may be a direct impact on emotions, whereby social interaction generates some degree of positive affect, and thus suppresses depression and anxiety. (3) External stresses may be perceived as less stressful, in the knowledge that support and help are available, so that problems can be dealt with. In long-standing relationships it could be expected that these benefits could be relied upon and would continue to be available.

CONCLUSIONS

1 Social relationships are a major source of happiness, relief from distress, and health.
2 The greatest benefits come from marriage and other close, confiding and supportive relationships.
3 Relationships increase happiness by generating joy, providing help, and through shared enjoyable activities. They buffer the effects of stress by increasing self-esteem, suppressing negative emotions and providing help to solve problems.

3

·WORK AND UNEMPLOYMENT·

JOB SATISFACTION

Overall job satisfaction can be assessed by simple questions like 'Choose the one of the following statements which best tells how well you like your job: I hate it, I dislike it, I don't like it, I am indifferent to it, I like it, I am enthusiastic about it, I love it' (Hoppock, 1935). Or a number of similar general questions can be put together and the replies averaged. Using a four-point scale, fifteen national surveys in the USA between 1972–78 found:

	%	
very satisfied	51.8	
somewhat satisfied	36.1	
a little dissatisfied	9.0	
very dissatisfied	3.1	(Weaver, 1980)

A recent British survey using rather different alternatives obtained the results shown in Figure 3.1. It seems that 36 per cent find their work 'rewarding and interesting', and a further 3 per

Figure 3.1   Job satisfaction in Britain

	dislike job	quite enjoy job	work interesting and rewarding	the most important part of my life	don't know
all	12%	45%	36%	3%	4%
men	15%	41%	36%	4%	4%
women	8%	51%	37%	1%	3%
ABC1	7%	37%	50%	2%	4%
C2DE	17%	52%	25%	3%	3%

Source   Whitehorn, 1984.

cent think that it is the most important part of their life. Of course work may be just as rewarding for others who rate their social relationships or leisure more highly.

Another way of finding out how people feel about their jobs is to ask them whether they would work if it was financially unnecessary. A recent British national survey obtained the results shown in Table 3.1. It can be seen that only about 32 per cent would carry on at their present job but that about 65 per cent would want to work at something. Another survey asked why people would go on working. The most popular answers were 'to avoid boredom', 'would be upset if didn't work' or 'would go crazy if no work', while only 12 per cent would work because they liked the work they were doing or simply liked to work (Veroff, Douvan and Kulka, 1981). These results suggest that the proportion of people who genuinely enjoy their work is rather smaller than the 52 per cent of the first study cited.

Finally we can see how well overall satisfaction can be predicted from different domains. The statistically independent

Table 3.1   People who would work if it were financially unnecessary

	men	women
	%	%
would work, stay in present job	31	34
would work, try to change job	35	29
would stop work, might work later	10	12
would never work	15	18
don't know	9	7

Source   Warr, 1982.

predictions in the *Quality of American Life* study were shown in Table 1.2 (p. 7). Work satisfaction came well below marriage and family as a predictor of overall satisfaction. Benin and Nierstedt (1985) found that while marital happiness was the greatest source of happiness, job (dis)satisfaction was the greatest source of unhappiness.

Taking these and other results together, we can see that satisfaction with work is less important than with marriage, family or standard of living, that job satisfaction is less than that in several other areas, and that it is a greater source of dissatisfaction and worry than of satisfaction.

We have so far discussed overall job satisfaction. Another approach is to measure the separate aspects of work: pay, social conditions, and so on. Many scales have been devised for this purpose: one book reviews no less than 249 scales of various kinds (Cook *et al.*, 1981). However the most widely used is the Job Description Index, which contains five scales, 72 items in total, all answered 'yes', 'no' or 'uncertain' (Smith, Kendall and Hulin, 1969). The five scales are designed to measure satisfaction in the following areas:

work on present job
  e.g. fascinating
present pay
  e.g. income inadequate for normal expenses (–)
opportunities for promotion
  e.g. fairly good chance for promotion
supervision on present job
  e.g. lazy (–)
people on your present job
  e.g. talk too much (–)

The minus signs show reversed items, that is ones that show *dis*satisfaction.

There has been a great deal of research on these scales. They predict overall job satisfaction, especially the 'work on present job' scale, but this is the only one of the five scales that is about intrinsic satisfaction. Additional scales have been devised for use with managers to measure satisfaction with subordinates and with the firm (Warr and Routledge, 1969).

WHAT IS JOB SATISFACTION?

Job satisfaction is a domain of satisfaction with a number of sub-domains, as suggested by the scales of the Job Description Index.

Intrinsic satisfaction with the work

The earliest studies were concerned with the effects of the physical conditions of work. The Human Relations school drew attention to the importance of social factors – of which more later. It was a study by Herzberg and colleagues (1959) that first drew attention to the importance of the work itself in job satisfaction.

A number of scales to measure intrinsic job satisfaction have been developed, typically with items like 'I feel a sense of personal satisfaction when I do this job well' (Warr, Cook and Wall, 1979). These scales are mainly about feelings of achievement, accomplishment, recognition and success at work. This is in keeping with the Herzberg findings. Other studies have tried to discover which features of jobs make them intrinsically satisfying.

It has been suggested that work produces positive emotions for people who do it under certain conditions. There are several ways in which this can happen. Hackman (1977) suggested that five features of jobs produce satisfaction. Many studies have investigated this issue, and the latest meta-analysis found the following average correlations with job satisfaction:

task identity – completing a clear and identifiable piece
of work   .32
task significance – the degree to which the job has an
impact on lives of others   .38
skill variety   .41
autonomy – the degree to which the job provides
freedom, independence and discretion   .46
feedback – the extent to which information about
effectiveness is available   .41
(Loher *et al.*, 1985)

These results show that workers are happier with jobs which are more varied and autonomous. However, this effect is considerably stronger for those with a strong 'growth strength need', i.e. people who enjoy complex and demanding jobs. While most managers and professional people may enjoy jobs that are complex, challenging and autonomous, how far is this true for manual workers? One estimate is 15 per cent, though others have put it higher (Hulin and Blood, 1968; Hackman, 1977). It has been found that many car assembly workers do it for the pay, and that the main satisfactions at work for many female workers are social. On the other hand there is some relationship between satisfaction and the five job characteristics listed above, even for those low in growth strength need (Loher, *et al.*, 1985; Spector, 1985).

Work also becomes a source of intrinsic satisfaction when individuals believe that work is one of the main things in life, that it is morally desirable to work hard, that one should lead a life of self-discipline, and that a person's worth should be judged by his or her work. These ideas came originally from the Protestant reformers, Calvin and Luther, and came to be known as the Protestant Work Ethic. People acquire this outlook if home and school encourage it. Many in the modern world still do think in this way, especially those who are young and well-educated; they are found to be less alienated and to hold more conservative political attitudes than those who have not been influenced by the Protestant Work Ethic (Furnham, 1984c).

Many people come to attach great importance to doing particular kinds of work, and derive great satisfaction from it. This applies to a range of occupations, from doctors, scientists, clergymen and social workers, through craftsmen of all kinds, miners and sailors. Not only the work, but also the sight, sound and smell of the place of work, the other people and the regular rituals, all acquire special significance and value.

Laboratory experiments suggest a further way in which task performance becomes intrinsically motivating. A typical measure of intrinsic motivation is the amount of free time subjects will spend on a task such as a problem-solving game. If they are paid to play the game, their intrinsic motivation is greatly reduced. Intrinsic motivation is greater for a task which is freely chosen and where there is evidence of one's own competence; it is reduced by external rewards, unless their main function is to provide evidence of successful performance (Deci and Ryan, 1980). Success produces greater enjoyment of the task and motivation to carry on doing it. For those with a high need to achieve, success leads first to their placing greater value on this particular kind of competence. This in turn results in greater enjoyment and task involvement (Harackiewicz, Sansome and Manderlink, 1985). A contrast has been made between 'instrumental' behaviour, typically work, which is goal-directed, and 'expressive' behaviour, typically leisure, which is done for its own sake (Apter, 1982; Graef, Csikszentmihalyi and Gianinno, 1983). However it seems very likely that work, for some, *is* a source of intrinsic satisfaction. There are people who enjoy flying planes, driving cars, operating computers, writing books, making furniture, or working in the garden. After all, a lot of them do these things in their spare time, without payment.

Pay

In a number of studies people have been asked to rank various sources of job satisfaction, and pay has usually come out among the first three (Lawler, 1971). It is more a source of dissatisfaction than satisfaction: in some studies as many as 80 per cent of employees were discontented with their pay. In job-satisfaction scales, satisfaction with pay is always one of the main components, and gives a reasonably good prediction of overall satisfaction.

Pay matters more to some individuals than others. Those who are most concerned about it are men, younger workers, and those at lower levels in organizations, i.e. those who are paid less (Lawler, 1971).

People are more satisfied with their pay if they are paid more, though the actual relationship is astonishingly small – typically .25 (Campbell, Converse and Rodgers, 1976). However, this correlation holds up when other variables like level in the organization are held constant. But with pay held constant, more senior individuals are *less* satisfied with their pay, as are those who are older, better educated, more highly skilled, better at their job, and men compared with women (Lawler, 1971; Schwab and Wallace, 1974).

These findings raise issues of central importance for this book. Satisfaction with pay is affected by how much people are paid in relation to what they believe is fair, what they think they should receive. It is widely believed that performance, seniority, age, education, etc. should be recognized and rewarded by higher pay. If there is a discrepancy between what employees think they should be paid and what they are paid, they are dissatisfied. People compare their present pay with what they were paid in the past – though inflation makes accurate comparisons difficult, and probably increases satisfaction with current pay a little. Finally, some allowance is made for other non-monetary rewards received from the job (Lawler, 1971). Employees compare their pay with that of others, perhaps checking that their own balance of inputs and rewards compares sufficiently favourably. A recent study found that about 65 per cent of people sometimes do this, 22 per cent frequently, especially with others in their own organization. However, whether or not they make such comparisons makes little difference to their own satisfaction (Fraser, 1984). These findings are all of great importance for theories about the causes of satisfaction, such as the theory that need satisfaction is the main cause of happiness (p. 143f).

Co-workers

Many studies have found that this is one of the most important components of job satisfaction. The Human Relations movement emphasized the importance of social factors at work, and while they underestimated the importance of other factors, like pay and the work itself, their findings are still valid. Co-workers provide both material and social rewards. Tangible rewards consist mainly of help with the work and co-operation towards joint goals, which in turn may lead to achievement, recognition and financial rewards. There can also be dissatisfaction due to competition and friction, and there are strong rules about fairness to avert these difficulties (Argyle and Henderson, 1985).

Co-workers are a source of social rewards. Job satisfaction correlates highly with popularity or acceptance by group members, .82 in one study (Van Zelst, 1951). Workers enjoy the informal social life of gossip, games, jokes, and general fooling about. The fooling about may be partly to relieve tension – this is one source of industrial sabotage – and partly to relieve boredom. In a group of workers on a repetitive task 'banana time' was when one man would steal and eat another's banana at a certain hour;

another would open a window, creating a row about the draught, and so on. They said 'If it weren't for the talking and fooling you'd go nuts' (Roy, 1959). Social support from the group is a major source of defence against outside threats, from the supervisor or elsewhere, and reduces the effect of such stresses on anxiety and depression (Caplan *et al.*, 1975).

Job satisfaction is higher for those who are accepted by their co-workers and who belong to cohesive groups. By cohesiveness is meant the extent to which members of the group are attracted towards the group. Cohesive groups have greater job satisfaction, less absenteeism, and less labour turnover, sometimes by a ratio of 1:3 (Mann and Baumgartel, 1953). Productivity is greater if co-operation is needed, because the members of cohesive groups help each other more (Van Zelst, 1952). Cohesiveness provides social support and buffers the effect of stress, so is related to both physical and mental health (Payne, 1980).

People at work benefit most in these ways if they have good opportunities for social interaction – not too much noise or spatial isolation, for example. The Tavistock Institute of Human Relations found that groups functioned better if frictions due to internal status differences and to lack of communication were removed. A number of successful field experiments have demonstrated the importance of properly designed working groups. Productivity was increased and accidents and absenteeism greatly reduced by a change in the arrangements for Longwall coal mining. Instead of three shifts doing different jobs, who never met, the jobs of cutting, filling and stonework were done in each shift, so that cohesiveness and co-operation could develop between the men doing the different jobs (Trist *et al.*, 1963).

Relations in working groups can be rather weak. In a British car factory, for example, it was found that although workers talked to each other quite a lot, most said they would not be bothered about being moved away from their workmates. Forty-five per cent had no close friends at work, and only 16 per cent visited other workers at home (Goldthorpe *et al.*, 1968). Some working groups may be closer than this. Members of certain kinds of team – crews of ships and aircraft, and those engaged on dangerous work – become very dependent on one another. Whole working communities may have strong cultures of their own, where people meet after hours to talk shop, as happens with universities. And

'Railroading, like music and thieving . . . is a world by itself'
(Caplow, 1954).

We have suggested elsewhere that people at work can become
friends, who are seen at home as well (A); friends-at-work, who
are seen at coffee breaks at work, but not outside (B); or acquaint-
ances, with whom it is perfectly pleasant to interact, but whose
company is not sought out particularly (C) (Henderson and
Argyle, 1985). We found high levels of interaction with category
A work-mates. Workers who had a type A friend were under less
stress, but job satisfaction was not affected. The activities shared
more with people in closer relationships at work were:

1 joking with the other person
2 chatting casually
3 discussing work
4 having coffee, drinks or meal together
5 teasing him/her
6 helping each other with work
7 asking or giving personal advice
8 discussing your feelings or emotions
9 discussing your personal life
10 teaching or showing the other person something about work.
                                            (Henderson and Argyle, 1985)

Supervision

Satisfaction with superiors is the second source of social satisfaction at work, ranked as less important than co-workers, typically
third to seventh in order of importance. Supervision was mainly a
source of periods of *dissatisfaction* in the Herzberg studies (Herzberg, *et al.*, 1959), and we found that there was a great deal of
conflict with supervisors (Argyle and Furnham, 1983). Supervisors may make demands for more or better work, may be felt to
treat different subordinates unfairly, may be seen as distant,
hostile or unsympathetic. Supervisors can provide benefits that
are partly material, partly social (Locke, 1976); they are a greater
source of instrumental, tangible help than co-workers (Argyle
and Furnham, 1983). They can help with promotion, pay rises
and conditions of work; they can do more to solve difficulties at
work than either co-workers, or spouses. On the other hand, they

can also create difficulties. The social rewards which supervisors can provide include praise and encouragement, and the creation of a pleasant social atmosphere. Support from supervisors can reduce the effects of stress on anxiety and depression (Caplan *et al.*, 1975). Most foremen feel that helping people in this way is part of the job (Kaplan and Cowen, 1981). But the social side of the relationship is made difficult by the gap in power, status and salary (Argyle and Henderson, 1985).

Supervisors who are high on 'consideration' or 'employee-centredness' have more satisfied subordinates and lower levels of absenteeism and labour turnover. In addition, they need to be sufficiently technically competent to help their team to be effective. Evidence shows that people are more satisfied when they are consulted and are allowed to participate in decisions affecting them (Argyle, 1972; Gruneberg, 1979). Clearly supervisors *can* be an important source of job satisfaction, but unfortunately they often lack the social skills to do this.

Opportunities for promotion

In the Herzberg studies it was found that achievement and recognition were the two most commonly given sources of satisfaction, and responsibility and advancement were not far behind. Workers need to feel that they are doing well at their work, and need external recognition of this (Gruneberg, 1979). Promotion is the most important kind of recognition, and carries with it two further rewards: more pay and more status. However, it is a potential source of dissatisfaction too, in the form of separation from co-workers, more responsibility, longer hours of work, and doing different, possibly less interesting work. Consequently some individuals desire it more than others. Managers and administrators are particularly keen to be promoted – they are in long-term careers where promotion is the main index of success. British academics are dissatisfied with the promotion system, since it is very hard to evaluate academic performance. Shop-floor workers do not think that their promotion prospects are very good (Goldthorpe *et al.*, 1968) as indeed they are not – if there are fifty men under one foreman, for example. Their main hope of advancement lies outside the firm, in starting their own businesses.

Other satisfaction factors

There are a number of other factors, such as satisfaction with working conditions and satisfaction with the company or organization, but these are ranked as less important than those which we have discussed, and are included in measures of general job satisfaction.

Research on the unemployed has found a number of 'latent' sources of job satisfaction – things which are not noticed until they have been lost. These are:

structuring time
providing status and identity
transcendent goals
shared experience and
enforced activity

(Jahoda, 1981)

These are features of work which are missed by many when they lose their jobs. However, as we show later, not everyone finds that work is satisfying in all these respects, and a few discover greater satisfaction during unemployment (p. 62).

THE EFFECTS OF JOB SATISFACTION

Satisfaction with life

As we showed earlier, there is a strong connection between job satisfaction and overall life satisfaction. Since work is a major part of life this is not surprising. But does job satisfaction influence life satisfaction, or vice versa? A statistical analysis to establish causal models found that *both* directions of causation operated, though neither was very strong (Schmidt and Bedeian, 1982). Another possibility is that the areas of work and non-work have a lot in common, such as friendships, status, similar styles of behaviour, and that they jointly affect satisfaction with life as a whole (Near, Rice and Hunt, 1980). Another study concluded that 'we suspect that how one affectively evaluates various life concerns relates to essentially *one* phenomenon at the global level . . . perceptions of general well-being' (Andrews and Withey, 1976). At least part of the link between the two kinds of satisfaction is a 'top-to-bottom' one, i.e. general well-being affects job satisfaction.

Health and mental health

Low job satisfaction is correlated with high rates of anxiety, depression, psychosomatic symptoms, and coronary heart disease. And (poor) mental health is more closely associated with (low) job satisfaction than it is with features of the job, suggesting that job satisfaction is an intervening state in the causal chain (Wall, Clegg and Jackson, 1978). However, job satisfaction and mental health are probably both to some extent affected by similar features of work: repetitive, machine-paced work, bad supervision, conflict with co-workers, and other forms of stress (Cooper and Marshall, 1976). In particular the combination of low status and low-grade work is associated with dissatisfaction and with poor health, but there could be several reasons for this, including a tendency for those in poor health to gravitate to poor jobs. On the other hand, clerical workers also have rather poor health, as do those in certain stressful jobs like airfield controllers and TV workers (see Kasl, 1973).

Social support, from co-workers and supervisors, is a major source both of job satisfaction and positive mental health. It can buffer the effects of stress at work more effectively than other sources of social support. People in stressful jobs are in particular need of support from cohesive working groups or socially skilled supervisors.

Another investigation found that job satisfaction was a predictor of length of life among workers. It correlated .26, better than physical functioning (.21) (Palmore, 1969). There is a high correlation between job dissatisfaction and coronary heart disease (r = .83), with other variables held constant (Sales and House, 1971).

It has been found that job dissatisfaction among nurses predicted tension on the job, particularly for dissatisfaction with the work and with the doctors. On the other hand, tension also predicted job dissatisfaction – it worked both ways – particularly dissatisfaction with supervision and pay. This is an interesting example of pay dissatisfaction being affected by non-economic variables (Bateman and Strassen, 1983). Another investigation used causal modelling on the relations between some of these variables, and concluded that job dissatisfaction and boredom caused anxiety and depression, which in turn led to bodily complaints (French, Caplan and Harrison, 1982).

Finally it has been pointed out that whether or not repetitive, boring jobs affect mental health, they do not do much for positive psychological well-being (Warr and Wall, 1975).

For a full discussion of the links between happiness and health, see Chapter 10.

Labour turnover

A correlation is found between job satisfaction and labour turnover. The correlation tends to be small, but job satisfaction is predictive of turnover. A high rate of turnover is generated by some of the main sources of dissatisfaction: pay that is perceived as too low, poor supervision, boring work, and lack of support from co-workers. The relationship between satisfaction and turnover is greater when there is high unemployment; under these conditions, when other jobs are hard to get, people leave mainly because they are dissatisfied. Under full employment some people drift in and out of jobs just for a change, not because they are dissatisfied (Shikiar and Freudenberg, 1982). Field experiments have shown that measures designed to increase job satisfaction, such as job enrichment, reduce the level of labour turnover (McEvoy and Cascio, 1985). It is possible to calculate the probable reduction in turnover from a given increase in pay, and to estimate whether the costs involved in recruitment and training would be greater or less (Gruneberg, 1979). When people are dissatisfied this starts off a chain of events which may or may not result in their leaving: evaluating their chances of finding a better job, looking for one, comparing it with the present one, and in some cases quitting (Mobley, 1977).

Job satisfaction is not the only factor affecting labour turnover. It has been found that there have often been recent changes in their commitment to the organization among those who decide to leave, caused by a fall in rewards, an increase in costs, less 'investment' and better alternatives. 'Investments' here include pension arrangements, local friendships, spouse's job and community ties (Rusbult and Farrell, 1983).

Absenteeism

It is widely believed that low job satisfaction is a cause of absenteeism, and a number of studies have found correlations between them. However a recent meta-analysis of no less than 707 separate analyses obtained an overall correlation of only −.09, so the effect appears to be rather a minor one. If absenteeism is measured for periods of time before and after job satisfaction is measured, it is found that absenteeism is predictive of job satisfaction, and vice versa (Clegg, 1983). The relationship is stronger for women, manual workers, workers in larger firms and younger workers (see Metzner and Mann, 1953). The explanation is probably that the commitment to work is less for these groups; they are less socialized into work, so that they respond to minor illnesses or problems by being absent more readily (Gruneberg, 1979).

It has been argued that labour turnover, absenteeism and lateness are among four general responses to job dissatisfaction: *exit*, i.e. leave, look for another job; *voice*, i.e. talk to supervisor, write letters; *loyalty*, i.e. stick it out, wait patiently; *neglect*, i.e. absenteeism and lateness (Farrell, 1983).

Job performance

It was once regarded as a major discovery that there is *no* relation between job satisfaction and productivity or rate of work (Brayfield and Crockett, 1955). However a recent meta-analysis of seventy-four studies, of 217 separate correlations altogether, found an overall correlation of .17 (Iaffaldano and Muchinsky, 1985). And some recent studies have found correlations which are higher than this, under certain conditions. An overall correlation of .35 was found in one of them, but it was as high as .60 when there was little pressure for performance, i.e. when hard work was more voluntary (Bhagat, 1982). It seems likely that this is because productivity leads to satisfaction, rather than vice versa, because good performance leads to rewards, such as bonus payments and recognition from supervisors (Lawler and Porter, 1967). There should be a positive relationship when such rewards are contingent on productivity (Locke, 1976).

Job satisfaction does result, however, in less counter-productive behaviours such as sabotage, stealing, doing work badly on purpose, and spreading rumours or gossip to cause trouble (Mangoine and Quinn, 1975). This effect was stronger for those over thirty-five, probably because they would only engage in such behaviour if they had a strong sense of grievance. It is very likely that low job satisfaction will lead to more strikes for the same reason. It has also been found that managers who are happy with their work behave with greater consideration and sensitivity towards other people at work (Motowidlo, 1984). We shall show later that the induction of good moods results in more positive social behaviour (p. 139f).

OCCUPATIONAL DIFFERENCES

It has been widely found that job satisfaction is greater for those in more highly skilled, higher status jobs. The most satisfied people at work are university teachers, scientists, clergymen, and other professional people like doctors and lawyers; the least satisfied are those in repetitive, unskilled jobs. One study found that 91 per cent of mathematicians would choose the same work again, compared with 16 per cent of unskilled steel workers (Blauner, 1960). Part of the explanation is no doubt that some jobs are paid more, but managers are often found to be less satisfied than the less well paid university teachers, scientists and clergymen (Gurin, Veroff and Feld, 1960; Sales and House, 1971). More to the point, perhaps, is that these jobs have most of the properties which have been found to be sources of intrinsic satisfaction: autonomy, significance, skill variety, task identity.

It is difficult to separate the components of job satisfaction between occupations in job satisfaction. The *Quality of American Life* study (Campbell, Converse and Rodgers, 1976) found that challenge was highest for professional workers, managers and farmers, lowest for operatives and service workers. Managers enjoyed their co-workers, though farmers did not. Satisfaction with pay was highest for managers and professionals, least for farmers and service workers. Comfort was greatest for farmers, least for skilled and unskilled workers.

Occupations also vary in their stress levels, and we have shown that both stress and dissatisfaction are sources of ill-health, bodily and mental. Table 3.2 shows the ratings for stress made in a recent British survey (Cooper, 1985). The ratings are from 10 to zero: the higher the rate, the greater the pressure.

It is sometimes possible to isolate the feature of jobs which are

Table 3.2 Stress and occupation

miner	8.3	farmer	4.8
police	7.7	armed forces	4.7
construction worker	7.5	veterinarian	4.5
journalist	7.5	civil servant	4.4
pilot (civil)	7.5	accountant	4.3
prison officer	7.5	engineer	4.3
advertising	7.3	estate agent	4.3
dentist	7.3	hairdresser	4.3
actor	7.2	local government officer	4.3
politician	7.0	secretary	4.3
doctor	6.8	solicitor	4.3
taxman	6.8	artist, designer	4.2
film producer	6.5	architect	4.0
nurse, midwife	6.5	chiropodist	4.0
fireman	6.3	optician	4.0
musician	6.3	planner	4.0
teacher	6.2	postman	4.0
personnel	6.0	statistician	4.0
social worker	6.0	laboratory technician	3.8
manager (commerce)	5.8	banker	3.7
marketing/export	5.8	computing	3.7
press officer	5.8	occupational therapist	3.7
professional footballer	5.8	linguist	3.7
salesman, shop assistant	5.7	beauty therapist	3.5
stockbroker	5.5	vicar	3.5
bus driver	5.4	astronomer	3.4
psychologist	5.2	nursery nurse	3.3
publishing	5.0	museum worker	2.8
diplomat	4.8	librarian	2.0

Source Cooper, 1985.

stressful. A study of student nurses found that they reported more anxiety and depression when working in medical than in surgical wards, and when in female than in male wards. The death rate of patients is higher in medical wards (Parkes, 1982).

INDIVIDUAL DIFFERENCES

Different people want different things. We have already seen that some working-class people are more concerned with pay than intrinsic satisfaction, partly no doubt because their work does not offer much skill variety or autonomy. Women have usually been found to be most concerned with social aspects of work and working conditions. Variations in motivation, abilities or other aspects of personality also affect what kinds of work make people happy. More generally, satisfaction is higher when there is a good fit between person and job. If an individual's profile of needs matches the profile of rewards offered by the job he or she will be more satisfied (Furnham and Scheaffer, 1984). The most obvious fit which is needed is between an employee's knowledge and skills, and those required by the job. It does not matter from the organization's point of view if an employee is over-qualified, but it does matter for the employee. Figure 3.2 shows that depression results if the job is too complex or not complex enough. Those with a need for 'growth' are more satisfied doing complex work in an open, non-hierarchical organization (Vecchio and Keon, 1981). Similarly those high in achievement motivation prefer more challenging jobs, and show more correlation between performance and satisfaction (Steers, 1975). Those with strong social needs are happier as members of close-knit, co-operative groups.

Figure 3.2   Job complexity and depression

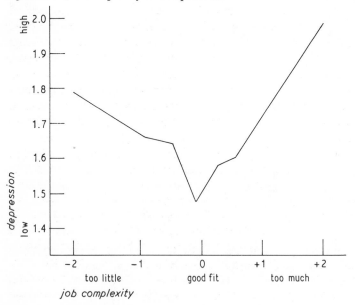

Source   Caplan et al., 1975.

ENHANCING JOB SATISFACTION

A great deal of thought has been devoted to ways of increasing job satisfaction, and a lot of experiments have been tried out. The main alternatives are as follows.

Redesigning jobs

Some jobs are so unsatisfying that nearly everyone is discontented in them, despite the individual differences mentioned above. Job enlargement and enrichment consist of increasing the variety of jobs done, so that a meaningful unit is completed, sometimes including inspection of the job, and increasing the length of the work cycle. Many people would like jobs that are to some extent more interesting and responsible. Many programmes of job enrichment have been carried out, usually with very positive results (Jenkins, 1981), for example leading to reduced labour turnover (McEvoy and Cascio, 1985).

Improving social relationships at work

This can be done in several ways, including the formation of natural co-operative work-groups, improving supervisory skills, increasing participation in decisions, creating contacts between workers and clients, and reducing status and pay differentials in the hierarchy. Some of the most discontented workers are those on assembly lines. Volvo and Saab managed to replace their assembly lines with ten-man bays linked by a conveyor system, using much longer work cycles. This has resulted in reduced absence and turnover (Kahn, 1981).

Training and selection of employees

Early programmes of counselling for workers were long ago abandoned as expensive and ineffective. Large-scale use of T-groups (training groups) appears to have suffered a similar fate. What *can* be done, however, is to match individuals to jobs more effectively. This is done by selection, promotion and transfers based on skills, though there are still many people in the wrong jobs from this point of view. Matching personality and needs to jobs is done in vocational guidance for those who receive it, and in the process of choosing and changing careers, but it is not a prime concern of personnel departments.

CONCLUSIONS

About 50 per cent of people claim to be satisfied with their jobs, though only a third of people would continue to do their jobs if they didn't have to. There are large differences between occupations.

Job satisfaction can be divided into several components, of which the most important is intrinsic satisfaction with the work itself. This is stronger when the work has skill variety and autonomy, when it is felt to affect the lives of others, and when there is evidence of successful performance. Other sources of job satisfaction include pay, co-workers and supervision.

Job satisfaction affects overall life satisfaction, as well as health and mental health (see Chapter 10). Labour turnover is less, absenteeism somewhat less, job performance a little more when people are satisfied with their work.

THE EFFECTS OF UNEMPLOYMENT

This book is supposed to be about happiness, so why discuss unemployment? The reason is that studying the effects of losing jobs has enabled us to understand better the satisfactions obtained from working. And research into how different people cope with unemployment has provided valuable information about the psychological basis of happiness.

Unemployment has greatly increased throughout the industrialized West, and shows no signs of decreasing. It is regarded as a major social problem because its effects are believed to be so negative. Let us first examine exactly what these effects are.

In Britain a person counts as 'unemployed' if he or she is claiming unemployment or related benefits, that is if they do not have a paid job and are actively trying to obtain one. This does not include the retired, most married women without jobs, or students in vacation. In 1985 in Great Britain 3.346 million people, 14 per cent of the work force, were unemployed in this sense, and at least 12 per cent of families contained one or more unemployed members. The rate is highest for young males, members of ethnic minority groups, and those with poor educational qualifications (*Social Trends*, 1986). Many unemployed people are between jobs – the median gap is 3.4 months. However, 40 per cent of them have been out of work for over a year; these tend to be the old, the young, the unskilled or disabled, ethnic minorities, or those who had been in prison (Smith, 1985–6). A study of the predictors of individual unemployment found that young people were also more likely to be out of work if they had a smaller desire to be at work, if their father was out of work, and if they were of lower social class (Stafford, Jackson and Banks, 1980). Some young people accept periods of voluntary unemployment as part of life, and this gives them the opportunity to sample different kinds of work (Kelvin and Jarrett, 1985).

UNEMPLOYMENT, HAPPINESS AND SATISFACTION

The causes and effects of unemployment vary according to different economic conditions. During the period 1950–70, for example, the rate of unemployment was very low in Britain, compared with other historical periods; the reasons for unemployment then were largely individual. During the 1980s the rate has been much higher, and unemployment now reflects the decline of whole industries, like coal-mining and steel (Kelvin and Jarrett, 1985).

Recent studies have found a very clear difference between the happiness of those with and without jobs. A national survey in Britain (Warr and Payne, 1982) investigated how far people reported that they 'felt pleased with things yesterday'. The results are summarized in Table 3.3. It can be seen that the unemployed and those in part-time work reported much more unpleasant emotional strain, but were just as pleased with things yesterday, as those in full-time work; more of the retired were pleased with things yesterday. In an Australian study of school-leavers those who did not find jobs became less happy, and more bored, angry with society, lonely and helpless (Tiggemann and Winefield, 1984). A British survey found that 19 per cent of an unemployed sample said that they had become miserable or unhappy since they became out of work, 17 per cent had become restless and bad-tempered, 13 per cent easily upset or snappy

Table 3.3 The emotional state of the employed, unemployed and retired

	full-time employment %	part-time employment %	unemployed – looking for work %	unemployed – not looking for work %	retired %
'felt very pleased with things yesterday (all of the time)'					
men	23	24	21	20	36
women	17	28	19	24	35
'unpleasant emotional strain yesterday (all or most of the time)'					
men	6	16	16	17	12
women	9	11	21	13	14

Source Warr and Payne, 1982.

(*Social Trends*, 1984). In a study of 1655 British steel workers, six months after closure of their plant, the positive affect scores (on the Bradburn scale) were 3.05 for those who had found jobs, 2.30 for those who had not. There was a smaller difference in negative affect, the unemployed scoring higher (Warr, 1978). In American surveys, 10–12 per cent of the unemployed describe themselves as 'very happy', compared with 30 per cent of the general population (Campbell, 1981). Unemployed people are also more angry than those with jobs (Stokes and Cochrane, 1984).

Many investigators have examined those who have lost their jobs, and describe states of shock, apathy, hopelessness, bereavement, as well as higher rates of divorce and emigration. Although reduction of earning occurs in many cases, when income is held constant the unemployed are still less happy than those at work (Campbell, Converse and Rodgers, 1976). Retired people are in a similar position to the unemployed, but they are more happy, not less.

Unemployed people had on average lower qualifications, more psychological problems, poorer health, and worse jobs before they lost them. However, longitudinal studies, for example of the closure of entire factories, show that their unhappiness is at least partly, and probably mainly, the result of the unemployment.

Among young people there is an almost universal desire to work: being on a Youth Opportunities Programme in Britain prevents the loss of satisfaction and self-esteem which follows from not finding work (Breakwell, 1984). We discuss the satisfaction of work for women elsewhere; in general the effects of unemployment for women are less than for men, unless they are the chief wage earner. Women are also affected, though not so much, by the unemployment of their husbands (Bradburn, 1969).

Unemployment hits some domains of satisfaction more than others. One of the main areas is, of course, money and standard of living. In Britain 13 per cent say they have been very badly affected materially, and another 24 per cent fairly badly affected. These percentages were higher for those who had been out of work for two years or more (*Social Trends*, 1984). It is true that some lower paid workers become better off by being out of work, if they have families and can claim both unemployment and supplementary benefits, but only 6 per cent received more, and in all cases very little more, in 1978 (Davies *et al.*, 1982). The majority are worse off, especially after they have been out of work for a year. The average family income where the head was unemployed, in 1982, was £109 per week, compared with £160 where the head was employed (*Social Trends*, 1984).

There is also less satisfaction with health and housing. The satisfaction and the stresses due to work are less, but those due to the family are greater (Campbell, 1981; Warr and Payne, 1983).

The unemployed are discontented in special ways.

Self-esteem

Many studies, though not all, find that the unemployed are lacking in self-esteem, feel that they have failed, are inferior (Feather, 1982). It has recently been found that while general self-esteem may not be affected, there are clearer effects on feelings of personal efficacy and achievement (Jackson, 1984).

Apathy

The unemployed often become bored and apathetic, especially if they find they cannot organize their time, and just sit around doing nothing (Feather and Bond, 1983). They have even been found to walk more slowly, to show a lowering of physical and psychological alertness; sitting about aimlessly can lead to deterioration.

Failure to mature

If school-leavers fail to find a job, they tend to stay at the same level of psychological growth as those still at school (Gurney, 1980).

MENTAL HEALTH

Some people do not like their work or are under severe strain at work. Nevertheless, there is no question that those without jobs are in a worse state of mental health, especially depression, and are more likely to commit suicide or become alcoholics than those at work. Table 3.3 showed more unpleasant emotional strain for the unemployed, least for those in full-time jobs. However, some unemployed people have lost their jobs because of illness, mental illness, alcoholism, etc. (Smith, 1985–6). The question is: does unemployment also cause poor mental health? There have been a number of longitudinal studies which provide a clear answer. For example, in a survey of 954 men who had been unemployed for different periods, mostly under a year, 20 per cent were in worse mental health than before (anxiety, depression, irritability, etc.) and 8 per cent better, as a result of the removal of occupational pressures (Warr and Jackson, 1984).

A follow-up study of school-leavers was carried out to see whether unemployment causes psychological ill-health, or vice versa. This used several thousand school-leavers in Leeds, their GHQ scores being found before they left school, and one to two years later. (See Table 1.3 for the General Health Questionnaire.) The average scores for those with and without jobs are shown in Table 3.4. Higher scores indicate greater emotional disturbance.

This table shows that the GHQ scores of those who did not find jobs *increased*, while for those who did find jobs it *decreased*. Those who found jobs also had lower GHQ scores in the first place. This kind of longitudinal design shows that unemployment affects mental health. It suggests in addition, however, that poor mental health has a small effect in making unemployment more likely.

Other research shows that unemployed people who do not succeed in finding jobs are more likely to be alcoholics, or to have had a history of psychiatric treatment. There is clearly a two-way link between unemployment and mental disorder (Furnham and Lewis, 1986).

It usually takes some time for the effects on mental health to appear. An Australian study of 400 unemployed young people

Table 3.4 Unemployment and mental health

	before leaving school	6–15 months after leaving school	16–23 months after leaving school
unemployed			
boys	11.4	13.6	
girls	11.2		13.4
employed			
boys	10.6	8.4	
girls	10.5		7.7

Source Banks and Jackson, 1982.

found that 56 per cent of them were clinically disturbed, and that in most cases this happened after the unemployment started, typically five months later (Finlay-Jones and Eckhardt, 1981). A British study found that mental and physical health were worst at about six months (Warr and Jackson, 1984). Another American study found that many wives became depressed, anxious and sensitive about their social relationships two to three months after their husbands lost their jobs (Liem and Atkinson, 1982, reported in Furnham and Lewis, 1986).

A British study of the changes in behaviour after people lost their jobs found that some of these changes were linked with a decline in psychological health, as shown by GHQ scores. It was found that sitting around at home, watching TV, and looking at the shops without buying anything go with poor mental health, while more active ways of spending time such as seeing friends, going for trips and going to the cinema or theatre are correlated with good mental health, though which causes which is not clear (Warr, 1984).

We can begin to trace the process whereby unemployment produces depression. A follow-up study of 2300 Americans found that those who lost their jobs become more depressed, and also reported marital, parent-child and economic difficulties (Pearlin *et al.*, 1981). A series of studies in Australia found clear effects of unemployment on the Beck depression inventory – a well-known scale for measuring depression. It was found that after a long period of unemployment people increasingly blamed themselves, were in a state of 'learned helplessness', in which they felt that the main cause of their unemployment, i.e. aspects of themselves, was uncontrollable (Feather and Davenport, 1983). However Catalano, Dooley and Jackson (1981) argue that economic changes really uncover existing cases of mental disorder, whose symptoms were previously regarded as trivial; families can no longer afford to support a marginal member.

Suicide is very clearly linked with unemployment. A high percentage of people who commit suicide are unemployed: 69 per cent in one series, five times the national average in another. They commit suicide after losing their jobs, and there is a positive correlation between unemployment rates and suicide rates across geographical areas, and from comparing rates in different years. How does unemployment affect suicide attempts? One route is via depression, or other aspects of poor mental health. Another is via poverty, reduced social support, and alcoholism (Platt, 1984; Smith, 1985–6).

A number of investigators have correlated rates of suicide and mental ill-health across time with level of unemployment. One such analysis found that a 1 per cent increase in unemployment in the USA, if sustained over five years, results in:

	%
suicides	+ 4.1
mental hospital first admissions	+ 3.3
prison admissions	+ 4.0
murders	+ 5.7
death from alcoholism	+ 1.9
total death rate	+ 1.9

(Brenner, 1976, reported by Cochrane, 1983)

INDIVIDUAL DIFFERENCES

However, not everyone is equally affected by being unemployed; as we saw above, about 10–12 per cent of American unemployed report that they are 'very happy'.

Being committed to work

This is associated with more distress for those out of work, though they are also more likely to find work. It is particularly distressing for those who have accepted the Protestant Work Ethic, and believe that their value as persons and their identity depends on the work that they do.

Length of unemployment

Distress increases during the first few months and then levels off. The effects of prolonged unemployment are worst for men in their forties (Jackson and Warr, 1984).

Age and sex

Middle-aged men are affected more than younger or older men, and men are affected more than married women, though no more than single women. However, as we showed earlier, married women with small children and without jobs are likely to become depressed (p. 27). Young mothers are affected most of all.

Social class

Working-class people are more upset despite the fact that they are believed to be 'used to it', mainly because middle-class people are better at filling time, and have less acute financial problems (Payne, Warr and Hartley, 1984).

Social support

The negative effects of unemployment on health, mental health and happiness are greatly reduced for those who have strong social support from spouse, family or friends, (see Chapter 2 and Table 10.3).

WHY DOES UNEMPLOYMENT MAKE PEOPLE UNHAPPY?

There is one very obvious explanation: it makes most people worse off financially, though it makes a few better off too. And the effects of unemployment on happiness, mental health and health appear to be rather greater than the effects of income, so we must turn to other explanations.

Attitudes and beliefs about work

For a long time many people in the West have had ambiguous attitudes to the unemployed – a combination of contempt and sympathy. The unemployed have been regarded as inadequate, idle scroungers, while at the same time unemployment has come to be seen as largely the result of industrial developments and new technology, combined with factors such as overseas competition and political decisions. A widely accepted theory is that attitudes to the unemployed are widely influenced by the Protestant Work Ethic. Recent studies in Britain have found that some people still endorse the Protestant Ethic, and those who do so think that the reason people are unemployed is that they are lazy, unintelligent, poorly qualified, or are scroungers who find they can do better on social security (Furnham, 1982a, 1984d).

The unemployed themselves think that unemployment is mainly caused by government, trade unions, or other societal factors, while the employed think it is also the fault of the unemployed (Furnham, 1982b).

However, there are arguments against the influence of the Protestant Ethic. Kelvin and Jarrett (1985) have pointed out that both manual workers and owners were often fairly idle in earlier centuries. Even in the nineteenth century, entrepreneurs spent a lot of time eating and drinking, and really wanted to be country gentlemen. The influence of the church during this period was very small for working-class people. In any case the Protestant Ethic would not have supported approval of some becoming rich at the expense of the unemployment of others (see Pahl, 1984). Of course, many people do become very involved with their jobs, and derive great satisfaction from them, as we have seen; but is this due to the teachings of Luther and Calvin? Kelvin and Jarrett suggest that the stigmatizing of the unemployed has a quite different basis in the language of law and administration, which prohibited the support of 'sturdy beggars' and 'idle rogues', and developed a picture of the unemployed as dependent, inadequate or even criminal. The importance of technological changes in destroying jobs was easily overlooked.

In the current climate of opinion, to be out of work may be seen as a sign of failure, it is a social stigma, a form of deviance.

> 'And if you can't find any work to do, you have the feeling that you're not human. You're out of place. You're so different from all the rest of the people around you that you think something is wrong with you.' (Kelvin, 1981)

Unemployment has now become very widespread, however, and includes people from all sections of society, including many who are highly qualified, and who have held responsible jobs in the past. Among the young, very large proportions cannot find work in some areas. Among the middle-aged, unemployment can be seen as 'early retirement'. The result is that many of the unemployed now feel less responsible for their plight, and more accepting of it. If you know a lot of other people who are also out of work, this part of the identity problem is greatly eased.

There is still the problem that most people base their self-image, and are categorized by others, primarily in terms of the work they do. To be unemployed is to lose this central component of the self-image.

Filling and structuring time

Out-of-work people are less distressed if they are able to plan, organize and fill their time (Feather and Bond, 1983). They are happier if they perceive their time as occupied. How do unemployed people spend their time? A recent British survey of a representative sample of 1043 of them asked about what they had done the day before, a weekday, with the results shown in Table 3.5. Their main activities were housework, shopping, job hunting, visiting friends and relatives and watching TV. The unemployed also entertain less but smoke more than other people (Warr and Payne, 1982). Among males aged 25–44, 44 per cent are 'heavy drinkers', compared with 28 per cent for those at work (Smith, 1985–6). Middle-class unemployed read more than before. Working-class people show a reduction in forms of entertainment which have to be paid for (Warr and Payne, 1983). There is more 'unstructured' time – watching TV, chatting, reading the paper, hanging about (Smith, 1985–6).

Table 3.5 How the unemployed spend their time (UK, 1982)

	morning		afternoon		total
	men %	women %	men %	women %	%
housework	19	49	7	21	19
shopping	20	26	9	17	16
job hunting	22	16	12	13	16
visiting friends or relatives	6	10	12	17	10
gardening	14	2	13	3	11
TV	4	2	14	12	8.5
reading	9	5	8	10	8
decorating	7	3	7	2	5.5
walking	5	3	8	2	5.5
nothing/sitting around	3	3	9	6	5.5
staying in bed	8	8	1	0	4.5
visiting town	5	7	3	4	4.5
playing sport	4	1	4	0	3
drinking	2	1	3	1	2

Source *Social Trends*, 1984.

Some unemployed people keep up their skills, for example setting up an office or workshop at home, and this is good for the self-image as well as filling time. Some take part in the informal or 'black economy', which both helps financially (though illegally) and maintains a social network. About 16 per cent of the unemployed do some unpaid work for good causes; this is less than for the employed, but the difference may be because the out-of-work include a lot of young and unskilled, who do less voluntary work (*Social Trends*, 1984).

After a long period of unemployment some adapt in a way which is not very satisfying. They stay in bed late, kill time, and give up bothering to apply for jobs. And of course they watch TV a lot – which was not possible during earlier economic recessions.

It is clear that there are plenty of things for the unemployed to do with their time, just as there are for the young, the retired and many married women at home. If they succeed in working out an organized pattern of life, they enjoy a greater sense of well-being.

Another example of happy 'unemployed' people can be found among those middle and upper-class people of an earlier era who did not need to work, and did not do so. As far as we can see they were perfectly happy, in part perhaps because they had never heard of the Protestant Ethic. Perhaps it was also because they had a fairly ordered way of life, with extensive duties and country pursuits.

Loss of social relationships

The unemployed suffer serious losses in one of the most important areas of life satisfaction, relationships with other people. There is loss of all relationships at work, i.e. loss of a co-operative network and of informal friendships. At work people are part of a complex set of complementary relationships which convey identity and status: a teacher feels he is a teacher as a result of the interaction with pupils. All this is lost.

There is usually some withdrawal from friendships, partly because the unemployed often cannot afford to pay for drinks or entertaining or to go on outings. They may feel inferior and stigmatized, and withdraw from the company of employed people, thinking rightly or wrongly that they are being ostracized. The bonds between unemployed people are weak: this is a group that they do not want to belong to.

Finally, the amount of social support at home often declines. Family relationships are damaged, there is increased tension in marriage, violence and divorce; there is increased trouble with the children and child abuse (Kelvin and Jarrett, 1985; Smith, 1985–6).

The hidden benefits of work

There is at first sight some contradiction between the finding that many people dislike their work – those in boring, repetitive jobs, for example – and the findings reviewed in this chapter, showing that people dislike losing their jobs even more. The explanation is probably that work provides a number of hidden benefits, in addition to being a source of livelihood. These include providing a structure to the use of time and social contacts outside the family; linking the individual to broader goals and purposes; giving status and sense of identity; and providing a raised level of activity (Jahoda, 1981; Warr, 1983). These factors are probably important for many people. On the other hand some unemployed people succeed in obtaining *more* of these forms of satisfaction after losing their jobs. A recent study described eleven people who had used unemployment in an unusually positive way. They preferred their own organization of time and self-discipline to an imposed one, they had not liked hierarchical authority and found enriched social support elsewhere, they chose their own goals in tune with their own values, they found their own identities, in one case as leader of a community project, and had as much opportunity as before for the daily exercise of competence and skill (Fryer and Payne, 1984).

Clearly it is possible to organize non-work activities in a very satisfying way. But which activities do this? Sitting around, doing nothing obviously does not. Gardening, hobbies, and decorating involve the same activities as certain kinds of work, except that they are unpaid, they are done when and how one wants, and may not provide contacts with other people or broader goals. In order to provide satisfaction similar to that of work, leisure should have certain properties, such as commitment to long-term goals, co-operation in a group and use of skills. In Chapter 4 we will see how far leisure can provide such satisfaction.

CONCLUSIONS

Unemployment makes most people very unhappy. There are serious effects on levels of mental ill-health, such as depression and suicide, and on health, which are discussed in Chapter 10. The effects are worst for people who are committed to the work ethic, for middle-aged men and for working-class people.

The explanation is partly that unemployment is often regarded as a sign of failure or idleness, partly the loss of various hidden benefits of work, like structuring time, providing status and identity, and social contacts.

A positive adjustment to unemployment is made by those who find things to do with their time, keep up their skills, and keep up their social relationships.

4

·LEISURE·

If you want to be happy for a few hours, get drunk. If you want to be happy for a few years, get a wife. If you want to be happy for ever, get a garden.   Anon

Leisure is an important component of overall life satisfaction. It is of special interest to us: since what people do in their spare time is much less constrained than work, leisure should be able to give us some important clues about what people want, what makes them happy. Leisure choices are not totally free; they are limited by what is available, by what people can afford, and by what is socially acceptable. But as work declines in quantity – shorter working hours, earlier retirement – there is evidence that work values and the Protestant Ethic are no longer all-important to so many people. If we can find out which leisure activities are most satisfying, this should help in planning for leisure, as well as helping us to understand the roots of happiness.

It is possible that leisure activities are more fundamental to human life than work, although the antithesis could also be argued:

> The first optimal experiences in each person's life include nurturance, feeding and play; these intrinsically rewarding experiences establish a benchmark to which later events are compared. As a person matures, the most rewarding experiences still tend to occur in expressive leisure contexts such as games, sports, intimate interactions, artistic, and religious activities. . . .
>
> Thus it could be argued that the most basic meaning of work and other instrumental activities is naturally determined by reference to meanings developed in leisure settings rather than vice versa.   (Csikszentmihalyi, 1981, p. 333)

WHAT IS LEISURE?

Which activities are we going to include as 'leisure'? The simplest way would be to include everything that an individual does during the hours when he or she is not sleeping, working, eating, or looking after self and family. For a long time leisure was regarded as what was done in the time left over from work. It is now recognized that this is a mistaken emphasis, since some people are not at work, and for many people leisure is more important than work. And some kinds of leisure are intermingled with work. Some psychologists have made a sharp contrast between work as goal-directed or instrumental, and leisure as expressive, done for its own sake, for intrinsic rewards. However, the more serious forms of leisure also involve the pursuit of goals: people swim not just to splash about and have fun, but also to improve their style or speed, or to keep fit. A better approach is to define leisure as those activities which people do simply because they want to, for their own sake, for fun, entertainment, self-improvement or for goals of their own choosing, but not for material gain.

Several surveys have been carried out on the meaning of leisure. It was seen as pleasure, self-realization or fulfilment, spontaneous activity, without constraints. Work was seen in terms of duty, efficiency, restraints and subordination (Tokarski, 1985).

SATISFACTION WITH LEISURE

An American national survey asked about leisure satisfaction on the 7-point 'delighted–terrible' scale, and found that 11 per cent were 'delighted', 32.5 per cent were 'pleased' and 36.5 per cent 'mostly satisfied'. Overall satisfaction with leisure was somewhat less than job satisfaction, and quite a lot less than marital satisfaction (Andrews and Withey, 1976).

In a later survey respondents were asked whether leisure or work led to more fulfilment of their basic values. Leisure did not produce as much fulfilment of values like security, moral respect or self-actualization as work, but it did more for hedonism and about the same as work for sociability (Veroff, Douvan and Kulka, 1981). For most people leisure is a less important source of satisfaction than job, marriage or family, but for a minority leisure is *more* important (see Table 4.1 based on US data). It is a greater source of satisfaction than work for a lot of single men (28 per cent).

Other studies have examined the satisfaction derived from different leisure activities. The percentages expressing great satisfaction (point 5 on a 5-point scale) in an extensive American study carried out in 1965–66 were as shown in Table 4.2. It can be seen that satisfaction from reading, sport, TV-watching and other leisure activities is less than that from social relationships, though leisure is often shared with other people.

Leisure satisfaction can be measured by means of scales designed to tap the main underlying motivations. This approach depends on knowing what those motivations might be. There is a fair degree of agreement on this point between different studies, as we shall see, and the different areas of satisfaction correlate

Table 4.1 Satisfaction from work and leisure

	employed men %	employed women %	housewives %
work > leisure	49	45	34
work = leisure	32	36	32
work < leisure	19	19	34

Source Veroff, Douvan and Kulka, 1981.

Table 4.2   Satisfaction with leisure activities

activity	great satisfaction %
your children	79
your marriage	75
your house (or apartment)	40
religion	34
being with friends	33
helping others	33
reading	32
being with relatives	27
making or fixing things	27
sports or games	26
housework	25
relaxing, sitting around	27
car	25
cooking	23
shopping	17
TV	17
clubs	13
politics	9

Source   Robinson, 1977.

quite well with one another to produce a general leisure satisfaction factor.

However, it is clear that the amount of satisfaction with different forms of leisure is not very closely related to the amount of time spent. The most frequent leisure activities are watching TV, walking, reading and listening to music; these are less fun than travel, mountain-climbing or skiing (Bammel and Bammel, 1982), but watching TV and reading involve less effort, they are much cheaper, and need no special skills, equipment, physical environment or weather.

LEISURE AND WELL-BEING

Part of the definition of leisure is that it consists of activities which are done for their own sake. They may involve immediate goals, like having fun or enjoying something, or longer-term goals like acquiring competence at a skill or sport, extending knowledge or education, writing a book, seeing the world. These can all be regarded as acceptable ends in themselves, and do not require any further justification, but we may still enquire whether or not leisure enhances general well-being and physical or mental health.

Leisure satisfaction is one of the components of the index of general well-being developed at the University of Michigan (Campbell, Converse and Rodgers, 1976). A more restrictive definition of leisure which stressed 'hobbies' was not found to be a very good predictor of well-being, nor was it rated as a very important domain. However leisure defined as 'life outside work' was one of the best predictors of global well-being.

Leisure also affects marriage and other aspects of social life, which we have seen are important sources of well-being. Shared leisure is associated with greater marital satisfaction, especially in the early years of marriage and after the children have left home (Wilson, 1980). We shall see later that one of the main sources of leisure satisfaction is the social interaction and strengthening of social bonds that it involves. Friends, especially male friends, often engage in joint leisure (p. 76f).

THE EXTENT OF LEISURE ACTIVITIES

The most satisfactory way of finding out exactly how much time people spend on different kinds of leisure activity is to persuade a sample of people to keep a diary for a week or longer. An American diary study carried out in 1965–66 found that men had 4 hours 46 minutes of free time per day, while employed women had 4 hours 2 minutes. This is time which is not taken up by work, travel, personal care or domestic duties. Of this, 2 hours 28 minutes for men, 1 hour 36 minutes for women were occupied with TV and other mass media. One hour 40 minutes for men, 1 hour 57 minutes for women were used in leisure activities in a more restricted sense – social activity, sport, entertainment, etc. (Robinson, 1977).

There is no comparable recent study in Britain using time budgets. However the *General Household Surveys* interview 25,000 households regularly, and have produced a great deal of information about leisure. I shall use these as my main source in this section. They show that in 1982 the hours of free time for different categories of people were as follows:

	weekdays	weekend days
employed males	4.0	11.4
employed females	3.6	9.2
housewives	7.0	8.0
retired	9.9	11.2

This free time occurred mainly between 6 and 10 p.m. on weekdays. In 1978 the proportions of evenings spent on broad categories of leisure in England and Wales were as shown in Figure 4.1. Watching TV was now the main leisure activity, followed by social activities away from home (clubs, dancing, church, evening classes, etc.), drinking, and social activities at home.

The frequencies with which people in Britain of both sexes and all ages engage in various leisure activities are shown in Table 4.3. This study was carried out in 1977. The first column shows how many people took part in each, during the past four weeks, during the most popular quarter. The second column shows how many times a month those who pursue each activity at all do so, in the most active season.

We shall examine some of the main leisure activities, starting with the one which now occupies most time: watching TV.

Figure 4.1 Proportion of evenings spent on various leisure activities

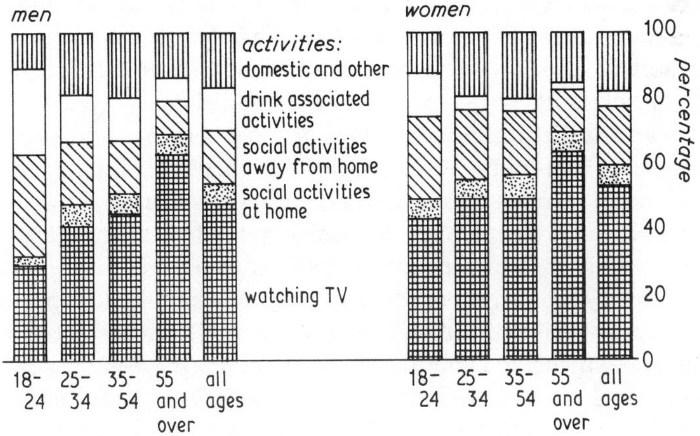

Source *Social Trends*, 1982.

Table 4.3   Participation in leisure activities

	Participation during most popular quarter %	Days per month in most active quarter
games of skill (cards, chess, Scrabble, etc.)	22.3	7.0
betting/pools	20.4	5.4
clubs/societies	12.3	3.6
social and voluntary work	9.6	5.6
bingo	9.3	5.6
visits to countryside	8.9	2.2
hobbies/crafts/arts	7.6	7.6
visits to parks	6.5	2.2
amateur music/drama	3.7	9.9

Source   Birch, 1979.

Watching TV

The amount of time people spend watching TV continues to rise, perhaps as a result of more channels and improved programmes. In 1970 British people watched for two and a quarter hours a day; in 1985 women in Britain watched TV for four and a half hours a day on average; men three and three-quarter hours, though rather less than this for adults aged between 16 and 64 who watched three hours six minutes, females three hours 39 minutes a day, (children and the elderly watch a great deal). They mainly watched BBC1 and ITV and at certain times in the evening. Figure 4.2 shows viewing patterns in the UK, in February 1981, for children and adults on different days of the week. It can be seen that at certain times of the week nearly 80 per cent of children (i.e. under sixteen) were watching, and at other times over 50 per cent of adults were. In fact sets are switched on for over five hours a day, and different members of the family watch different things or use it as background. Even so they admit to watching for about 45 per cent of their free time (Tunstall, 1983). There are several groups who watch TV a lot: in addition to the young and the old, women, members of lower social classes, and members of racial minority groups watch a great deal (Comstock *et al.*, 1978), as do those who are housebound and some of the unemployed

Figure 4.2   Television viewing habits of adults and children

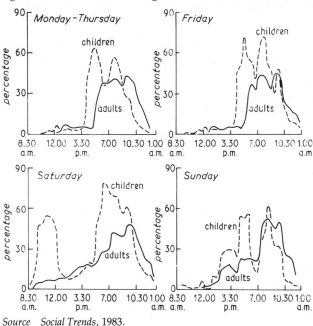

Source   *Social Trends*, 1983.

(Roberts, 1981). In the USA people watch TV more than in any other country: sets are switched on for seven hours a day.

A lot of this 'watching' is very casual – the set is left on rather like pop music or muzak, as part of the background, and is attended to more if and when it gets interesting. Collett (1986), at Oxford, has developed a technique for filming families at home while the TV is switched on. He has found that some of the time they are not even in the room, and a lot of the time they are not watching at all, or doing something else at the same time – housework, eating, talking or knitting. On the other hand most people do watch particular programmes (Bower, 1973). The most popular programmes are soap operas, of which the most watched in Britain are *Coronation Street* and *East Enders*. TV programmes help to organize the timetable, to 'structure' time, and indeed to define which parts of the day are devoted to leisure.

A lot of research has been carried out on why people watch TV so much, and the gratifications which they get from it. Several factors have been found:

1 Entertainment, diversion, escaping boredom, 'to get away from the ordinary cares and problems of the day'.
2 Keeping in touch with the world, information, advice.
3 Social needs, including vicarious social contact, 'parasocial' interaction with TV characters and presenters; as a social event with the family; something to talk about at work and with friends.
4 Identity, seeing people like oneself, comparing oneself with others.   (Murray and Kippax, 1979)

If such needs are measured in individuals this gives some prediction of which programmes they will watch. And the viewing patterns of different groups can be understood in these terms: for example, educated and middle-class people watch the news a lot, and ethnic minority groups watch soap operas, as one study suggests, partly to find out how to behave in common social situations (Comstock *et al.*, 1978).

As we said before TV is available, cheap, requires no effort, special skills, equipment, environment or weather.

Watching TV has immediate effects on emotional state. While watching programmes in general people are found to be relaxed, cheerful and sociable; they are more drowsy, weak and passive than for reading or any other activity, for instance, work, other leisure, eating, talking (Csikszentmihalyi and Kubey, 1981).

Other media

Radio

British people listen to the radio for about one hour 5 minutes a day on average. However, even more than in the case of TV they are likely to be doing something else at the same time. The most popular programme in Britain is Radio 1, the popular music channel, followed by Radio 2. Young people of course are particularly devoted to the sound of continuous music. Some older people listen to a great deal of classical music in the same way.

Reading

In the American study reported in Table 4.2, men spent an average of 39 minutes a day reading, women 26 minutes. In Britain 72 per cent of people read a daily paper, 76 per cent a

Sunday paper in 1983; in the USA people spend on average 22 minutes a day reading the paper (Szalai *et al.*, 1972). In Britain, they also read of lot of magazines: in 1983 42 per cent read a weekly magazine (though the most popular ones were the *Radio Times* and *TV Times*); 43 per cent of women read a woman's magazine, as did 9 per cent of men; each copy was read by 3–4 people on average (*Country Life* is read by 21.6 people – mainly in dentists' waiting rooms, no doubt); another 29 per cent read a monthly magazine, of which *Reader's Digest* is the most popular. In the USA most people spend five minutes a day reading magazines, many of them containing romantic stories, success stories, etc.

The average person does not spend much time reading books. Nearly one Britain person in two had not read a book in a four-week period in 1983. However, those who do read books get through quite a lot – 650 million a year borrowed from public libraries alone in Britain, i.e. about 26 each for those who read books at all, apart from books bought or borrowed from others. Among those who are seriously into books the figure is far higher. The books that are borrowed from public libraries are mostly fiction, and the most popular books are about detectives and spies. As Table 4.2 showed, 32 per cent of people expressed great satisfaction with reading – nearly twice as many as for TV, nearly as high as being with friends.

Sport

In 1980 in Britain the percentages of people engaging in outdoor sport over a four-week period were 38 per cent for men, 23 per cent for women. The figures for indoor sports show an even bigger sex difference: 32 per cent of men against 16 per cent of women. The rates are considerably higher for younger people. The most popular sports are shown in Table 4.4, based on a study carried out in 1977; these are the percentages who engaged in each sport, during the last four weeks, and the number of times. The two columns, respectively, give an idea of how many people take part in each sport, and how often they do it: for example, 11 per cent go dancing, and they go three times a month. This does not include gardening, which is a lot more strenuous than darts.

Table 4.4   Participation in sport (UK, 1983)

	Percentage participating during last 4 weeks	*Average number of times in 4 weeks*
walking (2 miles +)	19.0	8
dancing	11.0	3
billiards/snooker	8.0	7
swimming (indoors)	7.2	3
darts	6.9	6
watch football	3.1	3
keep fit/yoga	3.0	6
play football	2.7	5
squash	2.5	4
golf	2.2	5
table tennis	2.2	4
athletics	2.0	8
fishing	2.0	3
cycling	1.8	10
tennis	1.1	4

Source   General Household Survey, 1985.

Among the more energetic 'sports', the most popular are swimming and walking (for both men and women) and football and golf (for men). An increasing number of people are jogging every day in order to keep fit. In the USA it is estimated that as many as 10 per cent of the population engage in regular exercise of some kind in order to keep fit or lose weight. However, many of those who start by jogging switch to some other form of exercise like swimming or tennis (Bammel and Bammel, 1982).

Just as people watch TV because it is convenient, so they will take more exercise if the facilities are readily available. It was found in a British study that people were three times as likely to visit a park if it was within a quarter of a mile of where they lived, than if it was between a half and three-quarters of a mile (Burton, 1971).

Only a minority take part in active sports, and these are mainly younger persons. For those who do, this is clearly a source of great satisfaction. Table 4.2 showed that 26 per cent reported great satisfaction with sport – higher than watching TV (17 per cent). In addition a lot of people watch and take a great interest in sport, especially football. As a commentator on the American scene wrote:

> Each morning the American seats himself at the breakfast table, glances at the headlines in his newspaper, and turns quickly to the sports page. . . . He performs his weekly tasks in perfunctory manner, but when it comes time for sports he comes alive and is transformed by his enthusiasm. Perhaps ours is more nearly the sporting nation than an affluent nation, a capitalist country, a political democracy, or anything else.
>
> (Beisser, 1967, pp. 226–7)

Attending football matches, and to a lesser extent cricket matches, is a major leisure activity: about 8 per cent of men watch football regularly. Football fans are particularly enthusiastic, and this is clearly a very important part of their lives (Marsh, Rosser and Harré, 1978).

Home-based leisure

'Leisure and family life are thoroughly interwoven' (Roberts, 1981, p. 71). Diary studies show that well over half of adults' spare time is spent in or around the home, though a lot of domestic activities are regarded as mixed work and leisure (Young and Wilmott, 1973). Some of the main leisure activities are pursued in the home; we have already discussed TV, radio and reading. The rates of participation in Britain, over a four-week period in 1983, for a number of others are shown in Table 4.5.

Table 4.5 Home-based leisure

	men %	women %
gardening	50	39
games of skill	20	15 (for 1980)
needlework/knitting	2	48
house repairs/DIY	51	24
hobbies	11	3 (1980)
reading books	50	61
listening to records/tapes	65	62

Source *Social Trends*, 1985.

Many women have very little leisure – those with jobs and children for example. They spend more time in the house, and most of their leisure is there. Some housework is regarded as being partly leisure – shopping and cooking, looking after pets and plants. Women watch TV more than men, and do knitting and needle-work; men do more gardening and DIY.

A major home-based activity is looking after children, which is a combination of work and leisure. Some of it is more like leisure (going to the zoo, playing games); sometimes it is work (e.g. feeding infants in the middle of the night). It has effects on the whole pattern of life, including making other leisure activities less accessible.

At some ages, people spend more time at home. Young couples with small children, often with little money to spare, have limited leisure, which tends to be home based. In middle age, when children have become independent or left home, few take the opportunity to expand their leisure. Some become active in church, politics or social clubs, or go out for meals or concerts, but more simply stay at home. After retirement, despite the need to replace work with something with similar rewards, most older people spend more time at home and watching TV, though for some there is an increase in gardening and reading (Rapaport and Rapaport, 1975).

SOCIAL LEISURE

A great deal of leisure is spent partly or primarily in the company of other people. There are considerable differences between the sexes, however. Outside the home women see friends and relatives more, go to church, dancing and bingo, but go drinking less than men. There are also differences in the patterns of social leisure at different ages. Adolescents and young people engage in the greatest variety of leisure outside the home, experimenting with different activities and relationships, especially with the opposite sex. The main forms of social leisure at all ages for a four-week period in Britain in 1983 are shown in Table 4.6.

In addition a lot of sport is social – it can take two or 22 to play. TV is partly social too, though the level of social interaction drops a lot while people are watching. Home-based activities usually involve some co-operation, e.g. over gardening and DIY. The

Table 4.6   Social forms of leisure

	men %	women %
visiting/entertaining relatives and friends	90	93 (1980)
going out for a drink	64	46
going out for a meal	41	40
dancing	10	12

Source   Social Trends, 1985.

survey reported in Table 4.2 found that greatest satisfaction came from contact with family and friends.

A lot of social leisure involves drinking – in pubs and clubs, and in homes, as Table 4.7 shows (using British data for the 1980s). A lot of men, especially young men, can be classified as 'heavy drinkers', that is they have seven or more drinks once a week or several times a week. Data in Table 4.7 are for a four-week period in 1981.

Table 4.7   Drinking habits

	men %	women %
evenings spent in drink-associated activities, e.g. going to pub	13	3 (1977)
went out for a drink in the last 4 weeks	64	45 (1980)
heavy drinkers (7 glasses once a week or more)		
aged 18–24	35	5
25–44	29	2
45–65	16	1

Sources   General Household Survey, 1982; *Social Trends*, 1983.

Clubs, classes and voluntary work

Some of the most serious and organized leisure is carried out in clubs or other groups. This is theoretically interesting since some of it is rather like work, except that it is unpaid, and evidently done because it is satisfying for its own sake. It is a kind of work which receives no external rewards, only intrinsic rewards, including social ones. A lot of people do voluntary work, 'unpaid work of service to others apart from immediate family and friends': 25 per cent of British adults did some, about 10 per cent once a week or more in 1984. There are big class differences: professional-class females are most active (48 per cent), for organizations like the British Legion, Women's Institutes, Mothers' Union, Citizens Advice Bureau, the St John's Ambulance and the Samaritans. The main recipients are children, teenagers, the elderly and the sick and disabled. Some studies of the needs met by leisure include 'service to others' – this appears in Havighurst's list (1961), but not in Kabanoff's (1982).

Many people belong to social or sporting clubs: 53 per cent of employed men belong to one, and 16 per cent are officers (Young and Wilmott, 1973). The percentages of the population who had attended clubs of different kinds during a four-week period in 1977 are given in Table 4.8. The 'clubs and societies' include sporting and purely social clubs. Cultural activities, like music and drama, and evening classes, can also be regarded as clubs. So can church, though of course it is more than a club. A very popular activity in Britain is bingo, played by 22 per cent of working-class women.

Table 4.8   Participation in clubs of various kinds

	Population participating in most popular quarter %	Days per month in most active quarter
voluntary work	9.6	5.6
amateur music and drama	3.7	9.9
leisure classes	3.1	2.4
clubs and societies	12.3	3.6
bingo	9.3	5.6
religion	about 13% attended church weekly	

Source   Birch, 1979.

Holidays

About 39 per cent of British people do not have a holiday each year. In recent years 38 per cent had one holiday, and 20 per cent had two or more in 1984. Sixty-eight per cent of these holidays were in Britain, the remainder mostly in Spain and France. The most common places to stay were hotels, followed by friends' or relatives' houses, camping and caravanning, rented accommodation and holiday camps. Most were taken in the months June –September. The most typical length of a holiday in Britain was between four and seven nights; those abroad averaged fifteen nights.

A survey of over 10,000 readers of the American journal *Psychology Today* (a very large but rather odd sample) produced further information about holidays. Most people went with family or a friend, most wanted primarily to relax, though women wanted to indulge themselves, as did some men. The workaholics were eager to return to work (Rubenstein, 1980).

In addition many people go for day trips, to visit friends, fairs or shows, parks, zoos, the seaside or historic buildings – 593 million such trips in 1982.

SOCIAL CLASS

There are quite extensive class differences in leisure, as are shown in Figure 4.3, which shows patterns in the numbers participating in leisure activities in the previous four weeks, averaged over the year. The number given in brackets is the average percentage of respondents of all ages who pursued these activities. As the figure shows, professional people and non-manual workers, but not employers or managers, engage in more leisure activities of most kinds, especially active sports, hobbies, outings and cultural pursuits. Some of these differences are quite large: examples of the ratios of participation rates for male non-manual to male manual workers aged 30 to 59 are as follows:

squash	6:6
tennis	4:1
golf	3:2
swimming	2:2
leisure classes	2:7
social and voluntary work	2:0

(Birch, 1979)

Some leisure activities are more popular among working-class

Figure 4.3   Men's leisure activities by socio-economic group

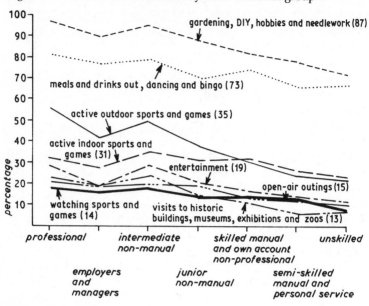

Source   Birch, 1979.

people, including bingo, darts, betting/football pools, billiards and snooker. Above all, working-class people watch more TV, 20 hours a week compared with 15 for middle-class people. Twenty per cent of unskilled workers enjoy TV more than any other leisure activity, while almost none in other social classes say this (Young and Wilmott, 1973).

Part of the reason for the greater leisure activity of middle-class people is that they have more money. They also have more space and facilities in their houses, and they have cars to get them to leisure facilities. Later we will consider how far leisure is a reaction to or a continuation of work, and shall conclude that for most people it is not a reaction to work. So what is the further explanation of these class differences? It looks as if there are simply cultural differences between classes, partly due to money and facilities, but partly due to historical factors and different attitudes and values. The result is that only certain leisure activities are acceptable in each social class.

The upper and middle classes of earlier times valued leisure above work, indeed many of them did no work at all. Veblen, in his famous *Theory of the Leisure Class* (1899), showed how rich people engaged in conspicuous consumption and time-wasting, to show that they had no need to work, and had plenty of money and time to burn.

Working-class youth today provide another example of such cultural processes. In the Britain of the 1980s, some of their popular leisure activities include dressing up as punks, skinheads, football hooligans, etc., and engaging in noisy and sometimes aggressive group activities. Sociologists have interpreted this in terms of group attempts to solve the difficulties which each group faces, and the development of symbols which express rejection of the established order, and help to provide a sense of identity. One explanation that has been put forward is that

> the Teddy Boy sub-culture can be 'read' as the theft of an upper-class style to celebrate heavy working-class masculinity; that skinheads' rolled-up jeans, cropped hair, industrial boots and preoccupation with 'trouble' can be understood as an attempt to recover and assert the virtues of the traditional working class community; that the mods' cool style with neat suits and pointed shoes can be interpreted as expropriating the consumption ethic, and extracting individuals from their true class locations. (Roberts, 1983, p. 121)

Some of these ideas were confirmed in a study of the clothes worn by football supporters. They saw boots and jeans as symbolizing toughness; scarves and flags stood for loyalty to the supporters' group (Marsh and Harré, 1978).

WHY DO PEOPLE ENGAGE IN LEISURE ACTIVITIES?

In other words, why do people watch TV, play sports and see their friends, instead of either working all the time, or going to sleep? Why do they engage in these particular activities? I shall consider the theories for which there is the best evidence.

There have been many investigations of the needs that leisure activities may satisfy, and there is no agreed conclusion as yet. The list of leisure needs has been extended and refined in a number of studies. In the following one 11 needs were used, with two items for each; the average ratings of satisfaction for each item are given in Table 4.9. The study was carried out in 1980 on 210 people living in Adelaide, fairly representative of the city's population. The list in the table suggests what the 'intrinsic' motivation for leisure may consist of: 'doing your own thing'; relaxing; getting away from things; excitement; using skills; and keeping fit.

Table 4.9   Different leisure needs

leisure needs	items	item means
1 autonomy	organize own projects and activities	2.78
	do things you find personally meaningful	3.39
2 relaxation	relax and take it easy	3.20
	give mind and body a rest	2.94
3 family activity	bring family closer together	2.81
	enjoy family life	3.30
4 escape from routine	get away from responsibilities of everyday life	2.85
	have a change from daily routine	3.12
5 interaction	make new friends	2.35
	enjoy people's company	2.55
6 stimulation	to have new and different experiences	2.66
	for excitement and stimulation	2.89
7 skill utilization	use skills and abilities	2.89
	develop new skills and abilities	2.61
8 health	keep physically fit	2.47
	for health reasons	2.46
9 esteem	gain respect or admiration of others	2.11
	show others what you're capable of	2.15
10 challenge/ competition	be involved in competition	1.87
	test yourself in difficult or demanding situations	2.31
11 leadership/ social power	organize activities of teams, groups, organizations	1.79
	to gain positions of leadership	1.48

Source   Kabanoff, 1982.

Later we shall present the theory that there are two contrasting motivational states: goal-directed and seeking satisfaction from the activity itself (p. 131). Much leisure is of the second kind, but goals are chosen 'to act as an excuse for the activity, an end-point for it, a way of structuring it, or a way of enhancing it' (Apter, personal communication).

Use and development of skills

Intrinsic motivation for leisure is particularly striking for those who are deeply into absorbing activities like rock-climbing, chess and disco-dancing which demand a great deal of effort and energy. Csikszentmihalyi (1975) found that the most satisfying elements were enjoyment of the experience and use of skills, the activity itself (the pattern, the action, the world it provides), and development of personal skills. Similar conclusions came from a sociological study of amateurs in drama, archeology and baseball, who were found to be deeply devoted to a disciplined and demanding form of activity which was the very opposite of relaxing (Stebbins, 1979). In addition to the expressive satisfaction obtained, there was gratification from the close social ties established, and in the social identity created. We shall discuss social ties and identity later, but in these instances they appear to be closely linked with the use of skills and the attainment of a high level of competence.

Satisfaction from use and development of skills is similar to the 'intrinsic motivation' experienced by people who really enjoy their work: a meaningful task is completed, over which they have some autonomy; it has a significant effect on others; and they are able to use their skills successfully.

Included in the factor is the desire to develop skills, ability and knowledge – a design for growth, enjoying facing a certain amount of challenge. This was a central part of Maslow's theory of motivation (1968): when lower needs have been satisfied, including social needs, a rather weak motivation for growth and 'self-actualization' begins to operate. Havighurst (1961) found that 'new experience', 'chance to be creative', and 'chance to achieve something' were common reasons given for leisure activities, and the Adelaide survey found similar factors (Table 4.9). This is reminiscent of the need for growth and the desire for more complex and demanding jobs found in some people at work (p. 35f).

This factor of skill use and development could explain some of the main varieties of leisure. Sport and exercise are about the use and development of bodily skills and fitness. Many hobbies and intellectual interests are about mental or artistic skills. A study of holidaymakers found that one of their main motivations was 'self-discovery' or 'personal growth', particularly for young people going to remote places (Pearce, 1982).

Social motivation

Every study of leisure motivation or satisfaction has found that a social-motivation factor is one of the main components. It includes contact with family, friends and the opposite sex, and it involves being able to help others, and being powerful as well as affiliative. Sometimes it is given as the most important reason for leisure activities, or as one of the most important. In at least one large-scale study the social component was the best predictor of overall leisure satisfaction ($r = .33$), and was best predicted from satisfaction with things done with friends ($r = .48$) (Crandall, Nolan and Morgan, 1980). Being engaged in co-operative projects is a major source of life satisfaction (Palys and Little, 1983). We saw that TV-watching is usually done with the family; it may also provide imaginary or 'parasocial' interaction with characters and presenters, and provides a major topic of conversation at work and with friends (p. 72).

Holidays are greatly affected by the social factor. Most people go on holidays with spouse, family or friends, and one of the main reasons they go is to visit friends or relatives (Pearce, 1982).

But what do people actually *do* together? Primarily other people provide companionship – someone to share experiences and activities with, to talk to, help solve problems, act as partner in games. As we saw earlier, other people are necessary for fun. People also eat and drink together. They have meals together at home, or they go out to eat. They go to the park with members of the family, they play games with groups of friends (Cheek and Burch, 1976). They drink together: nearly all the drinking which was shown in Table 4.7 is also social activity.

Identity and self-presentation

Providing a sense of identity and self-esteem is a source of job satisfaction which became evident from studies of the unemployed (p. 61f). It is also a component of leisure satisfaction, for example Havighurst's 'chance to achieve something' and 'self-respect' (1961), and Kabanoff's 'gain respect or admiration of others' and 'test yourself in difficult or demanding situations' (1982) (see Table 4.9). There are two factors here: establishing and augmenting the self-image or identity, and displaying it to others, i.e. self-presentation. If it is accepted by others, this reinforces the self-image.

Leisure activities can do this in several ways, such as:

1 dressing up (for sport, dancing, etc.);
2 acquiring status by holding offices in clubs, or informal status in sporting or other groups, especially by
3 acquiring new skills and competencies (in sport, music, dancing, pottery, etc.);
4 special styles of performance (e.g. dancing, art);
5 expressing distance from common styles, showing individuality;
6 acquiring membership of a special social group; and
7 talking about the activity to outsiders.

> A potter finds meaning not only in the product and in the experience of creating something, but in *being* a potter whose skills are exercised. (Kelly, 1983, p. 119)

These aspects of identity can be tried out in leisure situations, with little commitment or risk, but they may become central life concerns.

Earlier we gave an interpretation of the considerable class differences in leisure activities in terms of different forms of self-presentation, such as conspicuous consumption and other kinds of symbolism. A study of the followers of Musica Viva (i.e. chamber music) in Sydney found that they were a rather self-consciously élite group, proud of their musical sophistication (S. Kippax, lecture at Oxford).

While paid work is the main source of identity for many people, it is not for all, in particular not for the retired, the unemployed, housewives, or those for whom work provides little satisfaction.

Mass forms of leisure do not help to give a sense of identity, with the exception of supporting sports teams, which certainly does. It is the more engrossing and less common forms of leisure that do most for identity: amateur archeology, drama and amateur but high-level sport, for example, especially when public performances are involved (Stebbins, 1979). In fact the number and variety of leisure activities is very large – each meets the needs of a small group and offers a distinctive identity.

Relaxation

All studies of leisure motivation have found that the desire to relax is one of its main components. One scale contained the items 'relax and take it easy' and 'give mind and body a rest'. These had some of the highest ratings as motivations for leisure (see Table 4.9).

Holidays are particularly motivated by the need to relax: 37 per cent gave this motivation, the highest number, in the *Psychology Today* survey (Rubenstein, 1980). If people are asked why they watch TV, 60 per cent say 'entertainment or relaxation', 41 per cent 'because it's a pleasant way to spend an evening' (Comstock *et al.*, 1978); 46 per cent 'because I feel like watching television'; and 27 per cent 'because there's nothing else to do at the time' (Bower, 1973). However, TV-watching may work in the opposite direction as well, to provide stimulation for people when they are bored. Several theories of play have suggested that the function of play is to control the level of arousal, either by increasing or reducing it. Certain drugs, like nicotine, can also do this. Perhaps TV is like a drug in being able to help us achieve an optimal level of arousal. An American experiment induced different moods, after which subjects could choose between different programmes to watch. Those who were bored chose to watch exciting programmes, and this had the effect of increasing their level of arousal. Those who had been stressed chose relaxing and exciting programmes equally, and each reduced their level of arousal (Bryant and Zillman, 1984).

The need to relax or otherwise is partly produced by the experience of work. We turn later to theories of leisure as a reaction to work.

The creation of leisure worlds

There are other motivations for leisure, such as those listed in Table 4.9. However, I think that there is a further important component, hinted at in the item: 'The activity itself, the pattern, the action, *the world it provides*' (my italics).

We started this chapter with a quotation about the joys of gardening, but we have not really explained why people enjoy it. It is not very sociable, apart from chats over the garden fence. It is relaxing perhaps, but also hard work. It does involve the use of a variety of skills and the development of expertise. But it is a lot more; it is a world of its own, an enduring interest and concern. It also includes some of those sources of joy described in Chapter 7, of simply being in the garden on a nice afternoon.

Let us take another example: Scottish country dancing. This is very social, it involves the use and development of skills, and is relaxing in the sense that tensions can be discharged. It is in addition a complete world of its own, with special costumes and rituals, and it includes the arousal of a great deal of joy, partly through the music.

A similar story could be told about almost every leisure world – sailing, skiing, horse-riding, ballroom dancing, greyhound racing, pigeon fancying, video games, ham radio and so on.

LEISURE AS A REACTION TO WORK

We have seen that leisure provides forms of satisfaction very similar to some of those provided by work. In addition it is a source of some quite different ones. We have already discussed relaxation. In addition there are Kabanoff's needs 'to escape from routine' and for 'stimulation' (1982) (see Table 4.9).

In most simpler societies there is no clear distinction between work and leisure, there are no defined periods of leisure, and there is a lot of singing and story-telling at work (Thomas, 1964). Leisure, as opposed to work, has often been said to have started or become more salient in Britain from the time of the Industrial Revolution, when people started to work in factories, for set hours, often under unpleasant conditions. It was Engels who first proposed that leisure is a kind of compensation for work. Leisure certainly became separated from work, and became confined to non-work time for most people (see Pahl, 1984).

Figure 4.4   Leisure activities by age and sex

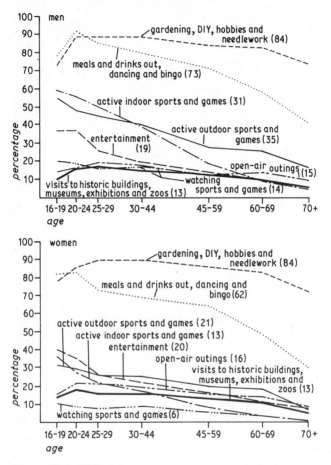

How far is leisure a reaction to or compensation for work, or deliberately unlike work? It has been found that unskilled manual workers are tired, and want to relax and watch TV at the end of the day; deep-water fishermen and some construction workers seek 'explosive compensation' for their demanding work, in drinking, fighting, drugs and promiscuous sex; advertising men and dentists play a lot of sport, perhaps to relax. The compensation pattern seems to apply most to those whose work is either very stressful, or boring and unsatisfying, and to uneducated manual workers (Parker, 1983). However, studies of the overall importance of compensation in leisure suggest that this is the main goal for only 5 per cent of people, and a secondary goal for 25 per cent (Kelly, 1983).

The opposite theory is that work spills over into leisure. People may take up leisure activities similar to their work – farm workers doing gardening, bank managers being treasurers of clubs, intellectuals reading or writing books. For some people work spreads into their leisure: social workers, managers, academics, writers and artists not only take their work home, and mix their work and leisure, but for them there is no clear distinction between the two – as before the Industrial Revolution. They have no set hours of work, they work at weekends and while on holiday, and mix their social life with work. Businessmen have a lot of social life at work, which could also be regarded as leisure. Colleagues become friends, work and leisure are seen as similar, and one of the main motivations for leisure is a desire for personal growth and development (Kabanoff, 1980; Parker, 1983). For many of these people work is very satisfying because it has some of the characteristics of leisure: a large measure of freedom and autonomy, being able to do jobs at their own speed and in their own way, and being in some sense the owner of the product. It is a mistake to call them 'workaholics', since they are really at play as well.

However, the spillover theory accounts for only a small proportion of leisure, and a third theory is that leisure is quite independent of work. This theory has gained ground in recent years as a result of the relative failure of attempts to predict leisure activities from occupational variables. For many people, perhaps the majority, work and leisure are simply unrelated; they are different, but not deliberately so. This is found for bank and clerical workers, for example, who quite enjoy their work, but are not deeply committed to it as the second group are: '(they) are neither so engrossed in their work that they want to carry it over into non-work time, nor so damaged by it that they develop a hostile or love–hate relation to it' (Parker, 1983, p. 91). Their colleagues are less likely to become friends, and the main function of leisure is entertainment, though for some of them leisure may become more important and more satisfying than work.

Conclusions

Leisure is more important and more satisfying than work for many people. It is a major source of life satisfaction.

The main forms of leisure are watching TV, other media, sport, home-based activities, social life, clubs, classes and voluntary work, and holidays. Middle-class people engage in more and different leisure activities.

Leisure is a source of satisfaction because it becomes intrinsically motivating, through the use and development of skills, provides social satisfaction, identity, relaxation, and it can be a reaction to work or a spillover from it.

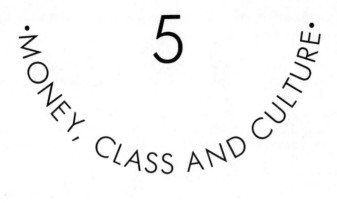

5
MONEY, CLASS AND CULTURE

Are richer people happier, and do they have better health or other aspects of well-being? It might be generally assumed that the answer is 'yes', but the detailed answer to this question is of considerable theoretical, and indeed political, interest. As before, we will look at different aspects of well-being one by one.

Happiness and satisfaction

American studies have considered the separate effects of income, education and occupation, while British studies have usually studied the effects of social class, which is highly correlated with income, but is mainly based on occupation. This scale is used by the British Census for classifying occupations.

I *Professional, etc.*, e.g. accountant, architect, chemist, company secretary, doctor, engineer, judge, lawyer, optician, scientist, solicitor, surveyor, university teacher;

II *Intermediate*, e.g. aircraft pilot or engineer, chiropodist, farmer, laboratory assistant or technician, manager, proprietor, publican, member of parliament, nurse, police or fire-brigade officer, schoolteacher;

III(N) Skilled non-manual, e.g. auctioneer, cashier, clerical worker, commercial traveller, draughtsman, estate agent, sales representative, secretary, shop assistant, typist, telephone supervisor;

III(M) Skilled manual, e.g. baker, bus driver, butcher, bricklayer, carpenter, cook, electrician, fireman, hairdresser, miner (underground), policeman, railway engine driver/guard, upholsterer;

IV Partly skilled, e.g. agricultural worker, barman, bus conductor, fisherman, hospital orderly, machine sewer, packer, postman, roundsman, street vendor, telephone operator;

V Unskilled, e.g. charwoman, chimney sweep, kitchen hand, labourer, lorry driver's mate, office cleaner, railway porter, van guard, window cleaner.   Reid, 1980.

A recent British study, using a similar classification system, found class differences in how pleased people felt with things yesterday (see Table 5.1). The main difference is that more of those in the lowest two classes did not feel very pleased with things yesterday, though the differences are quite small. Similar results are found in other countries including India, Cuba, Israel, Brazil and others (Cantril, 1965).

An American study in 1983–84 found that income made more difference to positive than to negative affect, and that the positive effects were more marked at the upper end of the income range, while the reduction of negative affect was more marked at the lower end. See Table 5.2, in which positive and negative affect are reports of extent of good and bad moods, on scales from 0 to 1.

Table 5.1 Class differences in feeling 'very pleased with things yesterday'

	classes		
	ABC1	C2	DE
all or most of the time	60	62	55
just a little of the time or not at all	12	15	23

Source Warr and Payne, 1982.

Table 5.2 Income and happiness

income	positive affect	negative affect
less than $2,000	.32	.56
$2,000–$2,999	.40	.58
$3,000–$3,999	.39	.54
$4,000–$4,999	.38	.51
$5,000–$5,999	.46	.52
$6,000–$6,999	.45	.52
$7,000–$7,999	.46	.53
$8,000–$9,999	.50	.49
$10,000–$14,999	.52	.46
$15,000 or more	.57	.46

Source Bradburn, 1969.

There is evidence that money can reduce distress, for instance caused by cold or hunger, and it can add to joy, for example by making possible expensive forms of leisure.

Those people who have larger incomes are a little more satisfied with their incomes, their standard of living and so on, than other people. However, this is a surprisingly weak relationship – corresponding to a correlation of .15 or .20, or less in different studies (Campbell, Converse and Rodgers, 1976; Liang and Fairchild, 1979; Michaelos, 1980). And in the *Quality of American Life* study, people rated their financial situation as one of the least important factors affecting their overall satisfaction with life (Campbell, Converse and Rodgers, 1976). Money does not make people happy, or at any rate it has a very small effect (much less than that of social relationships, for example). So what does make people feel satisfied with their incomes?

The first clue to the solution to this problem came from an earlier British study by Runciman (1966) who found that manual workers, in the top third of all salaries, were more satisfied with their pay than non-manual workers at the same salary level. The explanation was that manual workers compared themselves with other manual workers, not with the better-paid non-manual workers. More recent studies have shown that satisfaction with pay, housing and other domains depends more on comparisons with what other people have, and on comparisons with own past experience, than on the actual amount of pay received. This will be pursued further in Chapter 8.

To test the effects of extreme wealth, an American survey was carried out on 49 people, most of them earning over $10 million a year, who were compared with 62 people chosen at random from the same areas (controls). Some of the differences are shown in Table 5.3, which includes average scores for the very rich and the controls, on a number of different self-rating scales. It can be seen that the very rich people scored a little higher on a number of measures of happiness, and were quite a lot lower on negative affect.

Richer people are also more interested in money and score higher on a factor of obsessional concern with it ('I firmly believe that money can solve all of my problems', 'I worry about my finances much of the time', 'I put money ahead of pleasure', etc.), and on a factor of seeing money as power ('I sometimes buy things that I don't need or want to impress people because they are the right things to have at the time', 'I sometimes buy friendship by being generous with those I want to like me', etc.) (Furnham, 1984a).

It seems likely that those who are very poor will be unhappy, and from within-country studies this is found to be the case. However, as we shall see later, there is very little difference in the levels of reported happiness found in rich and very poor countries, e.g. Japan *v*. India, North America *v*. South America (p. 103f).

There is quite a lot of evidence that the effect of income on happiness is decreasing. For instance, it has become weaker in the USA over recent years. This may be because most people in

Table 5.3 Happiness of the very rich

	very rich	*controls*
% of the time happy	77	62
life satisfaction	4.77	3.70
positive affect	15.35	13.97
negative affect	4.92	7.65
self-esteem	.66	.46
self-actualization	.71	.55

Source Diener *et al.* 1985.

Table 5.4   The effects of income and education on happiness

education	income		
	less than $5000	$5000 –7999	$8000 or more
less than high school graduate	.35	.44	.52
high school graduate	.47	.47	.56
some college	.51	.53	.55

Source   Bradburn, 1969.

the USA are now quite well off materially (Campbell, 1981). On the other hand there are marked differences between the top 25 per cent and the next 25 per cent in most of the surveys of income and happiness, so there is still some effect of income. None the less, for better-educated people the effect of income on happiness is considerably reduced. See Table 5.4, which uses Bradburn's 'affect balance' scale based on the difference between the positive and negative mood items.

Finally, the effect of income on happiness seems to be less for younger people than for the old. This could be because older people are harder up, or because they belong to an earlier generation which was more concerned about money.

To sum up, class and income have a definite, but quite small effect on happiness. This effect appears to be decreasing over time, at least in the USA, and is less for the young and for the better educated.

Education is another component of social status. Data are available from the USA, where the separate effects of education and income have been examined. Education has a stronger effect for the less well off. Among people with high incomes education appears to make no difference to happiness, but for those with low incomes it does. It has been suggested that among this second group

> the educational experience and occupational advantages of college graduates have freed them in part from the demands of purely material needs, and broadened their concern with values relating to social relationships and self-evaluation.
>
> (Campbell, 1981, p. 65)

US data suggest that people with more education are happier than those with less, and this effect also has decreased over time. In 1957 44 per cent of college graduates and 23 per cent of those who had not been to high school in the USA were 'very happy'. In 1978 the corresponding figures were 33 per cent and 28 per cent (Campbell, 1981).

Income and social class affect other domains of satisfaction in several ways.

Work

In Chapter 3 we looked at job satisfaction in detail. Occupational status is another determinant of happiness, though it is compounded with income and education. Generally speaking those in the better paid and more prestigious jobs are happier. However there are different components of job satisfaction, and some jobs, while satisfying, can also be very stressful, or require very long hours of work, as in the case of doctors, senior managers and people with their own businesses. Nevertheless the social status of jobs is an important source of job satisfaction, independently of either pay or the nature of work.

Leisure

In Chapter 4 we showed that there are considerable class differences in the use of leisure. Middle-class people are more active in most kinds of leisure, especially sport, hobbies and cultural pursuits, though working-class people watch more TV. It follows that those of greater social status or wealth obtain quite a lot more satisfaction from leisure.

Social relationships

In an earlier book (Argyle and Henderson, 1985) it was shown that there are a number of class differences here. More middle-class people are happily married, they have closer friendships, and their work relations spill over into social life more. Working-class people on the other hand see more of their relatives, since they often live nearer, and they know more of their neighbours. Middle-class people belong to more clubs and organizations, and are more likely to be officers in them. On balance, middle-class people receive more support from their social net-works.

The self

As Table 5.3 shows, the very rich have somewhat higher levels of self-esteem and self-actualization than other people. Other sur-veys, of the normal range of wealth, have not found much effect of wealth on self-esteem, though they have found that education does have an effect (Veroff, Douvan and Kulka, 1981). The unemployed have low self-esteem (see Chapter 3), as do those with alternative life-styles, most of whom are fairly poor (Ginandes, 1977).

The effects of changes in wealth

It does not need to be proved that when people lose their jobs, or become worse off in some other way, this make them unhappy. But what about those who become better off? This can be disrup-tive too, especially if a large and sudden change in way of life is involved, as with winning the football pools. A study of 191 British pools winners, all of whom won £160,000 or more, found that many of them claimed to be a little happier than before, but there were some quite serious problems too. There was hostility and envy from neighbours and relatives; the winners were pestered with requests for money; those who moved house encountered snobbish rejection by middle-class neighbours; and some were more lonely, as a result of giving up work (70 per cent) and moving house. At any rate, they had better houses, cars and holidays (Smith and Razzell, 1975), but it is far from clear how many were really more satisfied with life. An American study of twenty-two winners of large lotteries found no clear difference between their happiness and that of controls (p. 153).

Many repeated surveys have been carried out in the USA since 1946. Despite continually rising prosperity, there were consider-able fluctuations in the percentage of those who said they were 'very happy'. In 1946–47 the percentage was 38–9 per cent, in the late 1950s it rose to 53 per cent, falling in 1971–74 to 27 per cent, and rising to 35 per cent in the late 1970s (Easterlin, 1974; Smith, 1979). There appears to be very little relationship with economic prosperity when we look at such changes over time, although there is a small positive relationship if rich and poor are compared at the same point in time.

An American study compared survey responses from 1957 and 1976. It found that there was an increase in anxiety, in self-awareness and self-expression, and a shift from integration with organizations to a concern with interpersonal intimacy (Veroff, Douvan and Kulka, 1981). It is not clear how far these changes are due to increased prosperity or education in the USA. Education can create wider horizons and aspirations, as well as more self-awareness and introspection. Greater wealth can lead to the removal of material worries, but perhaps the focus of worry shifts to personal and interpersonal problems, which cannot be solved by money (see p. 99).

Strain and mental disorder

A recent British study found that 11 per cent of people in the top three social classes reported unpleasant emotional strain for about half of the time or more yesterday, compared with 14 per cent in the bottom two classes (Warr and Payne, 1982); American surveys of negative affect show similar class differences (Bradburn, 1969) (see Table 5.5). There is also a tendency for poor

Table 5.5   Class differences in strain and worry

UK	class		
	ABC1	C2	DE
reported unpleasant emotional strain yesterday: most or all of the time	7	8	14
had experienced strain for more than a month		14.5	23.5

USA	education		
	college	high school	grade school
worry a lot	30	38	40
feelings of impending nervous breakdown	16	19	20

Sources   Bradburn, 1969; Warr and Payne, 1982.

people to worry about problems which are soluble, and for richer people to worry about insoluble problems – like satisfaction with self and interpersonal problems (Lane, 1983).

We turn now to class differences in minor degrees of mental disorder. In Britain 4 per cent of employed men in classes I and II have to take time off each year because of mental troubles, compared with 13 per cent in social class V (Reid, 1981). An Australian study found that there were fewer high scorers on the General Health Questionnaire in social class I (9.7 per cent) than in classes V (19.8 per cent) or VI (17.0 per cent) (Finlay-Jones and Burrill, 1977). A recent American study looked at the separate effects of income, education and job status. For men the best predictor of symptoms of mental disorder was (low) income, while for women it was (lack of) education. Income was important for the self-esteem of men, but not for women (Kessler, 1982).

Many studies in Britain, the USA and elsewhere have found that there are much higher rates of schizophrenia, depression, alcoholism, drug addiction and crime among the working classes. Middle-class people, on the other hand, are more prone to anxiety disorders and psychotic affective disorders (Dohrenwend, 1975). One of the best-known studies of depression was carried out among women in London (Brown and Harris, 1978). It was found that working-class women were much more depressed than middle-class women, especially if they had young children at home (see Figure 5.1 and p. 119f).

What is the explanation for the higher levels of strain and mental disorder among working-class people? One possibility is that they are under greater stress. While very little class difference has been found in the frequency of stressful life events, there are greater everyday difficulties of life for working-class people. Health problems in the family, financial problems, drunken husbands, inconvenient hours of work, and so on were cited for 61 per cent of the working-class and 38 per cent of the middle-class women in the Brown and Harris study. However, these difficulties are not sufficient in themselves to explain the class differences in depression, which were due more to other, class-associated factors: lack of a supportive husband, not having a job, early death of own mother and having several young children at home (Brown and Harris, 1978). So part of the explanation for the greater vulnerability of working-class women to stress lies in the

Figure 5.1 Female depression as a function of social class and age of children

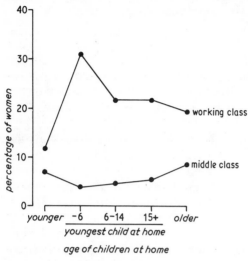

Source Brown and Harris, 1978.

smaller amount of social support they receive, and especially in the availability of a close confidant (Turner and Noh, 1983).

A number of studies have shown that the effect of stressful life events on mental ill-health is greater for working-class people (Liem and Liem, 1978).

One explanation is that working-class people, having fewer resources and less social support, find that they cannot control events, and become fatalistic, prone to learned helplessness. This makes them more likely to become mentally disturbed in the face of stress (Kohn, 1972; Wheaton, 1980). Working-class people are more likely to withdraw – a step towards psychosis; middle-class people are more likely to become anxious – the beginnings of neurosis (Langner and Michael, 1963). One version of the working-class withdrawal theory is that individuals act as if their behaviour at work is nothing to do with their real self, and are more concerned with acceptance by their friends at work than with approval from those in authority. However, this emotional withdrawal makes it more difficult to cope with real problems at work (Sennett and Cobb, 1972).

Table 5.6 shows some American class differences in styles of

Table 5.6 Class differences in ways of coping with worries and unhappy periods

	education		
	college	*high school*	*grade school*
	%	%	%
passive reactions	28	31	41
prayer	11	14	21
direct coping reactions	24	15	8
informal help-seeking	27	32	17

Source Gurin, Veroff and Feld, 1960.

coping. It can be seen that working-class people are much more likely to use passive methods of coping rather than trying to tackle problems directly – partly no doubt because they may not be in a position to do so. The study in Table 5.6 was carried out in 1957; a replication in 1976 found that the use of prayer for coping in the USA had declined quite a lot (Veroff, Douvan and Kulka, 1981). In Britain it has been found that working-class people react to unpleasant emotional strain by smoking more (especially women) and taking medicines, while middle-class people eat more (Warr and Parry, 1982). Working-class people are also more likely to react in an aggressive way, including breaking the law. And, as we shall see in Chapter 10 (p. 188f), they are more likely to express their distress in bodily form, as somatic psychophysiological symptoms such as headaches. The most likely origin of such coping differences is in childhood socialization: there may be class differences in how children are handled, which result in the use of different coping styles. It is certainly possible that working-class styles of child-rearing could lead to more aggressive and more hopeless forms of response to stress (Argyle and Henderson 1985).

A further possible cause of working-class vulnerability is 'downward drift' – that mentally disturbed people drift downwards into less skilled jobs. This has been found to be true for cases of schizophrenia, but not for less severe disorders (Wheaton, 1978).

We now have three possible explanations for the high rate of working-class mental disorders:

1 a higher level of stress or everyday difficulties;
2 childhood socialization, training inappropriate styles of coping, e.g. fatalism and withdrawal; or
3 downward drift.

Various attempts have been made to find out which of these theories is most important, but the present position is that all three processes probably operate (Cochrane, 1983).

Changes in prosperity

One of the main ways in which economic depression is disturbing is through increased unemployment, which was discussed in Chapter 3. Studies of the effects of economic change show that, for most populations, economic depression is followed, after a lag of 3 to 12 months, by an increased rate of suicide, depression and mental-hospital admission. However, the findings are more complicated than this. Working-class men are also upset by increased prosperity, perhaps because others are now seen to be *relatively* better off, perhaps because they are upset by change *per se* (Dooley and Catalano, 1980). However, these increases in mental ill-health may be only apparent, since admissions to hospital increase while symptoms do not. It seems likely that under economic stress families become less willing or less able to support a mentally disturbed and unproductive member (Catalano, Dooley and Jackson, 1981).

NATIONAL, CULTURAL AND RACIAL DIFFERENCES IN WELL-BEING

Which nations are the happiest, and highest in other dimensions of well-being? This is a hard question, since 'happiness' may be conceived of somewhat differently in different cultures, and because it is difficult to construct equivalent forms of measuring instruments.

Happiness and satisfaction

Are people happier or more satisfied in some countries than in others? The most straightforward way of finding out is to carry out surveys asking the same questions. Gallup undertook this task in 1976, and some of the results are shown in Table 5.7. As the author notes, there are some puzzles about these results. Why are the impoverished Latin Americans so satisfied? Why are people in the Far East more satisfied with their standard of housing than Africans, but less satisfied in all other respects? Are Europeans really less happy than Americans and Canadians?

Table 5.7   Percentages 'very happy' in different parts of the world

| | very happy | highly satisfied with | | |
		standard of living	housing	family life
N. America	40	46	55	73
Australia	37	–	–	–
Europe	20	35	49	64
Latin America	32	36	37	60
Africa	18	5	14	18
Far East	7	8	14	18

Source Gallup, 1976.

Surveys of satisfaction and happiness are regularly carried out for the Common Market countries. The most satisfied countries in Europe are Belgium, Denmark and the Netherlands, the least satisfied are France and Italy, according to these surveys (*Euro-Barometre*, 1983).

The trouble with such international surveys is that questions must be translated, and may not have quite the same meaning in other languages. A serious attempt to solve this problem was made by Cantril (1965) using his 'ladder' method (see Figure 1.1, p. 6, for a version of this). People were asked to imagine the 'best possible life' and the 'worst possible life' which they could lead; these were given scores of 10 and 0 on a ladder, and they were asked to say where their present life fell on it. The world average was about 5.0, and some of the national averages are given in Figure 5.2. This study suggests that international differences in happiness are very small, and are almost unrelated to economic prosperity. On the other hand the ladder method probably minimizes differences, since people would think of quite different comparison levels in each country. If you are living in a cardboard box and everyone else lives in a paper bag, you will be

Figure 5.2 Personal happiness and GNP in 14 countries as a function of economic prosperity

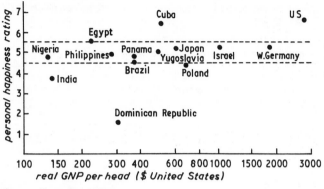

Source Easterlin, 1974.

quite pleased with your house (with acknowledgements to *Monty Python*).

Is it possible to study international differences in well-being more objectively, to get away from problems of translating questions, and cognitive biases and distortions on the part of respondents? There are a number of objective indicators which are relevant to unhappiness. Table 5.8 gives figures for suicides (which will be discussed later), divorce, alcoholism and crime. The 'anxiety' column is a statistical index based on these indicators, which correlate together quite strongly; the neuroticism questionnaire scores were scaled to give Britain a mean of 50 (Lynn, 1982). The least 'anxious' country is Eire, followed by the United Kingdom and New Zealand.

There is also evidence about ethnic differences in happiness within countries. Research inside the USA has found that blacks are lower in subjective well-being than whites. If income, education, occupation, age, and place of residence are held constant there is still a difference, especially for black women, though a smaller one. And blacks aged over 55 are happier than comparable whites (Campbell, Converse and Rodgers, 1976). Between 1952 and 1972, despite rising prosperity, the happiness of both whites and blacks declined, especially for better-off and better-educated blacks, perhaps because their rising aspirations had not been fulfilled (Diener, 1984).

Table 5.8 National differences in happiness and well-being

	satisfaction[1] (self-rated)	happiness[1] (self-rated)	suicide[2] (rates per 100,000)	anxiety[3] (see text)	neuroticism (from Eysenck questionnaires)	divorce (per 1,000 of the population)	alcoholism (deaths from cirrhosis of the liver per 100,000)	crime (number of prisoners in jail per 10,000)
Australia		2.87	11.0	47.6	50.6	6.5	4.8	6.6
Austria			25.7	66.3		11.3	23.3	11.5
Belgium	3.21		19.1	51.7	50.7	5.0	9.5	6.3
Canada		2.89	14.8	50.8		3.9	6.1	9.6
Denmark	3.48		31.6	44.9		14.6	8.4	3.1
Finland			25.2	46.9		8.2	3.3	15.4
France	2.79	2.37	17.2	61.5	54.1	6.6	29.3	5.9
W. Germany	3.00	2.46	20.9	60.9	51.8	8.8	19.0	8.6
Eire	3.21	2.77	4.9	31.4			2.0	1.3
Italy	2.62	2.01	6.4	57.1	50.5		17.3	7.8
Japan			17.6	61.7	53.9	7.4	9.7	7.7
Netherlands	3.33	3.03	10.1	44.5		4.9	3.5	3.4
New Zealand			9.7	44.4		6.9	2.3	7.7
Norway			12.4	45.0		6.6	4.2	4.4
Sweden			19.4	43.0	41.7	12.0	5.1	6.4
Switzerland			25.7	51.5		8.7	11.8	
United Kingdom	3.13	2.65	9.5	40.3	50.0	4.8	2.9	5.8
USA			12.5	51.6	50.1	21.8	11.3	11.8

Sources 1. *Euro-Barometre*, 1983; 2. WHO, 1983; 3. remainder from Lynn, 1982, for year 1960.

It was widely assumed at one time that members of immigrant and racial minority groups would suffer from low self-esteem as a result of their rejection by the wider society. In the USA this has not been found for blacks, who have self-esteem equal to or greater than that of whites. The reason is probably that they are well accepted in their own communities, and fairly insulated from the white majority (Simmons, 1978). The Japanese and Chinese Americans have rather high self-esteem, probably due to their stable families and their social cohesion (Cockerham, 1981). American Indians also have high self-esteem until they come into contact with white urban culture and compete, unsuccessfully, for jobs and income. They then become depressed, anxious, paranoid and alienated (Fuchs and Havighurst, 1973).

Does climate affect happiness? We show later that people are in a better mood on sunny days, and when the temperature is right and it is not too humid. However, research has shown that people adapt to different climates very rapidly, often within 2 to 3 weeks, for example, by perspiring more or getting tanned (Hobbs, 1980). And there is no evidence that people who live in more favourable climates are happier. It looks as if this is a case of adaptation (p. 152f), and climate has little or no effect on happiness.

Strain and mental disorder

It is very difficult to compare rates of mental disorders across cultures, because any given disorder takes a somewhat different form in different places. This was found to be the case with depression. It seems very likely that depression occurs in all cultures. Its origins are partly biological, partly from universal experiences such as loss of social bonds. The facial expression of sadness is also universal. However, the experience and symptoms of depression vary. One of the main findings is that in Africa and in most of India the suicide rate is very low, and ideas of guilt or sin are unknown. It has sometimes been reported that apparently depressed patients do not report depression, sadness or sense of inadequacy. However, recent studies, using the Present State Examination (p. 10f), *have* found evidence of depression, though not of guilt or suicidal ideas (Binitie, 1975).

What many African patients do have on the other hand are *bodily* feelings of tiredness and weakness, headaches, loss of appetite, insomnia, and a loss of interest in sexual or social activity. The situation is changing, however, and educated and westernized Africans are more willing to describe their condition in psychological rather than bodily terms (Marsella, 1980). It has been suggested that depressed Africans feel guilty and depressed only if they have come into contact with Jewish and Christian ideas (Littlewood and Lipsedge, 1982).

However, recent surveys of the evidence have concluded that there are some constant features of depression: sadness, disturbed sleep, fatigue, feelings of emptiness of life, and loss of interests (Singer, 1984). A number of cross-cultural studies point to the conclusion that depression is higher in western cultures. Feelings of guilt and concern with sin used to be more widespread in Britain and Europe than they are now, but they remain particularly strong among some groups, especially Jews and Protestants. Czechs, Swedes and Germans have particularly high rates of depression. It has been suggested that depression is less common in cultures with extended families, or with high levels of social cohesion (Marsella, 1980).

One major index of depression is the suicide rate. The World Health Organization publishes national suicide rates, and the latest figures for a number of countries are shown in Table 5.8. The main weakness of these figures is that suicide rates are known to be under-reported in Catholic and Moslem countries, and indeed may be as much as three times the official statistics (Stengel, 1964). Nevertheless there are still quite high suicide rates in several largely Catholic countries, such as Austria, Belgium and France. It can be seen from this table that suicide rates are very high in all of Eastern and Central Europe – West Berlin, Austria, Switzerland, Finland, Czechoslovakia and West Germany – perhaps reflecting the political uncertainties in those countries. The only country in that area with a lower rate is Poland, which is mainly Catholic. South America, which is also Catholic, comes out very low. Of the non-Catholic countries, Britain, the USA and Australia come out quite low.

While Catholicism probably reduces the rate of suicide, there are some cultures – including the Japanese – which may encourage it, by promoting the belief that under certain conditions suicide is a sure route to heaven. However, a problem with using suicide as an index of distress is that the suicide rate is *greater* in countries which are prosperous (r = .59), and in the same country during prosperous periods (Lester, 1984). Perhaps this is further evidence that wealth does not make people happy; or it may be because during times of prosperity the differences between people become greater and those who are doing badly become more distressed (Henry and Short, 1954).

One of the most extensive sources of international data on mental health comes from the use of the Eysenck Neuroticism scale in different countries. These have been collated by Lynn (1981; 1982) and the national averages calculated. A high percentage of those tested were students, which is probably a good thing for purposes of comparison. The main weakness with the data is that although the numbers involved are large, the samples were not particularly representative. Of course, this method overlooks cultural variations in the form neurosis takes. Despite doubts over the validity of the scale, or of its translations into other languages and cultures, however, this is a unique set of data. Some of the results were shown in Table 5.8, column 5. The neuroticism scores for several other countries not included in Table 5.8 are of interest (again, with scores scaled to give Britain a mean of 50):

Comparing these figures with column 5 of Table 5.8, we can see that certain countries come out rather high on neuroticism, especially countries in the Middle East (Egypt, Kuwait, Jordan,

Table 5.9   Countries with high and low neuroticism scores

highest		lowest	
Egypt	63.0	Sweden	41.7
Kuwait	60.8	Turkey	44.6
Syria	57.7		
Uganda	57.2		
Jordan	56.3		
Iran	55.2		
S. Africa(black)	55.1		
Poland	55.1		
Lebanon	54.6		
Greece	54.5		
Ghana	53.1		

Lebanon, Syria and Iran, but not Turkey). African countries also score quite high (Ghana and Uganda, though not Nigeria), as do some European countries (France, Greece and Poland) and Japan. Britain, the USA, Canada and Australia score towards the low end; the countries scoring lowest are Sweden and Turkey. A survey of 114,000 industrial workers in forty countries, asking only two questions, showed a similar pattern of results (Hofstede, 1980).

Can these national differences be explained in terms of the stresses to which the populations have been exposed? The Arab countries of the Middle East have very high neuroticism scores, and these may be the effect, or possibly the cause, of the high level of political instability and frequent social upheaval in these countries. There were sharp rises in indexes of neuroticism in Germany, Italy and Japan after the end of the Second World War following their defeat and military occupation; the scores returned to previous levels by 1965 (Lynn, 1981). This evidence is supported by a study of female German teacher-training students carried out in 1950. The Berlin girls, whose lives had been most disrupted, were by far the least happy, and they attributed their unhappiness to the war. Girls in Gottingen were happier, but less so than girls in England, the USA or Switzerland (Barschak, 1951). There are therefore two quite strong sets of evidence for the theory that national differences are due to stress. Conversely, there is no clear relationship between neuroticism and prosperity or lack of it.

There are considerable differences between the mental disorder rates of immigrants to Britain. The rates of mental-hospital admission, adjusted for age and sex, per 100,000 in 1971 were:

natives	494	
Irish	1110	
Scots	696	
Indian	403	
Pakistani	336	
West Indian	539	(Cochrane, 1983)

While Irish immigrants to Britain are very high in their rate of mental-hospital admission, especially for schizophrenia and alcoholism, the same is true in the Republic of Ireland. It has been suggested that this is due to the late marrying age, restraints on sex, and lack of emotional closeness in the Irish family, especially between men, leading to a distrust of other men made worse by alcohol. However, while the Scots in Scotland also have a higher rate of mental disorder than the English, and five and a half times the rate of admissions for alcoholism, for the Scots in England the rate of mental disorder is higher still. West Indians face problems of prejudice and disappointed expectations. They may turn to Rastafarian and Pentecostal groups, producing in some of them religious delusions, perhaps mistakenly diagnosed as schizophrenia. Indians are the best adjusted, partly because of selective immigration, a supportive family system and a cultural emphasis on education. Pakistanis do not do so well; their mental-disorder rate is higher than the figures above indicate, since families conceal their problems and underuse the medical facilities. Their rigid Moslem culture increases the difficulties of adjustment (Cochrane, 1983).

However, studies in the USA have found that while blacks have high rates of schizophrenia and alcoholism, this effect almost disappears if social class is held constant. Although blacks in the USA probably experience more stress than whites, as a result of prejudice, this is counterbalanced by emotional support from the group, and by beliefs which prevent self-blame for their problems (Kessler, Price and Wortman, 1985).

CONCLUSIONS

Subjective feelings of happiness or satisfaction are a little higher for individuals who are richer or of higher social class, *within* countries, especially for feelings of positive affect, though this effect is getting smaller with time and is less for more educated people.

There are considerable class differences in anxiety, depression and minor forms of mental disorder. This is partly due to greater everyday difficulties of working-class life, the use of ineffective styles of coping, to downward drift, and to less social support. There are larger differences in health, which are discussed in Chapter 10.

It has proved very difficult to find consistent differences in happiness between countries. The ladder method probably minimizes any differences unduly, because people use local comparison levels. Surveys, translated into different languages, find that North America, Europe and Australia are the happiest places. Within Europe, Belgium, Denmark, the Netherlands and Britain are happier than France, Germany or Italy.

Mental disorders take different forms in different cultures and it is hard to compare the rates. However, suicide rates vary a great deal, and are highest in Eastern and Central Europe. Questionnaire measures of neuroticism vary from country to country, and we have seen that it is greater in Middle Eastern countries, which have been politically unstable. Immigrants often have rather high rates of mental disorder, especially alcoholism and schizophrenia.

How should we evaluate the well-being of the British, compared with those in other lands? The British people rate very highly on polls of happiness, have a low suicide rate, low rates of divorce, alcoholism and crime, and a fairly low neuroticism score.

The happiest countries, on the various kinds of evidence available, appear to be Britain, Australia, New Zealand and the Netherlands. Here are some other comparisons, noting ratios with the British rates in some cases:

USA scores high on satisfaction surveys, but has very high rates of divorce (4.5:1), alcoholism (3.9:1) and crime (2:1).

Japan has high rates of suicide (1.9:1), alcoholism (3:3:1) and neuroticism.

France scores low on surveys of happiness and satisfaction, and has high rates of neuroticism, suicide (1.8:1) and alcoholism (10:1).

Belgium and Denmark score slightly higher than Britain on surveys of satisfaction and happiness, but have a high rate of suicide and alcoholism.

6

·PERSONALITY·

ARE THERE HAPPY PEOPLE?

We sometimes say that someone has a 'sunny' or cheerful temperament, and psychologists often decide that someone is depressed. How far is happiness or satisfaction a property of persons? Depressed patients are depressed most or all of the time. But the rest of us are in different moods depending on our situation. Does happiness depend on being a happy person, or on being in a lot of pleasant situations? The 'top-down' theory is that it is the person that counts: there is evidence that happy people interpret situations in a more positive way, that adding up pleasant events is not a good predictor of happiness. The 'bottom-up' approach says that happiness depends on the number of pleasant events and activities that an individual experiences (Diener, 1984).

One way of tackling this question is to see how consistent individuals are, and how much their feelings of happiness depend on situations. In fact both are important, but individuals are quite consistent between different times and different situations. It is possible to ask trait-type questions (do you usually feel happy?) and state-type questions (how happy are you feeling now?). The second type are, of course, more variable between occasions and situations. Let us concentrate on state questions.

Diener and Larsen (1984) found that more of the variation in positive and negative affect in various work and leisure situations was due to persons (52 per cent) than to differences between situations (23 per cent), and persons were especially consistent for negative emotions. Satisfaction with life as a whole was the most stable aspect of persons, positive affect the least, but there was still a lot of consistency in individuals' moods on different occasions.

Individuals may be consistently in a certain mood because they interpret, or cope with, situations in a characteristic style, or because they choose or avoid certain kinds of situations. People seek situations that are related to personality traits and motivations. For example, extraverts spend more time in social situations, and in physical pursuits, especially when these are freely chosen. Play-oriented individuals spend less time in work (Furnham, 1981; Emmons, Diener and Larson, 1986). Those who are low in social skills, or high in social anxiety, avoid many common social situations, including some which are commonly found very enjoyable, like dates and parties (Argyle, Furnham and Graham, 1981).

There are clearly depressed people, and to a slightly lesser extent there are people who are consistently in a positive mood. Who are these happy people? They tend to 'look on the bright side'; this has been described as the 'Pollyanna principle'. In support of this idea it has been found that some individuals score high on happiness and optimism, rate events as pleasanter, have a more positive view of others, recall more positive events and have pleasanter free associations (Matlin and Gawron, 1979). This fits in with research showing that we remember things which are associated with our present mood; when people are in a happy mood they remember happy events better (Teasdale and Russell, 1983). Some people may have richer networks of associations with positive emotions and tend to react positively to everything (Bower, 1981).

Self-esteem is also strongly correlated with subjective well-being. In some studies it has been found to be more strongly correlated than any other variable (Campbell, 1981). Depressed people evaluate their own performance at tasks more negatively and they underestimate the quality of their performance, though there is also evidence that their self-evaluations are sometimes more accurate and realistic than those of normals (Lewinsohn *et al.*, 1980). However, there is a fall in self-esteem during periods of unhappiness; perhaps happiness affects self-esteem as well as vice versa.

How about manic people? Are not manics very happy though mentally disturbed? In fact the main mood in mania is not happiness but excitement: they are in a state of high arousal, euphoria, they are often irritable when thwarted, and feel very carefree (Tyrer and Shopsin, 1982). They can be characterized as follows:

> Manics wear smart, striking but rather loud clothes, look extremely well and very pleased with themselves, are smiling and alert, and have a loud confident voice of robust, resonant quality. They talk incessantly and tend to monopolize the conversation with their hilarious jokes and outrageous stories, but are easily distracted and move rapidly from topic to topic. Their excitement and jollity are infectious, and they are good at being the life and soul of the party. Manics have a self-confidence and self-esteem for which there is no adequate basis, and they will not take criticism from others. They enjoy making speeches and writing letters to important people. On the other hand they are quite good at handling people. This, together with their energy and self-confidence, often leads to a successful career in one of the more colourful occupations such as politics or show business. Their chief failings in social competence are an inability to perceive themselves accurately and in annoying others by their dominance and unsuitable jokes. Their delusional self-importance, their constant talking and a tendency to bizarre behaviour may lead to their becoming a public nuisance.   (Argyle, 1983, pp. 218–19)

Unhappiness is part of a broader syndrome too. Neuroticism is a major dimension of personality, which has consistently been found to correlate with negative affect, at about .40 (Costa and McCrae, 1980; Warr, Barter and Brownbridge, 1983). This is such a strong connection that we have been taking neuroticism as an index or component of distress, negative affect. It goes without saying that depression is especially strongly linked with un-happiness.

Loneliness is strongly associated with unhappiness. This could be described as a close link between satisfaction in the social domain and general well-being. However, loneliness is a source of *negative* affect, which we have seen is not the same as lack of positive satisfaction. Lonely people have high scores on depression scales (Horowitz, French and Anderson, 1982). We consider above the causes of loneliness (p. 28f).

OTHER FEATURES OF PERSONALITY ASSOCIATED WITH HAPPINESS

Extraversion has been most consistently found to be related to happiness. It correlates with positive affect and with satisfaction, but not with negative affect (Emmons and Diener, 1985). The relationship is so robust that extraversion can predict happiness 17 years later (Costa, McCrae and Norris, 1981). If positive and negative affect are measured separately, extraversion is associated with positive rather than negative affect. If extraversion is divided into sociability and impulsiveness, it is the sociability component which predicts happiness. And these correlations are quite strong, typically .30–.40. Those high on 'sensation-seeking' (which correlates with extraversion) report intense experiences of joy (Tolor, 1978). Many studies have shown that 'sociability' and extent of social contacts are associated with happiness.

Headey and Wearing (1986) carried out a repeated panel study of 600 Australians, in 1981, 1983 and 1985. They found that extraversion predisposed people, especially young people, to have favourable life events, especially in the domains of friendship and work; these in turn led to a high level of positive well-being, and to increases of extraversion.

In a series of detailed case studies of happy and unhappy students, one study found that the happy ones had much better relationships with other people, while for the unhappy ones social relations were often 'sources of anxiety, anger and guilt that led to cautious withdrawal and empty isolation' (Wessman and Ricks, 1966).

People are said to be high on 'internal control' if they believe that events are under their own control, rather than due to other people or to fate or luck. Subjective well-being is greater in those scoring high on internal control, as also in those who believe that they have a lot of choice in what they do. We shall show that those strong in resources (which presumably affects control and choice) are also happier. However, the explanation could be that people who have experienced a lot of negative life events both become unhappy and believe themselves unable to control events (Diener, 1984).

People are happier if they have managed to resolve their inner conflicts, and achieve some degree of integration of their personality. It has been found that those with a smaller discrepancy between self-image and ideal self, or between aspirations and achievement, are happier (Wilson, 1967).

In a study that made detailed analyses of some happy and unhappy male students, their self-images were as follows:

> The composite self-picture presented by the nine happy men, both in depression and elation, was that of a warm, friendly, candid person, comfortable in intimate relationships, conscientious, inventive, capable of taking things as they come, and not pessimistic. . . . It appears that for these happy men a period of relative depression was a time of taking stock, self-searching, and looking for solutions to problems, with strong optimistic feelings that solutions would be found.
>
> (Wessman and Ricks, p. 110)

It was found that the happy students both had more satisfactory relationships with other people and coped better in the domain of work than the unhappy ones: their work had more meaning for them, they felt they could achieve their goals at work, and they found it highly satisfying – two of our three main sources of happiness.

We showed earlier that people get a great deal of 'intrinsic satisfaction' from work, i.e. from actually doing the work, using skills and achieving some sense of success or achievement from completing tasks. There is a similar kind of intrinsic satisfaction in the more serious kinds of leisure. Some individuals are more involved in goal-directed activities than others, and it has been suggested that satisfaction follows from being involved in such activity. In one study subjects were asked to list up to 10 'personal projects' in which they were engaged, and to rate these on a number of scales. Life satisfaction was greatest for individuals whose projects involved short-term goals, which were enjoyable and not too difficult, and which were done in collaboration with others (Palys and Little, 1983). A study of the amount of positive affect experienced in different situations found that this was greater in situations in which it was reported that goals were present, and where these goals could be attained (Emmons, Diener and Larsen, 1986).

Another feature of integration is the ability to organize and plan, to use time successfully. Happy people see time positively, it is filled and planned, they are punctual and efficient, the future is bright; for unhappy people time is unfilled, open and uncommitted, events are discrete, time is broken up, they postpone things and are inefficient, are anxious and apprehensive about the future (Wessman and Ricks, 1966). We saw earlier that the unemployed are happier if they succeed in planning their time (p. 60f).

Education, wealth, intelligence and other abilities, coping skills and physique are not parts of 'personality' in a narrow sense, but are nevertheless important properties of persons. We have already seen that education and wealth have a definite though rather small effect on well-being. It might be expected that happiness would be correlated with intelligence simply through the ability to solve problems better. Several studies, mainly with students, have not found much relationship, but in a large American adult sample a correlation of .13 was found, when other resources like income and education were held constant (Campbell, Converse and Rodgers, 1976). This is a very modest effect, but it is one of the strongest effects among different personal resources in this study (Table 6.1). This table shows that the resource variables (intelligence, health and so on) affect feelings of ability to control events in the same way. Again, these are correlations, showing strength of association between 0 and 1.

Physical attractiveness has a weak effect for the population as a whole, but a greater effect on happiness for women, especially for young women. This is to be expected, in view of the finding that attractive people are believed to have many other desirable properties, and are liked more, especially by the opposite sex (Berscheid and Walster, 1974). Attractiveness seems to convey

Table 6.1   The effect of different personal resources

	well-being	feelings of competence
intelligence	.13	.14
health	.13	.12
attractiveness	.03	.04
height	.05	.07
income	.14	.13
education	.10	.10
religious faith	.11	.05

Source   Campbell, Converse and Rodgers, 1976.

social status (Webster and Driskell, 1983). There is evidence that attractive people are more socially skilled (Goldman and Lewis, 1977), perhaps as a result of the easier social environment that they encounter. Height has an effect but only for men. Again this is to be expected since taller men are preferred for positions of leadership; height is a small factor in dominance.

Social skills, interpersonal competence, are another important resource. Those who are effective in this sphere are likely to have more friends, while those who are not are likely to become isolated and lonely. Students who report that they are low in social support are rated by others as less likeable, less socially skilled and less attractive (Sarason *et al.*, 1985). Most jobs entail dealing with other people, and in many jobs this is central (for example, the work of teachers, doctors, salesman, managers and policemen). We have seen that most leisure is social, so that those who can communicate and co-operate more easily will enjoy their leisure more. Loneliness is an example of the effects of poor social skills. Lonely people are depressed (Weeks *et al.*, 1980), and feel excluded, alienated and angry (Horowitz, French and Anderson, 1982). Their problem is primarily lack of social skills (p. 28f) Neurotic mental patients often suffer from inadequate social skills too, for example being cold and unassertive, poor conversationalists, low in rewardingness, and sometimes they play destructive 'games' designed to put other people down, or are difficult in other ways (Argyle, 1983).

Headey and Wearing (1986) found in their repeated panel study that low personal competence predisposed people to have negative life events, especially in the domains of work and material standard of living; these in turn led to 'ill-being' or unhappiness, which led to reduced personal competence.

Ability to cope with worries or problems is related to happiness. Those who talk to others, or who pray, when worried or unhappy, tend to be happier than those who do not (Veroff, Douvan and Kulka, 1981). Internal controllers are less affected by stressful life events, because they use better methods of coping. They try to alter the situation rather than avoiding it or trying to relax, as external controllers do. Internal controllers are also more flexible, and use methods of coping which are suited to the problem (Parkes, 1984). Elsewhere we explain gender and class differences in happiness and mental health in terms of the more constructive methods of coping used by men and by middle-class people (see also pp. 101, 171).

Personality turns out to be a rather important source of well-being, as is shown by the quite strong association with personality dimensions, like extraversion and internal control. These correlations are stronger than those between satisfaction and age, sex or social class.

PERSONALITY AND LIFE EVENTS: THE CASE OF DEPRESSION

This is a very important issue in the study of depression, because the outcome affects the form treatment should take. If depression is primarily a function of persons in some way, then therapy should be directed towards changing them. If depression is due to depressing events the solution would be to arrange for more cheerful ones.

Depression is often precipitated by stressful life events, such as being widowed, divorced, losing a job, trouble with the police, ill-health in the family. Losing a social relationship, or a set of relationships, is the most common case. However, some people become depressed without a precipitating stressful life event or major difficulties like bad housing. Table 6.2 shows some of the findings from a study of working-class women in London, 114 of them depressed and 382 non-depressed controls. It can be seen that 25 per cent of the depressed patients did not report any recent stressful life events. These people were found to be particularly high in vulnerability factors, to which we now turn.

Depression can be predicted from properties of persons, re-

Table 6.2   Stressful life events and depression

	depressed patients %	normal and borderline women %
severe life event in past 38 weeks, alone	30	13
severe event *and* and major difficulties	32	6
major difficulties alone	14	11
no severe events or difficulties	25	70

Source   Brown and Harris, 1978.

gardless of life events. The vulnerability factors in the study above were lack of spouse or similar confidant, being working class, not having a job, having young children at home, and early loss of own mother. However it was the *combination* of stressful life events and vulnerability factors that gave the best prediction of depression. Table 6.3 shows the percentages of women with depression who had experienced severe life events (first column) or not (second column), where they had strong social support (first row) or low social support (second row).

Table 6.3   Stressful life events, vulnerability and depression

	severe life event or major difficulty %	no severe life events %	
intimate social support			
high	10	1	
low	41	4	
loss of mother before 11	47	0	
no such loss	17	2	
employed	15	0	
not employed			excluding early loss of mother, or young children no
	30	11	intimate support

Source   Brown and Harris, 1978.

The vulnerability factors in this study (Brown and Harris, 1978) were mainly lack of social support and additional forms of stress. Interest has now moved to vulnerability based on faulty thinking processes.

One theory is that people become depressed if they learn that some things are uncontrollable, that they cannot obtain desirable goals or prevent undesirable events. They think that this failure is due to their own incompetence, that they have caused their own failure, and they become depressed (Abramson, Seligman and Teasdale, 1978). It was suggested that individuals would be prone to depression if they attributed negative events to themselves, and believed that such events were likely to happen again, and would occur in different spheres. The conclusion of many experiments is that part of this theory is correct: depressed people do attribute failure to themselves more than normal people do. However, there is little evidence that attributional style actually causes depression; the reverse now seems more likely. When people have experienced upsetting events they become depressed and then start blaming themselves for things (Coyne and Gotlib, 1983; Williams, 1984). On the other hand changing the attributions of patients has been found to be successful in relieving depression (p. 213).

Another possible vulnerability factor is that depressed people evaluate themselves more negatively. This has been found in experimental studies. However, it seems that depressed people distort their self-perceptions no more than normals do – whose perceptions err in the favourable direction. Similarly, depressed patients remember more negative than positive information about themselves, and remember more depressive adjectives. Subjects high in neuroticism remember negative information about themselves better (Martin, Ward and Clark, 1983).

Another theory is that depressed people hold a number of distorted beliefs, for example 'you can't be happy unless everyone likes you'; they generalize from single instances to concluding 'I am a failure as a mother', select negative interpretations of events, and expect failure and rejection (Beck, 1976). There is a certain amount of evidence that depressed patients do think in these ways (Coyne and Gotlib, 1983). However, in a longitudinal study no causal relation was found between depression and irrational beliefs or negative cognitions. It was concluded that negative thinking often occurs in depressed people, and makes recovery more difficult (Lewinsohn *et al.*, 1981). Distorted beliefs, like internal attributions, seem to wax and wane with the depression, rather than cause it (Persons and Rao, 1985).

Depressed people do something else that is relevant to the study of happiness: they reward themselves less, and this is probably one of the causes of their depression. A 30-item scale has been constructed with items like:

> 'When I do something right, I take time to enjoy the feeling.'
> 'There are pleasurable activities which I enjoy doing alone at my leisure.'
> 'I should be upset if I made a mistake.' (−)   (Heiby, 1983)

Happy people have higher scores, depressed people lower scores on this scale. And depressed people reward themselves less, for example by less self-praise, in laboratory tasks (Heiby, 1983; Heiby, Ozaki and Campos, 1984).

THE EFFECT OF RELIGION

Religion can be regarded as one of the domains of satisfaction. In the *Quality of American Life* study (Campbell, Converse and Rodgers, 1976) it was found that 38 per cent regarded having a strong religious faith as extremely important, and another 22 per cent saw it as very important. However, the relation between satisfaction with religion and overall life satisfaction with other factors held constant was rather weak. Other American surveys found the same thing, though the relation with overall satisfaction is sometimes as high as .27 (Andrews and Withey, 1976). The importance of religion is greater for some groups – women, the elderly, and of course religious people themselves.

Satisfaction with religion, or involvement with religion, appears to be closely linked with marital happiness. In an English study it was found that 91 per cent of married women who were regular church attenders said that their marriages were exceptionally or very happy, compared with 62 per cent of non-attenders (Chesser, 1956). On the other hand a strict religious upbringing can be a source of sexual problems in marriage (Masters and Johnson, 1970). The divorce rate is much less for religious people, partly no doubt because divorce is disapproved of or forbidden by most churches.

A recent US finding is that religious people feel less lonely than others. Several different questionnaire measures of religious belief were used, with the results given in correlations in Table 6.4. The strongest connection with (lack of) loneliness was with the 'existential well-being' scale, which consisted of items like 'I feel there is some real purpose in my life' and 'I don't know who I am, where I came from, or where I'm going' (scored negative). These items would not be particularly associated with church-going, and are more like the sense of meaning and purpose which were found to be connected with happiness in a study reported below. Religious well-being was measured by more traditional items like 'I believe that God loves me and cares about me'. While this scale was also associated with (lack of) loneliness, the correlation was much smaller (Paloutzian and Ellison, 1982).

In a large American survey of readers of *Psychology Today*, no direct relation was found between church membership and happiness – perhaps because readers of this magazine are a fairly irreligious lot. What was found, however, was that people were happier if they felt that life had meaning and direction, and that they had confidence in their guiding values. One person said:

My life has been terrific the last few years – lots of money, women, friends, all sorts of activities and travel. My job is good and I am good at it. There is even a good future – I will probably be promoted this year and make lots more money and have freedom to do what I want. But it all seems to lack any significance for me. Where is my life leading, why am I doing what I'm doing? I have the feeling that I am being carried along without ever making any real decisions or knowing what my goals are. It's sort of like getting on a road and driving along fine, but not knowing why you chose that particular road or where it is leading. (Freedman, 1978, pp. 195–96)

Table 6.4 Religious beliefs and loneliness

	loneliness
religious well-being	−.15
existential well-being	−.65

Source Paloutzian and Ellison, 1982.

This survey found that people who lack meaning in their lives tend to be less happy with almost every aspect of their life. They are less satisfied with the recognition they receive, with their financial situation, their home, job, love life, sex life, marriage, friends, where they live, and even their own physical attractiveness. Given two people with equal incomes and educations, the person who feels his or her life has meaning is more likely to be pleased with their income (Freedman, 1978).

There are two possible explanations for the benefits of religion. First, they may be due to the meaning and purpose, the integration, provided by religious ideas. The Protestant Ethic (p. 36) is an example of such integration and direction. Freedman's findings provide some support for this view – except that his church-going subjects did not have a greater sense of meaning and purpose. Many students of the psychology of religion have accepted this theory, and have offered support from case studies and experiments (Argyle and Beit-Hallahmi, 1975).

The other theory is that the church is simply a source of social support. It also provides support for the kinds of integrating values and commitment covered by the first theory. The benefits of church membership are greater for those who have retired and who are widowed – i.e. who have lost other important sources of social support (Moberg and Taves, 1965); it is also important for health (see p. 196f).

CONCLUSIONS

There are people who tend to be consistently happy, despite variations in mood caused by different events and situations, just as others are depressed. Happiness is part of a broader syndrome, which includes choice of rewarding situations, looking on the bright side, and high self-esteem. Unhappy people tend to be lonely and high in neuroticism.

Happiness is associated, quite strongly, with other aspects of personality: extraversion, internal control, absence of inner conflicts, good social relationships, involvement with goal-directed work and leisure, and ability to organize time. It has weaker associations with a number of personal resources, like intelligence and attractiveness.

Research on depression shows that it is jointly caused by

stressful life events and various vulnerability factors, such as lack of social support. Attribution of failures to self, and distorted beliefs, accompany rather than cause depression, though altering them can help to lift it.

Religion is a definite though minor source of happiness; it is more important for old people, and is more strongly linked with marital happiness and health.

7

•JOY•

There are several kinds of good mood and a large number of emotion words to describe them. One way to decide how to classify moods, good or bad, is to ask samples of subjects to group together a lot of different emotion words, and then to carry out a statistical procedure (factor analysis, or multi-dimensional scaling) to discover the underlying dimensions which the judges are using. A typical study is shown in Figure 7.1. Similar results were later obtained in a number of very different cultures (Russell, 1983). This and many other studies have found that there are *two* main dimensions of emotional expression, pleasant–unpleasant (or happy–sad) and arousal–sleep (or degrees of interest and excitement). The same two dimensions are found for emotional *expression*, for example in the face. And two quite separate neurophysiological systems have been found to be responsible for these dimensions. However, as we saw earlier, it is possible to find independent factors of positive and negative emotion, from studies of self-reported mood, under certain conditions (p. 4f, and see Watson and Tellegen, 1985).

Figure 7.1 Two dimensions of emotion

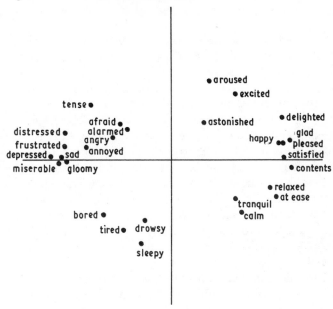

Several types of positive emotion can be distinguished. *Joy* and *elation* correspond to the main dimension of positive emotional experience. They are associated with a smiling face, with enjoying the company of other people, feeling accepted, self-confident and relaxed, and with problems being solved (Izard, 1977).

Excitement or, at a lower intensity, *interest* is the second dimension of emotion. The combination of excitement and joy is laughter, and a mood of happy excitement (Izard, 1977). There are some people who seek and value intense experiences; they have been called 'sensation seekers'. They particularly seek sensations based on speed, danger and variety of sexual partners. Extraverts and young people, especially males, are interested in sensation-seeking. There seems to be something about sheer arousal which is deeply satisfying, especially to this kind of person (Zuckerman, 1979). The reduction of anxiety following arousal is a source of joy, even euphoria, for example after landing from parachute jumping. In one way or another arousal seems to be able to contribute to joy; perhaps it is the 'spice of life'.

Contentment, relaxation and comfort correspond to a lower level of excitement, a lower degree of intensity, though they can still be very enjoyable.

In recent studies a third dimension of emotion has appeared: intensity or depth of experience. For example, *tender* and *disgusted* are of high intensity, while *pleasant* and *attentive* describe low-intensity experiences (Daly, Lancee and Polivy, 1983). Argyle and Crossland (in press) asked people to group positive emotions from 24 different activities on the basis of the similarity of these feelings. One major dimension found was depth. This kind of feeling was induced by music, reading and nature. It was described as 'inspiration, 'sadness yet joy', 'the smallness of my existence', 'tearful, spiritual, profoundly moved', etc. A second dimension was based on success, a third on commitment to others.

Depth has much in common with 'peak experiences' – 'moments of highest happiness and fulfilment' (Maslow, 1968). The characteristics of these 'peak' or 'flow' experiences include:

> absorption, focused attention
> awareness of power
> intense joy, value and meaning
> spontaneity, effortlessness
> integration and identity. (Privette, 1983)

It is also similar to what Csikszentmihalyi (1982) called 'flow', complete absorption in a work or leisure activity (p. 83); it has been suggested that the source of this 'self-rewarding involvement' is a balance between the challenge of an activity and the skills of the participant. If challenge is too great there is anxiety, if it is too little there is boredom (Chalip *et al.*, 1984).

THE CAUSES OF GOOD MOODS

One method of discovering the causes of good moods is to ask people when they last experienced positive feelings and what caused them. In a recent study with students in five European countries, the main causes of joy were said to be relationships with friends (36 per cent), especially by middle-class, female and psychology students, basic pleasures (food, drink, and sex) (9 per cent), and success experiences (16 per cent). In the British sample, basic pleasures were reported much more frequently as causes of joy (32 per cent), than in West Germany, France, Italy or Switzerland (Scherer, Summerfield and Wallbott, 1983). This may have been because the British students were more prepared to give frank replies, or because the question carried a slightly different meaning in the English version.

An American study with students, along similar lines but not specifying *past* experiences, also found that social relationships were a common source of joy – with family members, romantic partners, friends and sports teams. While task success, for example at sports, was described as reward for hard work, romantic rewards were not actively worked for; there was much anticipation of pleasure here, and some anxiety. 'The accounts of joy episodes with friends generally describe either reunions with long-lost friends or gatherings at which friends talk, laugh, relax and feel close' (Schwartz and O'Connor, 1984).

Which life events are the most positive? We made up lists of major positive events, and asked 467 subjects, adults as well as students, to rate each on a scale from 0 to 100 according to how much 'happiness, satisfaction or well-being' they believed each would bring to people in general. The most highly rated events are shown in Table 7.1.

It is possible to draw up much longer lists of pleasant events. The Pleasant Events Schedule contains 320 items; of these 49 were found to be associated with a good mood for the day on which they occurred for 10 per cent of people (MacPhillamy and Lewinsohn, 1976). The frequency of pleasant events correlates with positive mood for most people at .30 to .35. However, activities are only reported if they are experienced as pleasant, and people probably experience more events as pleasant if they are in a good mood to start with (Williams, 1984). Nevertheless this line of work has led to a form of treatment for depression which seems to be quite successful (p. 205f).

There have been different emphases in these studies. The one by MacPhillamy and Lewinsohn (1976) included a lot of items on pleasant outdoor activities. A study of girls in several countries in 1950 found that their major sources of happiness were sports and

Table 7.1   Positive life events

falling in love	78.0
passing an examination or gaining a qualification	75.5
recovering from a serious illness	72.1
going on holiday	68.9
making it up after an argument with your husband/ wife or boy/girl friend	66.0
getting married or engaged	65.0
birth of a child	64.6
winning a lot of money	64.4
getting promoted at work or getting a pay rise	59.9
going out with or visiting friends	58.0
getting a new job	56.1

Source   Henderson, Argyle and Furnham, 1984.

games (swimming, tennis and cycling) and cultural activities (music and reading) (Barschak, 1951).

In order to understand how positive experiences work, we need to classify the main sources. In the Henderson, Argyle and Furnham study (1984) (Table 7.1) we carried out a factor analysis to find such factors, and other investigators have done the same. It is possible to produce a list of the main sources of pleasure (not in order of importance), as follows:

eating, drinking, sex
rest, sleep
spouse, friends and other close relationships
success, promotion, satisfaction with self
physical activity, sport, feeling healthy
task performance, use of skills
reading, music, TV and other cultural activities
intense experiences, e.g. aesthetic, religious.

Particular occasions which create positive moods may involve a combination of these elements. For example, a successful piece of co-operative work involves social, success and skills components. Dancing may include social, success, skills, music and sex. A meal with friends perhaps includes social, eating and drinking, sex, and relaxation.

It is a very mixed list, which creates problems for psychologists. But a lot of different kinds of food will satisfy hunger, and a lot of different activities can lead to joy. There are differences between individuals in what gives them most joy: for some it is church, for some music, sport, work and so on. This is important to remember when trying to cheer people up by scheduling more frequent pleasant activities.

There are ways of classifying the various sources of pleasure, which are of some theoretical importance. One distinction is between direct physical sensations, like eating, drinking, sex, rest, etc., and satisfactions based on acquired drives of some kind, such as self-satisfaction and cultural activities. The less basic ones are major sources of satisfaction and enjoyment: an American survey found that music and reading came just below friends, but well above meals, home or work (*Public Opinion*, 1981).

It is very interesting that many of these pleasant activities do not involve the gratification of any known needs, or the reduction of arousal. On the other hand people often seek arousal and excitement when they are bored. This consideration has led to the theory that there are two basic forms of motivation and pleasure. In the 'telic' state people pursue serious goals, are concerned with the future, and prefer a low level of arousal. In the 'paratelic' state they seek excitement, in a playful way, and are interested in the behaviour itself, rather than what it leads to. There are two equilibrium points, not one, and frequent reversals between the two states are brought about by external events, frustration and satiation. There are consistent individual differences in preferring one mode to the other (Apter, 1982; 1984). This theory is not yet supported by very much empirical evidence, but it is useful in offering an account of two very different sources of gratification.

However, the origins of joy are more diverse still, and we will now examine some of them in more detail.

Social events

This is the most common source of positive emotions, but we do not fully understand why. Part of the story is that infants have an innate tendency to respond to people, derived from the evolutionary importance of sociability, to look and smile; this is developed in the course of early interaction with mothers (Malatesta, 1985). They are thus able to deliver powerful social rewards which encourage adults to care for them (Tomkins,

1962). In addition, smiling and other social signals are produced much more often when others are present, and via facial feedback this creates enhanced positive feelings in the person smiling.

Social relationships can be sources of joy and positive satisfaction in a number of ways, as described in Chapter 2.

Work and leisure

The ways in which work and leisure can provide joy and satisfaction were described in Chapters 3 and 4.

Exercise and sport

These produce a feeling of well-being mainly through their physiological effects, such as release of endorphins and other neurotransmitters, and later relaxation. There are psychological effects, such as regulating arousal, time out from routine activities, and self-esteem from successful performance. Sport can also produce feelings of euphoria during peak performance, when the performer has feelings of unusual power and control, and becomes unaware of his surroundings, the body seeming to perform on its own (Browne and Mahoney, 1984).

Drugs

A number of drugs are capable of producing positive moods, though they usually have other effects as well. *Amphetamines* (pep pills, 'speed', dexedrine, etc.) release dopamine and nor-adrenaline, resulting in greater rewards and activity. *Anti-depressants* also increase the level of these transmitters, especially nor-adrenaline and 5-hydroxy-tryptomine, and are thus able to relieve depression. *Marijuana* affects the central nervous system in ways not yet fully understood, producing a complex state of euphoria, anxiety and lassitude. It has been found in a sample of young people that it did not produce much positive affect, but did produce strong feelings of excitement and freedom (Larson, Csikszentmihalyi and Freeman, 1984). Users have to learn how to have the approved experiences. *Alcohol* is a central nervous system depressant, but, as it has been said, 'the super-ego is soluble in alcohol'. The result is some loss of inhibition, and increased social intimacy (Matheson and Davison, 1972; Iversen and Iversen, 1981). In the study showing that marijuana did not produce positive affect it was found that alcohol produced strong positive emotions along all scales – happy, sociable, excited, free, etc. *LSD* experience was once described as 'like 1000 orgasms'. Hallucinogenic drugs can produce religious experiences in people with religious beliefs in a religious setting. This happened at the 'Good Friday miracle', at which a number of theological students were given a pill before a two-and-a-half-hour meditation. Those who were given the psilocybin pill had what appears to have been classical mystical experience; those who had a placebo made of sugar did not (Pahnke, 1966).

Music

Music can produce a wide range of positive emotions, including joy, excitement and feelings of profound satisfaction. Some of the relevant properties of music are known; for example, joy goes with a faster pace, rhythm, a flowing melody and major keys (Valentine, 1962). When there is also singing the properties of the voice which express emotion become relevant. However, since it is impossible for us to tell which emotion is which in unfamiliar music, for example, Indian or Chinese, there must be cultural-learning experiences linking certain kinds of music to moods.

Weather

People are happier, and kinder to others, on days when the sun is shining, when it is warm but not too warm, and the humidity is low (Cunningham, 1979). It affects their reported satisfaction with life as a whole (Schwarz and Clore, 1983). Mental health is affected in a similar way (Briere, Downes and Spensley, 1983). These effects probably reflect some primitive response to the environment. However there must also be a high degree of adaptation to the weather, since there is no evidence that people who live in favourable climates are any happier (Chapter 5).

Nature

People experience strong positive feelings in the countryside, and in wild, natural settings. They enjoy vegetation, water, and prefer the natural to the man-made, some depth of view, an intermediate degree of complexity, and the peace and tranquillity of these areas. It has been suggested that there may be some evolutionary basis to, for example, the preference for scenes with water (Altman and Wohlwill, 1983).

In addition there are a number of 'mood induction' procedures which have been used in the laboratory, and these are described in Chapter 11.

THE PHYSIOLOGICAL BASIS OF POSITIVE EMOTIONS

The main emotions are happiness, sadness, anger, fear, disgust, contempt, surprise, interest and shame. There are three aspects to emotions: a physiological state, facial and other expressions, and conscious experience. The expression can be regarded as a 'read-out' for the benefit of others. The biological reason that we experience emotions at all is probably that they provide an internal read-out of what is going on in the system, indeed an amplified read-out. It is obviously very useful to be aware of pain – it signals a warning about dangerous aspects of the environment, and focuses attention on them. The signalling of pleasure and rewards is valuable in the same way, directing attention to positive and biologically rewarding aspects of the environment. It is useful to have a direct read-out of physiological, motivational states, like hunger and thirst, so that appropriate action can be taken.

General emotional arousal (increased heart-rate, etc.) is an important factor, and has the function of energizing the organism to cope with challenges, to engage in fight or flight. This is illustrated by experiments in which injections of adrenalin have been found to increase the intensity of different emotions like anger and euphoria, induced by environment events (Schachter and Singer, 1962). However, it is now known that different emotions have distinctive patterns of physiological arousal, as was first shown in the cases of fear and anger (Ax, 1953). In fact there are a number of different areas in the hypothalamus and limbic system corresponding to specific emotions like anger, fear and sex. And there are other areas which produce variations in the quality of emotion, along the two main dimensions of pleasant–unpleasant and degrees of arousal (Buck, 1984).

We turn now to the experience of positive emotions. The key here is the stimulation of the 'pleasure centres'. The discovery of these was one of the most exciting developments in recent research on the brain. It was found that if an electrode was inserted in this part of a rat's brain, electrical impulses were so rewarding that animals would press a bar as much as 10,000 times per hour for up to 26 hours. While we do not really know that rats experience 'pleasure', stimulation of these areas is evidently highly rewarding (Olds and Milner, 1954). This also works for other species, including monkeys. The part of the brain which registers reward in this way in rats is the septum near the hypothalamus, and the limbic system.

Activation of parts of the pleasure centres mimics the effects of food reward; a rat will not work for the electrical impulse in one area unless it is hungry. Activation of some areas mimics the effects of water or sex; others produce general rewards. In humans a variety of pleasant sensations can be produced from different parts of the brain, including pleasant tastes, sexual arousal, a relaxed mood, enjoyment and laughter (Rolls, 1979).

The passage of messages in the brain is facilitated by various neurotransmitters, and this applies to the activation of the pleasure centre. These include *dopamine* and *nor-adrenaline*: experiments have shown that they are released by amphetamine. Higher levels of them increase the rate of self-stimulation, showing that greater reward is being received. This may be why amphetamine is able to act as an anti-depressant and produce more positive moods. Another set of neurotransmitters are the *endorphins*, which act as analgesics among other things. Soldiers and sportsmen, under high stress, generate more endorphin and don't feel pain until later, and it is likely that they are having peak experiences of euphoria (Levinthal, 1983).

The experience of emotion is partly the subjective awareness of altered heart-rate, blood pressure, and other bodily changes involved in the emotion. It is also affected by facial expression. Emotions can be modified by asking people to adopt different expressions. In one experiment subjects who were asked to inhibit their expression found electric shocks less painful (and had less physiological reaction to them) (Lanzetta, Cartwright-Smith and Kleck, 1976). The conclusion of a long line of experiments is that facial expression can regulate the intensity of emotion experienced, rather than substitute one emotion for another (Laird, 1984).

Emotional reactions also depend on how situations are interpreted. This has been shown in an experiment with an unpleasant film of circumcision among the Aborigines, for which different sound tracks were prepared. The sound track which emphasized the painfulness of the procedure had more effect on heart-rate and skin-conductance than sound tracks which suggested that the operation was not painful, or which created a detached, intellectual attitude (Lazarus, Averill and Opton, 1970). There are different ways of perceiving the same stimulus. In one experiment subjects were asked to touch a vibrating board – an essentially neutral stimulus. Some were led to expect it to be pleasant, others for it to be painful, and that is how they perceived it (Anderson and Pennebaker, 1980). So the subjective experience of emotions is partly due to the appraisal of external events, and partly due to the awareness of general and specific bodily events, and of facial and other emotional expressions.

The same stimulus has very different significance depending on the expectations of the observer – the same meal, book, holiday, etc. may be appraised as good or bad, depending on what was expected. This in turn depends on what the observer has become accustomed to. We shall discuss this further in connection with 'adaptation levels', which we shall use to explain why it is that some people living at what is objectively a very low level of material prosperity say they are quite contented. We saw in Chapter 6 that depressed people interpret events differently from other people – they think that when things go wrong it was all their fault, and that there is nothing they can do to stop it happening again.

Emotional experience is affected by social factors in several ways. Emotional expressions are displayed much more when there are other people there to see them. This develops in infants, who from about 12 months start to inhibit crying in the absence of a recipient, and produce more facial expression when other people are there (Malatesta, 1985). Adults smile a lot more, to a pleasant stimulus, in the presence of others. Kraut and Johnston (1979) found that people smiled more on a sunny day, in the presence of others, and at a bowling alley after a good shot, when attending to their friends rather than to the skittles (Table 7.2).

Table 7.2 Facial expressions for joy in public
and private

at a bowling alley	hit	miss
		% smiling
at the skittles	4	3
at companions	42	28
in the street	sunny	cloudy
		% smiling
alone	12	5
with others	61	57

Source Kraut and Johnston, 1979.

The emotions that people feel can also be powerfully affected by the apparent moods of other people. In the Schachter and Singer (1962) experiment, subjects with a euphoric companion become euphoric, subjects with an angry companion became angry, both states being enhanced by the adrenalin injections.

Emotions can be affected by cultural traditions in a more subtle way. At any time and place a certain range of emotions is recognized, labelled and experienced. We no longer, for example, experience the emotions of 'melancholy' and 'accidie', which were familiar in the seventeenth century (Harré, Clarke and De Carlo, 1985). We have seen how depression takes different forms in different cultures. Do happiness or joy take different forms at different times and places? They probably do, but the basic experience and expression of joy appears to be universal to mankind. Positive affect and evaluation are probably very primitive biological responses (Zajonc, 1980).

THE EFFECTS OF POSITIVE MOODS

Good moods have a number of powerful effects on behaviour and thought processes.

Positive thoughts

When people are in happy as opposed to sad moods they think about things quite differently. In an experiment in which hypnosis was used to produce happy and depressed moods, it was found that happy moods led to positive free associations, cheerful TAT (Thematic Apperception Test) stories, charitable descriptions of social events, perception of self as socially competent, and feelings of self-confidence and self-esteem (Bower, 1983). Other experiments have found that individuals in good moods perceive more positive and fewer negative acts on videotapes both in their own behaviours and in that of others (Forgas, Bower and Krantz, 1984). We shall see later that induced positive moods lead to increases in judgements of satisfaction with life as a whole (p. 195). The thought processes of depressed patients differ from those of normal people in a similar way, in being more negative and pessimistic (p. 121).

Memory

Put people in a good mood and they can remember happy events or positive words better. An experiment in which subjects were put in happy or sad moods by hypnosis asked them to learn lists of words and later to remember the words. It was found that words could be remembered much better when subjects were in the same mood as when the lists were learned. The effects were quite large: subjects in a happy mood could recall 78 per cent of those learned in a happy mood, 47 per cent of those learned in a sad mood. Subjects could also remember more pleasant childhood events and fewer unpleasant ones (26 per cent *v.* 2 per cent) when in a happy mood (Bower, 1981). Other experiments have obtained similar results by other methods of mood-induction, such as allowing to succeed, receiving a gift, reciting positive self-statements and music (Isen *et al.*, 1978). Good moods enable people to remember words describing positive personality traits better; sad moods produce better memory for negative trait words (Teasdale and Russell, 1983). The effect has been found for depressed patients who have a daily fluctuation of mood. If tested at the time of day of their good moods they recall more happy events (Clark and Teasdale, 1982). Depressed patients in general selectively remember unpleasant events (Lloyd and Lishman, 1975). The generally accepted explanation for these results is that memories are based on a network of associations between events and concepts. These are linked to emotions, and when a person is in a certain emotional state his or her memory is activated for events associated with that emotion (Bower, 1981).

Problem-solving

People in good moods tackle problems in a different way from those in neutral or sad moods. They move more quickly, adopt the simplest strategy, and accept the first solution they find. In one experiment the problem was attaching a candle to a wall given a box of drawing pins and a book of matches. The solution is to use the drawing-pin box as a base, pinned to the wall; 75 per cent of those who had seen a comedy film found the solution, compared with 13 per cent who had seen no film and 20 per cent who had seen a non-humourous film (Clark and Isen, 1982). In another experiment subjects were asked to rank six fictitious cars, for which nine kinds of data were provided. Subjects who had been allowed to succeed on a previous task used fewer kinds of information, checked these items less often, and did the task much faster, 11.1 minutes as opposed to 19.6 for controls. They seemed to be efficient decision-makers, not impulsive or careless, and not risk-takers (Isen and Means, 1983).

There is evidence that positive mood induction leads to more unusual and diverse word associations, showing that a broader range of associations can be tapped (Isen *et al.*, 1985); more fringe items are accepted as members of categories, like furniture, vegetables and vehicles (Isen and Daubman, 1984). This would make for enhanced creativity and problem-solving.

Helping and altruism

Many experiments have shown that happy people are more helpful and generous. This also works for good moods induced by success experiences in the laboratory, by receiving small gifts, or by recalling happy memories. On sunny days, more people stop to help with sociological surveys, and they tip waitresses more (Cunningham, 1979). And happy subjects are willing to help in a variety of ways (Batson *et al.*, 1979). These effects are far from trivial. In one experiment 47 per cent of subjects who had been put in a good mood by recalling happy past events offered to give blood, compared with 17 per cent in a control condition (O'Malley and Andrews, 1983). In a study of more permanent moods 1,988 people were rated as happy or not, and selfish or not, with these results:

		happy	
		yes	no
selfish	yes	3.9%	37.0%
	no	41.6%	17.5%

Source Rimland, 1982

Negative moods can also lead to higher levels of helping, but the process involved is quite different. Sad subjects help more if they believe that their moods are changeable (Manucia, Baumann and Cialdini, 1984), or if the costs involved are low (Weyant, 1978); helping others does indeed produce a more cheerful mood. Cheerful people too find that helping others is a rewarding experience which will sustain their mood. However, they still help more than control subjects, even if they have been led to believe that their moods are not manageable (Manucia, Baumann and Cialdini, 1984), regardless of rewards and costs involved (Weyant, 1978), and in the case of young children who do not find altruism self-gratifying, even if the help is anonymous. There is strong evidence then that happy people do not help to enhance their mood, as sad people do.

Why do good moods lead to more helpfulness? Good moods produce positive thoughts, perhaps including thoughts of positive, helpful behaviour. We shall see below that good moods lead to liking for other people, so that the rewards for helping them would be increased. And when someone is in a happy state he or she may see an imbalance between their own condition and that of others, and hence want to redress the balance in the interest of fairness (Dovidio, 1984). If subjects are put in a good mood they help a lot more if asked to focus on themselves, perhaps because this makes them more aware of such equity considerations. (Saddened people help more if they are asked to focus on the *other*) (Rosenhan, Salovey and Hargis, 1981).

Liking other people

Several of the studies cited earlier found evidence that good moods lead to more positive evaluations of others. Another experiment found that good moods, produced by funny films or reciting positive self-statements, led to higher scores of rated attraction to mythical other people, who were presented by a report of their attitudes (Gouaux, 1971). If real people are met in a beautiful as opposed to an ugly room (Mintz, 1956), or in a comfortable room as opposed to a crowded or very hot room (Griffit and Veitch, 1971), they are liked more.

CONCLUSION

Two main dimensions of emotional states have been found: pleasant–unpleasant and arousal–sleep. There is also evidence of a third dimension: 'depth', 'flow' or intense absorption.

There are about eight main causes of joy, some based on need-satisfaction, some on quite different sources. The effects of social events, exercise, drugs, etc. are partly physiological, partly psychological.

The physiological basis of positive emotions is that subjective experience provides a read-out of emotions. The pleasant quality is provided by the pleasure centres, but is modified by facial feedback, interpretation of the situation and the behaviour of other people.

Positive moods produce positive thoughts, improved recall of happy events, better creativity and problem-solving, more helping behaviour and greater liking for other people.

8
SATISFACTION WITH LIFE

We saw in Chapter 1 that satisfaction is one of the main components of happiness. Satisfaction is a kind of cool, reflective appraisal of how well things are going, and have been going. There is satisfaction with 'life as a whole', with work, leisure, marriage and other domains. We saw that most people say they are pretty satisfied with things, for satisfaction with life as a whole, and with marriage. Are people really as satisfied as they say they are? This is the classical problem of validity, which often arises with information from interviews or questionnaires.

Some of the results are rather puzzling. We saw that there is very little difference in satisfaction with income or material prosperity between rich and poor people and between those living in rich and poor countries. So what is the real situation? Many ways of asking about satisfaction have been tried, scales, ladders, pie-charts, and so on. They agree quite well with one another (Andrews and Withey, 1976). It looks as if people are expressing a perfectly genuine subjective state of some kind. On the other hand, it also looks as if commonsense ideas of the cause of satisfaction may be wrong, and that the experience of satisfaction is the result of psychological forces and biases in addition to the actual satisfaction of needs.

We will now look at some of the main theories that have been put forward to explain variations in satisfaction. We shall be able to draw on findings which have been reviewed earlier, for example on the effects of money, and personality, on satisfaction.

THE EFFECT OF OBJECTIVE CIRCUMSTANCES ON SATISFACTION

We saw in Chapter 2 that marriage, family life, friends, and other social relationships are major sources of satisfaction. Those who are married, especially those who are happily married, have a higher level of life satisfaction. We showed that there is evidence that marriage has a causal effect on satisfaction.

We saw in Chapter 3 that for most people being at work is a source of satisfaction, being unemployed a source of discontent. Again there is evidence that loss of job is a cause of low satisfaction. And people at work are more satisfied when the work is interesting, when they can use their skills, and when other conditions of work are good. However, it is not only the best-paid jobs that are satisfying: clergymen and university teachers are more satisfied than managers.

We saw in Chapter 4 that leisure is a great source of satisfaction. Active and involving forms of leisure are the most satisfying, but there are other sources of satisfaction as well, including relaxing in front of the TV.

These three areas of life – other people, work and leisure – are the three main domains of satisfaction, and satisfaction is affected by the actual state of affairs (whether a person is married or not, at work or not, and so on).

In the *Quality of American Life* study (Campbell, Converse and Rodgers, 1976), the following correlations were found between objective circumstances (e.g. actual income) and satisfaction:

health	.66
friends	.40
income	.25
education	.23

Here it is possible that the causal pattern is more complex, and that overall satisfaction may affect satisfaction in particular domains. On the other hand, there are some domains in which objective satisfaction has little effect on subjective satisfaction. We saw earlier (see p. 93) that satisfaction with income is only slightly greater for the better paid (a correlation of .15 to .25). The effect of income on happiness is similarly quite small (r = .20, or less) within countries. There is almost no relation between wealth and happiness *between* different countries, and the rising prosperity in the USA since 1957 has been accompanied by a falling level of satisfaction. Studies of satisfaction and changing economic conditions have found overall no stable relationship at all (Easterlin, 1974). People who win large sums of money in football pools or lotteries are not found to be on the whole more happy afterwards, though this is partly due to the disruption of their way of life, and loss of social contacts (p. 97).

There is a similar small correlation between amount of education and satisfaction with education (r = .23, Campbell, Converse and Rodgers, 1976). Better educated people are somewhat happier, because they are partly freed from material concerns (p. 95). Mental health is worse at the lower end of the social scale, partly because of the high level of everyday frustration. Physical health is also worse, partly because of poor health habits (more smoking, less exercise), and less access to medical facilities. Perhaps the strongest relationship in this area is between jobs and job satisfaction.

Another test of the effects of objective circumstances comes from comparison of different cities or regions. In one such study *no* relationship was found between satisfaction with recreation facilities and the actual availability of such facilities (Wasserman and Chua, 1980). Many poor whites in the USA are 'very satisfied' with their housing (Michaelos, 1980). There is some relationship between fear of crime and the crime rate for large cities (Wasserman and Chua, 1980); on the other hand, violent crime rate in the USA is about five times as high as that in Canada, but the fear of crime is about the same.

Does the satisfaction of needs produce satisfaction? We do not yet know the full list of human needs, though there is little doubt that people need food and drink, sex, acceptance by others, success, and so on. As we saw in the last chapter, joy is produced by the seeking of goals, and the arousal of needs, for example by intense involvement in work or leisure, as well as by the satisfaction of needs, and also by a variety of events with no obvious connection with needs at all – music, the countryside, etc.

There is little doubt that conditions of life affect satisfaction: people who have a stable marriage, an interesting job, good health, etc. are happier (Freedman, 1978). But this is far from the whole story, and a great deal of satisfaction is derived from activities which are very enjoyable but which have nothing to do with the satisfaction of needs.

THE EXPERIENCE OF PLEASANT EVENTS

If satisfaction is not always affected by objective conditions, perhaps it is affected by the experience of pleasant events, which we know can produce positive emotions. It has been found that simply putting people in a good mood increases their reports of satisfaction with life as a whole. In one study, good moods were induced by asking subjects to think of pleasant events, testing subjects on a sunny day, or in a nice room, after the German soccer team had won a match, or by letting them 'find' a small coin. Some of the results are shown in Table 8.1. These experiments show that short-term moods have quite a large effect on judgements of satisfaction. Subjects seem to be using their immediate mood as a source of information about how satisfying their lives are.

Further experiments by the same group of German investigators found that thinking of a past pleasant event did not increase satisfaction, while thinking of a past unpleasant event

Table 8.1 Effect of mood on satisfaction

pleasant event	unpleasant event	pleasant room	unpleasant room
8.6	5.7	9.40	8.10
sunny day	rainy day	team won	team lost
6.57	4.86	+2.5	−2.8

Sources Schwarz and Clore, 1983; Schwarz *et al.*, 1984.

did (see p. 150), showing the operation of comparison processes. However, thinking of a past pleasant event in terms of detailed, concrete imagery did produce increased satisfaction. When recalled in this way, pleasant events provide evidence of how good life has been (Strack, Schwarz and Gschneidinger, 1985).

We have seen that positive life events produce joy, negative life events distress. Success has been found for a form of therapy based on discovering which activities are most closely associated with good moods for an individual, and then encouraging him or her to engage in these activities more often (p. 205f). One way in which these activities can affect satisfaction is that people use positive moods, past and present, as evidence for their level of satisfaction. So satisfaction is, at least in part, based on the experience of joy. But there is a further complication: joy is also based, in part, on cognition. The same event can be a source of positive or negative affect depending on how it is interpreted (p. 136). A more general point is that if someone has high hopes for an event, and these are not realized, he or she will be less pleased than if nothing was expected. This is the basis for another theory of satisfaction, to which we now turn.

ASPIRATION AND ACHIEVEMENT

According to this theory, satisfaction is greater when achievements are close to aspirations, lower when they fall short. Aspirations in turn are based on comparisons with other people and own past experience. To test this theory it is necessary to ask about the gap between aspirations and achievement. The model proposed by Campbell, Converse and Rodgers (1976) is shown in Figure 8.1. Later versions of this model have suggested that it is only realistic aspirations, or those which are thought to be

Figure 8.1 The effect of comparisons on satisfaction

comparisons with*
most liked previous
experience
relatives   → aspiration
typical Americans   → achievement
all others   → gap   → satisfaction with
                                                                domain (housing,
                                                                finances, etc.)

*comparisons are listed in order of their influence on aspirations

Source Campbell, Converse and Rodgers, 1976.

Figure 8.2 Satisfaction with life as a whole: the goal-achievement gap model

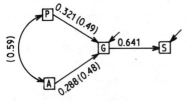

Source Michaelos, 1980. (Shows regression coefficients; zero-order correlations in brackets.)

deserved or are under one's own control, which work in this way (Taylor, 1982).

Various tests have been made of this model. An example is shown in Figure 8.2. It can be seen that the goal–achievement gap gives a good prediction of satisfaction (r = .64), and this is in turn predictable from comparisons with best previous experience (P) and with 'average people' (A). It is also found that P and A do not in themselves give good predictions of satisfaction. They have to be combined with achievements for the model to work.

In a later study (Michaelos, 1985) it was found that discrepancy measures predicted global satisfaction a little better than combining domain satisfaction scores. The discrepancy which predicted best was between aspirations and achievement, followed closely by comparison with others (see next section), and between what was achieved and what was thought to be deserved (equity). However it is by no means certain whether these gaps and aspiration levels cause satisfaction, rather than vice versa, or whether some more complex process is at work.

Job satisfaction has been found to depend on the satisfaction of needs, in relation to what is wanted or valued. Satisfaction with pay depends on the gap between what is wanted and what is received, and also on how much pay is valued. The same is true of other areas of job satisfaction, such as promotion and working conditions. Satisfaction is a product of the goal–achievement gap and the value of each particular goal (Locke, 1976). Work may satisfy higher-level needs or 'values' like growth, self-actualization, moral respect and security, and these same values can be satisfied in leisure (Veroff, Douvan and Kulka, 1981).

The goal–achievement gap theory has been used to explain

some of the historical results mentioned before. It has been noticed that improved economic conditions are often followed by discontent and political unrest. Several theories have been put forward to the effect that improved conditions produce expectations which rise too fast for the actual rate of improvement, resulting in discontent (Taylor, 1982). The falling satisfaction of Americans during the last 25 years may be because aspirations are rising faster than economic achievement can realize. The same process could explain the decline in the satisfaction of educated blacks over this period.

While there is some evidence that this theory applies to achievement, money, etc., it probably does not apply to more basic forms of satisfaction, like sex (Freedman, 1978). And we should not expect it to apply to intrinsic forms of satisfaction based, for example, on satisfying work or leisure. Aspirations may be very high, and tend to be revised upwards once a certain level has been achieved. High aspirations are a threat to happiness (Diener, 1984), and happiness therapy sometimes includes persuading people to lower their aspirations (p. 214).

COMPARISON WITH OTHER PEOPLE

In order to decide whether a person is 'tall' or 'short', we have to make comparisons with other people. Similarly, being 'intelligent', or 'good at tennis' requires social comparisons. How people make judgements or ratings depends on their understanding of what the points on the scale mean. Self-ratings of life satisfaction are likely to be based on comparisons with others, while reports of happiness depend more on immediate moods (McKennell and Andrews, 1980). It is possible to shift people's judgements by changing the way the scale is anchored at one end or the other. In one experiment subjects were asked to write a description of a day in Milwaukee in 1900, but were provided with materials with a 'good old days' or a 'bad old days' emphasis. They later rated their own present level of satisfaction; subjects who had the 'bad old days' manipulation said they were more satisfied now than those who had the 'good old days' materials (Dermer et al., 1979).

In another experiment subjects were tested in a very attractive room. Their general satisfaction was increased, but satisfaction with their housing was *reduced* (Schwarz *et al.*, 1984). One of the main ways of anchoring scales is by comparison with other people. We saw earlier that manual workers in the top third of British incomes were more satisfied than non-manual workers with the same incomes, because the manual workers compared their salaries with those of other manual workers, most of whom were paid less, while the non-manual workers were paid less than many other non-manual workers (p. 93f). In America college-educated people with a reasonably good income are less satisfied than non-graduates with the same incomes (Freedman, 1978).

In fact, a number of studies have found that the difference between, say, pay and the pay of others is a better predictor of satisfaction than pay itself. The best predictor of such satisfaction in one investigation was comparison with 'typical Americans'; the greater the positive discrepancy, the greater the well-being; averaging of discrepancies across 13 domains gave the best prediction of satisfaction with life as a whole (Carp and Carp, 1982). With whom do people choose to compare themselves? A study of workers in Wisconsin found that the majority did compare their pay with that of others, especially those in the same occupation (Fraser, 1984). Those most inviting comparison, and most visible, include people in the neighbourhood, relatives, and those who went to the same school or college.

There is another way in which people make social comparisons. Members of one group often compare themselves with members of rival or competing groups; they focus on attributes of their own group which can be used to show their superiority, thus enhancing their self-esteem (Turner and Giles, 1981). People who are objectively in an unfavourable situation can discover respects in which they are superior. Para- and quadriplegics for example think that brain is more important than brawn, and that they are good at social relationships (Schulz and Decker, 1985). This second kind of social comparison might be expected to enhance feelings of self-esteem, but perhaps increases the gap between what is achieved and deserved, i.e. feelings of inequity.

Many experiments have shown that when people are under stress, or have low self-esteem, they often choose to compare themselves with lower-status others. This has the effect of improving self-esteem, and even mental health, whereas the presence of more successful people can be a source of dissatisfaction and discomfort. We respond to the misfortune and failure of others in an ambivalent way. While we rarely accept that we are pleased about such events, they can nevertheless be a source of satisfaction (Wills, 1981). There is evidence that believing that others live in bad conditions can cheer up old people (Kearl, 1981–82).

People also use their own past for comparison purposes. There is evidence that those who were brought up in poverty during the Depression rate later periods of life rather positively (Elder, 1974). There may be an advantage in having had an unhappy childhood. Experimental data confirms that comparisons with the past can affect judgements of satisfaction in this way. In a German experiment, students were asked to think about three particularly positive and pleasant, or negative and unpleasant events in the past. They then made ratings, as points on a scale from 1 to 11, of their present level of satisfaction and happiness. The results were as follows:

	positive past event	negative past event
satisfaction	6.85	7.77
happiness	6.23	7.23

In a second experiment, subjects were asked to think about the past events either in an abstract way (why it happened) or in a very concrete way, evoking detailed memory images. The results were as follows:

	negative events	
	concrete	abstract
satisfaction	4.69	7.62
happiness	5.87	8.12

It can be seen that it is only their abstract memory of unpleasant past events which produced enhanced feelings of satisfaction; the concrete memories had a depressing effect (Strack, Schwarz and Gschneidinger, 1985).

An example of the comparisons made with other people and own past is given in Figure 8.3, which shows the results of an

Figure 8.3   Satisfaction with housing and neighbourhood

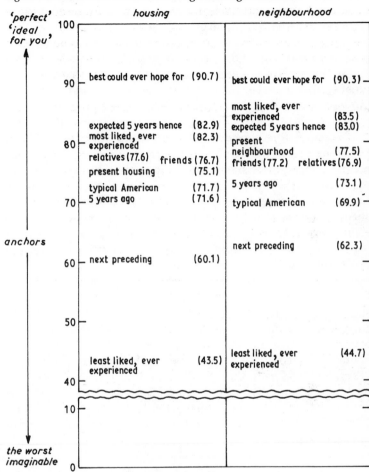

Source   Campbell, Converse and Rodgers, 1976.

American survey of people's perceptions of their housing and neighbourhood.

Social comparison theories offer an explanation of findings which are unexpected and puzzling, though the explanation tends to be post hoc and speculative. For example, the lack of differences in satisfaction between different countries has been explained in this way (Easterlin, 1974). However the differences are small only if the Cantril 'ladder' method is used, and this method deliberately asks people to think of comparison levels. India came out quite low (Figure 5.2), perhaps as a result of comparisons with the British or with very rich Indians. If absolute judgements of satisfaction are asked for the international differences are greater, though still rather puzzling (p. 103). For example Britain, USA, Canada and Australia come out as much more satisfied than Europe, and Africans as more satisfied as those in the Far East. Comparison levels are evidently only part of the story.

The lack of difference in satisfaction within countries has been given the same explanation. However we have seen that rich people are more satisfied than poor people, though not very much more; the main differences are at the bottom end of the social scale, though there is a trend in the USA for these differences in satisfaction to decrease. From comparison theory we should expect greater class differences in satisfaction.

Let us review the success of the social comparison theory. The evidence shows that comparison with others and with past experience is one source of judgements of satisfaction. On the other hand it is not the only factor: absolute ratings of satisfaction show greater differences than the ladder method between countries, and there are some differences in satisfaction within countries due to money or class. There must be limits to the operation of comparison processes: it is not the case that 'if everyone has a pain, then mine doesn't hurt' (Diener, 1984). It has been found that sexual satisfaction does not depend on beliefs about the inferior sexual activities of others (Freedman, 1978). Satisfaction does depend, to some extent, or direct appraisal of experience.

ADAPTATION

This is a familiar process in psychology. If someone is asked to judge the weights of a number of objects weighing between 2 and 6 ounces, a one-pounder will seem 'heavy', whereas if he had been judging 3 to 6 pound objects it would seem 'light'. Stimuli are judged against a standard based on the range of stimuli which have been experienced in the past. As applied to our present concerns, the same objective events or conditions could be sources of pleasure or pain depending on the previous adaptation level. A further implication is that adaptation does in fact take place, and perhaps people can get used to anything.

One of the main pieces of evidence cited in support of this theory is the claim that quadriplegic patients, who have lost the use of all four limbs, are just as happy as other people (Brickman and Campbell, 1971). However, in an extensive study of 100 para- and quadriplegics, it was found that after 20 years they were still a little less happy than the general population (Schulz and Decker, 1985). See Table 8.2, which shows self-report scales of subjective well-being and other measures of happiness. It can be seen that the patients reported lower present happiness compared with controls, which does *not* show adaptation, and greater past happiness, which suggests comparisons with the present.

The other evidence which has been thought to support adaptation theory is the finding that people who have won large sums of money on football pools or lotteries are no more satisfied than other people (see p. 97). In the Brickman *et al.* study, 22 lottery winners averaged 4.0 on the present happiness scale, compared to 3.82 for 88 controls. The results of research on winners of football pools and lotteries show that the effects are quite complex, often involving giving up work, moving house, and having awkward contacts with friends and relatives.

In any case adaptation takes some time, and there is a period of raised or lowered satisfaction before it sets in. If satisfaction depends on increases of rewards, this could explain why people often strive for more than they have already. Another way of increasing satisfaction would be via periods of abstinence followed by periods of satisfaction (Brickman and Campbell, 1971), though it is not clear that the overall satisfaction would be any higher.

Table 8.2 Happiness of para- and quadriplegics

	patients	general population
subjective well-being	10.76 (n=100)	12–13
depression	9.74	9.25
positive feelings	4.04	3.77 (1 is positive)
present happiness	2.96 (n=29)	3.82 (n=88)
past happiness	4.41	3.32

Sources Brickman, Coates and Janoff-Bulman, 1978; Schulz and Decker, 1985

Common experience suggests that basic satisfaction, from food, sex, the company of other people, interesting work, do *not* cease to satisfy because they have remained constant. As we showed earlier, some objective circumstances *do* affect satisfaction.

Adaptation theory can explain why the weather seems to have so little effect on satisfaction. Sunny and rainy days have some effect on mood and ratings of life satisfaction, as we have just seen (p. 145), but sunny and rainy climates make little difference, presumably because people get used to them. This would be an ideal sphere for research on adaptation theory. For example, 65°F should be experienced as 'hot' or 'cold' depending on the prevailing climate, and the extent of adaptation should depend on the consistency of the weather. The only exception is where the weather is exceptionally bad, for example in central Canada; then some of the population move away when they can. There are limits to what can be adapted to.

Adaptation theory provides a further explanation, if one is needed, for the small difference in satisfaction between countries and classes, and for the relatively high happiness of the seriously handicapped. It makes a number of interesting, and counter to commonsense, predictions about how to enhance satisfaction. There is one, possibly fatal, objection however. As we saw in Chapter 6, some people are very happy, others very depressed; why has adaptation not taken place (Freedman, 1978)?

LOOKING ON THE BRIGHT SIDE: THE POLLYANNA EFFECT

Are people really as satisfied as they say they are? In the surveys that we have reviewed most people claim to be very satisfied, or 'happier than most', or tick points 6 and 7 on 7-point scales of satisfaction. Perhaps they are not telling the truth, or perhaps they are not facing up to the truth. Take marital satisfaction for example: 68 per cent said they were very happily married (point 7 on a 7-point scale) and 22 per cent nearly as happy (point 6) (Abrams, 1973). Yet we know that over a third of marriages end in divorce, and that there is physical violence between many couples (Argyle and Henderson, 1985).

It looks as if there is some kind of systematic distortion of judgement going on. An explanation of how it may happen comes from the German experiments discussed above on the effect of experimentally-induced moods on reported satisfaction. In one experiment subjects were studied when in good or bad moods by being tested on sunny or rainy days, or in pleasant or unpleasant rooms. Some subjects had their attention drawn to the weather, or the room, offering an explanation for their mood ('We are interested in how weather affects a person's mood'). The results for life satisfaction were as follows:

	no priming	*priming*
sunny	6.57	7.21
rainy	4.86	7.07

Source Schwarz and Clore, 1983

It can be seen that it is only the negative mood which is affected by the priming, while those who were in a good mood were unaffected – a good mood needs no explanation. So positivity bias could be due to people searching for alternative explanations for negative moods, not for good ones.

CONCLUSIONS

Objective circumstances have a rather small effect on satisfaction, especially such variables as income and education. Marriage, work and leisure have a greater effect.

Pleasant events produce positive moods, and also increase judgements of life satisfaction. The gap between aspiration and achievement modifies the effects of actual need satisfaction, though it has little effect on biological satisfactions. The same applies to comparisons with other people. These processes explain a number of anomalous results, such as satisfaction falling as prosperity rises, and the lack of differences in satisfaction between rich and poor countries. Adaptation to any particular conditions sets in, within limits, though some genuine sources of satisfaction seem to persist in their power to satisfy.

9

AGE AND SEX

AGE

Happiness does not vary much with age. It depends on which measures are used. If the emphasis is on satisfaction or cognitive appraisal of well-being, there is a definite *increase* with age. In Figure 9.2 later we show the steady increase of job satisfaction with age. There is also some increase in the average level of reported happiness (Witt *et al.*, 1980). A recent British study confirmed this relationship for 'being very pleased with things yesterday' (Warr and Payne, 1982) (Table 9.1).

There is a problem with this kind of research, in that what appear to be age differences could be generation differences – between people brought up in different historical periods. The answer is to carry out longitudinal studies of the same individuals at different ages, and we cited some of these in the section above on unemployment (p. 55). However, there are no such studies for age differences in general, although very similar age differences are frequently found in researches which were carried

Table 9.1 Age and 'feeling very pleased with things yesterday'

	age			
	16–24 %	25–44 %	45–64 %	65+ %
all of the time	19	22	28	35
most of the time	38	39	30	25

Source Warr and Payne, 1982.

out at different dates and in different countries, which gives confidence that these probably are genuine age effects.

Measures of the frequency of joy, or positive emotions, show a progressive *decrease* with age. And the frequency of pleasant activities falls off quite appreciably with age (Lewinsohn and MacPhillamy, 1974). Table 9.2 shows this decline in both positive and negative affect. Figure 9.1 shows the average ratings of the frequency and the enjoyability of pleasant events, on a 0 to 1 scale, at different ages, from one American study. There is no significant decline in the enjoyability of events, just in their frequency. This is confirmed by the fall in participation in all kinds of leisure and in sexual activity. And the *intensity* of feelings, both positive and negative, declined with age, from 4.31 to 3.95 on a 1–6 scale in one study (Diener, Sandvik and Larsen, 1985). It needs no research to show that children laugh and cry a lot, and research on ageing has shown that older people have 'flattened affect'. Putting this together, older people are more satisfied, but experience less frequent and less intense feelings, both positive and negative.

There is some evidence that while men become happier when they get older, the opposite is true of women, who are

Table 9.2 Age and emotions

	age			
	21–29	30–39	40–49	50–59
positive affect	.55	.47	.41	.40
negative affect	.56	.51	.48	.48

Source Bradburn, 1969.

Figure 9.1 Number of pleasant activities and enjoyment at different ages

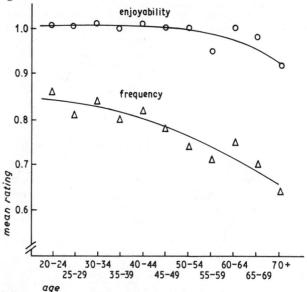

Source Lewinsohn and MacPhillamy, 1974.

happiest when young, at any rate before they have children. Satisfaction is greater than happiness for the elderly, but especially for those who are uneducated.

What is the explanation of these age changes? Older people have a smaller discrepancy between aspiration and achievement – they are more adjusted to their situation. Table 9.3 shows how much the gap between aspirations, expectations and present reality changes with age. The first line shows the differences, for people of various ages, between what they could ever hope for (aspirations) and what they have (actual), both on scales from 0 to 100. Expectations are what they realistically expect. The patterns shown by the figures are partly due to lowered aspirations, partly to rising achievement, so that the two almost meet in old age, while the very young have both low attainments, and wildly optimistic hopes of the future (Campbell, Converse and Rodgers, 1976). In addition there is a process of accommodation to things as they are; we shall discuss this in connection with the increasing level of job satisfaction. The reason for uneducated older people

Table 9.3 Aspirations versus reality as a function of age

	age						
	18–24	25–34	35–44	45–54	55–64	65–74	75–90
housing							
aspiration							
minus actual	23.7	23.6	14.5	12.7	7.4	8.8	4.2
expectation							
minus actual	12.4	17.8	8.1	4.1	0.7	0.2	0.7
neighbourhood							
aspiration							
minus actual	18.0	19.8	11.0	12.0	8.1	1.0	8.6
expectation							
minus actual	10.1	11.7	5.3	3.4	0.9	−2.7	1.2

Source Campbell, Converse and Rodgers, 1976.

being so satisfied – though not very happy – is perhaps because in their youth they had not developed very high expectations, and came to accept things as they were.

These age changes can be further understood by examining changes in the sources of happiness. These alter in importance during the life cycle. Another American study compared the sources of happiness of people at different ages. For young subjects (21–29) marriage was an important source of both happiness and unhappiness, as were other social relationships, with family, friends and children. (See also Chapter 2, 'Social relationships'.) Economic and material worries, and job worries were also important. However, this age group was the most optimistic about the future. The middle-aged subjects (40–49) reported the greatest 'zest', that is finding life interesting, feeling useful, seeing life as full and hopeful, being aware of the richness of their present life, though not quite as 'happy' or optimistic as the young. The older subjects (65+) were less happy and optimistic, less concerned with jobs, money or relationships and social acceptance, and more concerned with their health. But they felt more able to take problems in their stride than younger people, had a greater sense of perspective, and were less overwhelmed by problems. We can conclude that at different ages the problems which people face are rather different, so that they focus on different sources of well-being (Veroff, Douvan and Kulka, 1981).

Predictive studies of happiness among the elderly find that the most important factors are health, income and social contacts (e.g. Edwards and Klemmack, 1973). Health is important at all ages, but is especially so for the elderly, for whom it is often a problem and source of worry. Income is relatively unimportant for younger people, much more so for the elderly, again since they have less of it. Social contacts are important at all ages.

Age changes in *relationships* and satisfaction with them were discussed in Chapter 2. *Job satisfaction* is usually found to increase with age, and a typical pattern of results is shown in Figure 9.2, based on averaging several large-scale American surveys. Age changes in *health* come later (p. 162).

Leisure activities, and presumably satisfaction with them, also decline with age. The only leisure activity which increases with age is watching TV.

Income, and satisfaction with income, increase with age. After the children have left home, people are suddenly better off; after they have retired they may be worse off.

Physical attractiveness is a moderately important source of satisfaction, especially for women and particularly for young women, and it inevitably declines with age.

Older people are more religious, and there is a stronger link between *religion* and well-being among the elderly. The religious

Figure 9.2   The effect of age on job satisfaction

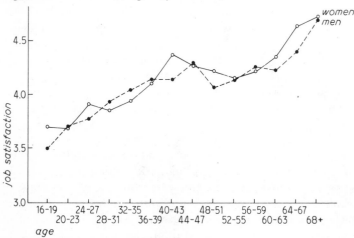

Source   Kalleberg and Loscocco, 1983.

are happier and in better health (p. 196f). Perhaps for this reason older people are more at peace, and more optimistic about the future than young people (Freedman, 1978).

Fear of ageing increases with age, and is quite strongly correlated with a low level of subjective well-being (Klemmack and Roff, 1984). This is partly fear of declining health and attractiveness, of loneliness, and of death; the last of these at least is offset by religious beliefs (Argyle and Beit-Hallahmi, 1975).

STRAIN, NEGATIVE AFFECT AND MENTAL DISORDER

Surveys of unpleasant emotional strain, or of minor degrees of mental disorder, show a steady decline with age, or a peak for the 30–40 age group, followed by a decline. This peak is probably caused by the presence of young children. A similar decline with a peak in the 30s is found in British studies (Eysenck, 1975; Crown and Crisp, 1979), and in Australia (Finlay-Jones and Burrill, 1977).

However, some of the sub-scales, measuring particular areas of symptoms, have obtained a rather different trend with age. A more rapid fall with age is found for hysterical symptoms (Crown and Crisp, 1979) and for immobilization (Gurin, Veroff and Feld, 1960) – both of which consist of withdrawal or giving up in the face of stress.

The chance of suffering from a definite mental disorder also varies with age. *Depression* is more common among people over 40, especially for women. *Schizophrenia* is more likely to start in those under 30. Some *psychosomatic symptoms* increase with age, especially indigestion, constipation, hypertension, colitis and weight trouble. Others however *decline* with age – headaches, nervous stomach, diarrhoea (Schwab and Schwab, 1978). Older people suffer less from nervous irritability, and other symptoms of strain, though they have more difficulty in sleeping, and they take a lot more sedatives and other pills (Dunnell and Cartwright, 1972).

At different ages people use different ways of coping with stress, as Table 9.4 shows, from both US and UK studies. It can be seen that younger people react to stress by seeking informal help from other people, and making direct attempts to solve the problem, though they also eat more. Middle-aged people are the most likely to eat and smoke more. Older people react more

Table 9.4   Age differences in ways of coping with stress

UK (1982) age		drink more %	eat more %	informal help-seeking %	smoke more %	take medicine %	see doctor %
16–24	men	10	9	12	9	3	1
	women	5	14	13	16	4	4
25–44	men	7	7	7	17	9	3
	women	7	20	5	21	14	4
45–64	men	8	4	9	18	19	10
	women	4	7	6	15	25	11
65+	men	5	4	5	10	32	8
	women	4	5	8	4	33	14

USA (1960) age		passive reactions %	prayer %	direct coping reaction %	informal help-seeking %
18–34	total	20	7	16	39
35–54	total	34	18	15	24
55+	total	38	23	12	14

Source   Gurin, Veroff and Feld, 1960; Warr and Payne, 1982.

passively, resort more to prayer, and more often see the doctor and take medicine.

HEALTH

The amount of illness slowly increases with age. The percentage of people with long-standing illness goes up from 22 per cent (age 15–44) to 51 per cent (age 65–74) and 60 per cent (70+) for males, and to 58 per cent (age 65–74) and 70 per cent (75+) for females (*General Household Survey*, 1980). The level of 'long-standing illness' increases rapidly to affect 23 per cent of the population by 15–44, but only about half of this illness is 'limiting'. And only 7 per cent of those aged 15–44 state that their health in the last year was not good; this increases considerably among older people. The number of days of restricted activity per year shows a similar steady rise. The frequency of going to the doctor more than doubles between childhood and old age.

The probability of dying is small until the age of 50, and then increases rapidly (see Table 10.1, p. 180). This is based on the British Census for those born in 1960–62, making predictions from earlier years. It can be seen that there is a steadily increasing number who die in each period, so that of males born in 1960, 10.4 per cent will probably die between the ages of 60 and 65; 13.7 per cent between 65 and 70; and so on. Forty-two per cent of the females and 23 per cent of the males will still be alive at the age of 80, in 2040, assuming no nuclear or other catastrophes.

Living or dying are partly dependent on the will to live, which can be assessed by asking people to rate their keenness to carry on living. The will to live is much reduced in those who are socially isolated, who are in poor health, or who feel that they have lost their usefulness (Ellison, 1969). However, the causes of death vary greatly with age: young people are most likely to die from accidents or violence, middle-aged men from heart disease, middle-aged women from cancer, and so on.

Health-related behaviour changes with age. The level of heavy drinking declines considerably, as Table 9.5 shows. 'Heavy' drinking is defined here as 7 or more units (i.e. glasses of wine, half pints of beer) once or twice a week or more; 'moderate' drinking is defined as 7 or more units once or twice a month, or 5 or more units once or twice a week. There are no corresponding

Table 9.5 Age and drinking

| | moderate | | heavy | |
age	men	women	men	women
18–24	37	4	19	9
25–44	31	3	16	6
45–64	17	1	14	2
65+	4	0	8	0

Source   *General Household Survey*, 1980.

changes in smoking. The heaviest smokers, however, are those aged between 25 and 60. The amount of exercise taken generally falls off with age, as Table 9.6 shows, summarizing the results of a British questionnaire which asked about exercise taken in the previous four weeks. It can be seen that, while the more vigorous forms of exercise fall off rapidly with age, walking falls off much more slowly.

CONCLUSIONS

Are older people happier? They are more satisfied and somewhat happier, but they experience positive emotions and engage in pleasant activities less often; conversely, they also experience negative emotions less often, and their emotions are less intense. There are increases of satisfaction in some of the most important domains – work, marriage (after the children have grown up), income, leisure and religion. There is a *decline* of satisfaction however in the areas of health, sex and physical attractiveness.

Table 9.6 Age and exercise

| | swimming | | football | walking (2 miles+) | |
age	men %	women %	men %	men %	women %
16–19	15	22	24	13	22
20–34	14	15	11	20	22
35–59	8	6	2	21	19
60+	1	1	0	18	12

Source   *Social Trends*, 1983.

Part of the explanation of the general increase in satisfaction is simply that older people are better off, and enjoy a better standard of living. In addition they succeed in accommodating themselves to their situation and environment, either by changing these or by changing themselves. And their aspirations and expectations are lower than they once were, almost in line with things as they are.

Strain declines and mental health improves, after a bad period in the 30s, which coincides with the rearing of young children. On the other hand, depression is more common among older people, as are some psychosomatic symptoms, like indigestion and hypertension. Older people worry less and feel less strain, but they take more pills. The general improvement is partly due to accommodation, and the gradual solving of major problems. Older people also have more resources for coping with stress – more money, more social contacts and more skills.

Health is the main area in which there is deterioration with age, especially after 50. The death rate from heart attacks and some other illnesses increases. This is partly due to a gradual biological decline, though it is largely due to accumulated problems, some of them avoidable and caused by bad health habits – lack of exercise, bad diet, drinking and smoking – and by stress.

SEX

HAPPINESS AND SATISFACTION

We start with studies of positive affect, or elation, as described in Chapter 1. The most recent British study, of 3077 adults, asked them how much of the time they felt pleased with things yesterday, and concluded that there was no overall difference between men and women (Warr and Payne, 1982). However studies of positive and negative affect find that women have more frequent negative affect, but also a little more frequent positive affect (Bradburn, 1969; Harding, 1982).

Women tend to feel emotions, both positive and negative, with somewhat greater intensity, at all ages. Women had an average score of 4.34, men 3.88 on a scale from 1–6 (Diener, Sandvik and

Larsen, 1985). Gender effects are different for old and young. For those aged under 45, and even more for those under 30, there is a statistical trend for women to be happier than men, especially if they have no children. For people over 55, men are happier than women (Spreitzer and Snyder, 1974; Campbell, Converse and Rodgers, 1976), see Figure 9.3.

As we discussed in Chapter 2 (p. 16), most single people are less happy than married people, but the difference is greater for men, who seem to get more out of marriage than women. The most unhappy people tend to be men who have never married, together with divorced or separated women (Campbell, Converse and Rodgers, 1976). The sources of satisfaction and happiness are different for men and women. Men are affected more by economic and material factors, and by their jobs; women are affected more by their children and the health of the family. Men are more concerned with the local community and with wider political affairs (Veroff, Douvan and Kulka, 1981; Warr and Payne, 1982), and, according to Campbell (1981), men are somewhat more satisfied with themselves than women, who are more self-critical. Men feel that they are more in control of their lives.

Figure 9.3　Gender differences in happiness at different ages

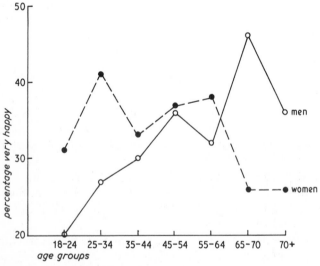

Source　Spreitzer and Snyder, 1974.

The sources of self-satisfaction are rather different for the two sexes. For men being tall is important; for women it is not, provided that they are not too far from the norm, preferably about 5′ 8″ (1.74m). For women physical attractiveness is much more important. Obesity is a problem here; more women are over-weight than men, especially working-class women, and over-weight women are very unhappy about their appearance. Few people over the age of 45 are judged attractive by others, so this is a source of dissatisfaction for older women.

STRAIN, NEGATIVE AFFECT AND MENTAL DISORDER

Warr and Payne's (1982) British survey found that 18 per cent of women and 13 per cent of men experienced 'unpleasant emotional strain yesterday', for about half of the time or more. A national survey of American mental health found that 37 per cent of women and 26 per cent of men worried for much or all of the time, while 25 per cent of women and 12 per cent of men felt that they were about to have a nervous breakdown (Table 9.7).

Other studies, in a number of countries, based on community surveys or on records from GPs and out-patient clinics, all show the same trend – that women suffer from symptoms of mental disorder, both minor and major, much more than men. In the USA, however, it has been found in successive surveys that in the years 1957 to 1976, the gap between women and men has been

Table 9.7   Sex differences in strain and mental health

	men %	women %
experienced unpleasant emotional strain yesterday for about half of the time or more	13	18
worried a lot or all the time	26	37
felt about to have a nervous breakdown	12	25
report nerves, depression or irritability	14	27
report sleeplessness	12	20
take tranquillizers, sedatives or sleeping pills	6	13
scored over 12 on GHQ	13.5	18.7
diagnosed by doctor as having mental disorder	7.4	14.9

Sources   Gurin, Veroff and Feld, 1960; Dunnell and Cartwright, 1972; Goldberg, 1978; Warr and Payne, 1982.

Table 9.8 Typical sex ratios for mental illness, alcoholism and crime

	men : women
depression	1:2
neurosis, anxiety, etc.	1:1.5
mental disorder, all kinds	1:1.7
schizophrenia	1:1
alcoholism	3:1
crime	8.5:1

Sources Gomberg and Franks, 1979; Guttentag, Salasin and Belle, 1980; Cockerham, 1981.

closing (Kessler and McRae, 1981). The ratio of female to male attempted suicide rates was about 3:1 in 1957, and has now declined to about 1.4:1 in the USA; more men and fewer women make the attempt (Kessler and McRae, 1983).

Part of the difference between men and women is that women decide more readily that they have an emotional or psychiatric problem, and seek help, on the basis of minor or vague signs of depression or lack of well-being – or that men decide less readily. Up to a quarter of the sex differences in mental health have been found to be due to this (Verbrugge, 1976; Kessler, Price and Wortman, 1981). The reason for this is that depression, anxiety and other symptoms of mental ill-health have been found to be more acceptable in women, while men who show such symptoms are rejected (Hammen and Peters, 1978; Cockerham, 1981).

However, the position is very different for the various kinds of mental illness, and for alcoholism and crime. Typical sex ratios are shown in Table 9.8, which uses US data. There is a great difference for depression (females:males 2:1), and the level of clinical depression among certain groups of women is rather high. Among working-class women in Camberwell those who were clinical or borderline cases of depression totalled 34 per cent for working-class women, and an even higher percentage if they had young children at home, did not have a supportive husband, did not have a job, or had recently experienced stressful life events (Brown and Harris, 1978). Another typical depressed person is a working-class woman who has recently lost a social attachment, such as a widow, or someone whose children have left home.

The sex difference is less for psychosis in general, while for schizophrenia there is no difference between the sexes. And there are some conditions for which men have the higher rates: alcoholism and drug-addiction. Men also have a far greater crime rate: about 8.5 times that of women (Guttentag, Salasin and Belle, 1980). This sex difference varies with marital condition: it is greater for the married than the single, from which some have argued that female ill-health is due to the frustrations of marriage for women (Gove, 1972). However, the sex differences in mental disorder, while high for the married, are still present for the single, divorced and widowed, including female heads of families (Fox, 1980; Guttentag, Salasin and Belle, 1980). I believe that the correct interpretation is that men get more out of marriage than women, in particular receiving more social support, as was shown in Chapter 2. Single men have a very high rate of mental disturbance.

Worry and strain vary with the life cycle. Women experience more strain before marriage, feel more frustrated and tied down when they have pre-school children, and are unhappy if in later life they have no children or if they are unmarried mothers – both seen as failures to meet popular expectations. Men are worried about money in the early years of marriage, and are more distressed in later life if unmarried (Campbell, 1981).

Why do women, on the whole, have higher levels of depression, anxiety, and other manifestations of stress? Is it because women are exposed to greater stress than men? We discuss below the theory that the female role is more stressful. In addition, there is evidence that women are more exposed to stress from unemployment and low incomes (Reskin and Coverman, 1985). Is it because women are more vulnerable, that is more upset by a given level of stress? We discuss below theories that the way girls are socialized and the resulting coping styles may be responsible (Kessler, Price and Wortman, 1985).

Does the strain of work make women mentally ill? On the whole women at work are *less* mentally ill than other women, partly because the more fit are able to do a job. However, having a job *and* small children can produce depression – the children offset the benefits of employment (Cleary and Mechanic, 1983). This is because women experience conflict between the two roles: married women with jobs do 5 hours a week more housework than their husbands and lower their career aspirations accordingly (Haw, 1982). Of course, the stress depends on the job; for example, women doctors have a high rate of suicide and depression.

One theory is that it is the roles which men and women play that are responsible. Fixed occupational roles, with clear demands, make it difficult to postpone things, take time off, or adopt the sick role; there is pressure to keep going. The domestic role lacks these demands and is unstructured, as well as being isolated and of low prestige (Gove and Tudor, 1973; Gove, 1984). This theory is supported by the facts that women with young children are more mentally ill and those with jobs less so, (although, where the domestic role is valued more, for instance, in countries like Mexico, there are smaller differences between the sexes), (Ross, Mirowsky and Ulbrich, 1983). It has been suggested that married women are confronted by a 'double-bind': if they become housewives they will be isolated, trapped and unrewarded; if they do a job they will be in conflict between the demands of work and home (Tavris and Offir, 1977). In fact, housewives find marriage restricting and burdensome and seem to be in worse mental health than either married women with jobs or single women with jobs (Birnbaum, 1975). Women sometimes say that what they really need is a wife (Rohrbaugh, 1981).

The explanation of these gender differences probably lies, at least partly, in socialization experience. Girls are reared differently from boys, to be more dependent, and become more likely to react to frustration in a helpless rather than an assertive manner; this could interact with later positions of lower power and status than men and produce depression (Radloff, 1980). Girls are also reared with a close attachment to their mothers, producing a greater need for social support and a greater sensitivity to loss of attachment in later life; this may interact with lower social support from husbands, a greater probability of being widowed, and more difficulties after divorce (Weissman and Klerman, 1979).

Another way of explaining these results is to contrast male and female ways of coping with stress. Where women give up and become depressed, men take to drink, or become aggressive and break the law. Surveys have found marked sex differences in how people cope with things that worry or bother them, or periods of unhappiness, as Table 9.9 shows. It can be seen that women are less likely to take constructive action, make more use of prayer, and get less help from their spouses. They also eat more and resort to medicines. On the other hand, men are more likely to do nothing, and receive less informal support from friends and others. It is not obvious that the male package of coping strategies is superior.

Table 9.9   Sex differences in methods of coping with worries

UK (1982)	men %	women %
take medicine or tablets	13	18
eat a bit more than usual	6	13
drink a bit more than usual	8	5

USA (1976)	men %	women %
positive coping (do something)	19	9
passive methods (do nothing)	27.5	21.5
prayer	16.5	29.5
seek informal help	43.5	52.5
(of these) from spouse (married only)	73	58
friends	32	34
children	2	6

Source   Warr and Payne, 1982; Veroff, Douvan and Kulka, 1981.

HEALTH

Different indices suggest that women are on average in worse health than men. As Table 9.10 shows, using British data, women have more short-term, acute illnesses: the difference is between 12 and 20 per cent at different times, greater than this for coughs, bronchitis, etc. Overall, however, there is little or no difference in long-standing illness. Working-class men aged 45 to 64 have a *higher* rate than women; women aged 65+ have a higher rate than men (Black, 1980; and see Figure 10.2, pp. 190–1). However, more women think they are in poor health, and there is a much greater difference in frequency of seeing the doctor, taking medicine and days off. Women are 'more attentive to bodily discom-

Table 9.10 Sex differences in health and illness (UK)

	men %	women %
long-standing illness	28	30
limiting long-standing illness	16	19
acute sickness in last 2 weeks	10	13
reported health in past year as:		
good	64	54
fairly good	26	32
not good	11	14
saw doctor in last 2 weeks	11	15
had 1 symptom, took prescribed medicine	22	37
average number of visits to doctor per year	3.6	4.8
average number of days of restricted activity per year	22.8	29.8
average number of symptoms	3.2	4.5

Sources Dunnell and Cartwright, 1972; *General Household Survey*, 1980.

fort', especially for minor illnesses, and that is perhaps one the reason why they live longer (Verbrugge, 1985).

A lot of female illness is due to problems of menstruation and pregnancy. Women also have more trouble with varicose veins and their feet; they have more disease of the blood and of the circulatory system. Men suffer more from heart disease and bronchitis, and from the effects of accidents, poisoning and violence (Reid and Wormald, 1982). If self-report surveys are compared with clinical data, it is found that women over-report their illnesses (or men under-report them) and, having decided that they are ill, seek medical help at a lower level of illness. Other studies have found that women take more medicine than men, with the same symptoms (Dunnell and Cartwright, 1972).

Although women appear to have worse health than men they also live longer, (see Table 10.1, p. 180). The percentages of men and women in Britain who do not live to collect their pensions at 65 are 31.5 per cent and 18.7 per cent respectively. What is the explanation of this apparent paradox? Part of the answer is that the minor and short-term illnesses from which women suffer, or think they suffer, are rarely fatal. The illnesses which men suffer from, especially the chronic ones, are more serious (see Table 10.2, p. 183).

The important differences between men and women lie in the rate of deaths due to heart attacks (due to stress), lung cancer (partly due to smoking), accidents (due to reckless driving and dangerous occupations), cirrhosis of the liver (due to drinking), and suicide (partly due to unemployment and failure at work). It is now clear that the main explanation for the shorter lives of men relates to behaviour which is encouraged in men – smoking, drinking, fast driving, competitiveness, all part of the way of life of men at work (Waldron, 1976). The female advantage has been declining in recent years, as women adopt a way of life more similar to that of men (Verbrugge, 1976). It is also possible that there are genetic differences in favour of women. One theory is that male sex hormones inhibit the immune system and make men less resistant to infection (Waldron and Johnston, 1976) but this is probably less important than the behavioural effects discussed.

It is also possible that women benefit from the stronger social support networks which they establish with family and kin, friends and neighbours (Argyle and Henderson, 1985) (see Chapter 2). The benefits which women receive from these networks include medical advice – health is one of the main things women talk about – as well as material help and social and emotional support. The one relationship in which women do less well than men is marriage.

Does having a job make women more prone to illness? As we saw earlier, on the whole, women at work are in better health than housewives, though this may be partly because only those who are well enough stay at work. And although women in general are more likely to see the doctor for a given degree of ill-health, this is only true of women who are not at work and who have a chronic rather than an acute illness (Marcus and Siegel, 1982). This last finding provides an explanation of why men go to the doctor less – it is because the demands of work make them less willing to waste time being ill, or the demands of masculinity make them less willing to admit to bodily weakness. It also depends on the job: highly educated women in good jobs have fewer chronic illnesses and live longer, while women in clerical jobs have a high rate of heart attacks (Wingerson, 1981; Haw, 1982).

The largest health difference between the sexes, and the most common cause of death, is coronary heart disease. The causes of this are known: smoking, high cholesterol, and high blood pressure, some of which in turn are due to stress, poor diet and lack of exercise. Women suffer less from heart disease partly because they smoke less. However, after the age of 55 these factors give much weaker predictions of heart disease for women – who are actually more at risk in these terms, and for whom other factors are more important (Johnson, 1977). Type A personality – the tendency to be aggressively hard-working, impatient and competitive – is more common among men, and is a predictor of coronary heart disease. More women with jobs have type A personalities, but the rate is lower than for men with jobs. Women who have young children at home and have jobs suffer more from coronaries: 11 per cent of working women with three young children had coronaries compared with 4.4 per cent of unemployed housewives with the same number of children (Haw, 1982).

CONCLUSION

There is little gender difference in satisfaction with life as a whole or in positive affect, but women have more negative affect and more intense feelings. Young women and older men are happier, single men are the least happy. There is not much difference in satisfaction with different domains, though more men are very satisfied with marriage and women have a more satisfying social network. Men get more satisfaction and dissatisfaction from their work, and enjoy different aspects of it. They also have more active leisure, and tend to be more pleased with themselves.

The differences in health are more interesting: women have somewhat worse health, mainly through gynaecological problems and minor ailments, but live longer than men, probably because women smoke and drink less, have less stress, live less dangerously, are less likely to have type A personalities, and look after themselves better.

Women have much higher levels of depression, anxiety and other signs of stress, though this is partly because women decide they are ill, or have emotional problems, more readily. It is partly because of the conflict between home and work, the stresses of looking after children, and may be a consequence of the way girls are socialized combined with their position of lower power in later life. It is interesting to note that these differences are smaller in the most recent studies. See Chapter 10 for a more general discussion of the links between health and happiness.

10

•HEALTH•

Health is an important aspect of overall well-being, indeed an *objective* aspect of it. It is closely linked with happiness, and is widely regarded as one of the main causes of happiness. Many investigations have been made of the connection between health and happiness, and a meta-analysis of such studies found an average correlation of .32. This was stronger for women, and was greater if subjective measures of health were used (Okun *et al.*, 1984). A strong connection is found between negative affect, feelings of distress or amount of worrying, and poor health (Tessler and Mechanic, 1978; Burchfield, Holmes and Harrington, 1981).

Not only are happiness and satisfaction affected by health, but this link is particularly strong for older people. The connection between life satisfaction and health holds up when other variables, for instance, social status and income, are held constant (Edwards and Klemmack, 1973). And if *health* is held constant, other variables affecting life satisfaction become less important, such as membership of voluntary associations for old people (Buck and Aucoin, 1975), and show an important causal network:

social networks
work   → health → happiness
leisure, etc.

However, happiness probably causes health, as well as vice versa, in other words, we can simply regard health as another component of well-being. In any case health is affected by all the variables we have discussed already, though the details are different. For example, stress is bad for both physical health and mental health, and social support offsets these effects – but the processes involved are quite different.

Health is rated, in Britain and the USA, as the second most important domain of satisfaction after marriage (p. 7). This is not, however, the case in all parts of the world. For example, the Koreans place health nineteenth in a list of goals and values. The World Health Organization definition of health is 'A state of complete physical, mental and social well-being and not the absence of disease or infirmity'. In this section we shall be concerned with physical well-being. How well do people feel? How many have symptoms of ill-health? Subjective feelings of ill-health go beyond formal medical diagnosis and have been described as the 'iceberg' of symptoms below the surface of normal medical diagnosis. For this reason we shall concentrate on surveys of self-reported health.

The best measure of an individual's health is a complete medical examination by a doctor, supported by a number of medical tests. This method has been used in surveys of GP lists, but there is a problem: 30 per cent of people or more have not seen a doctor in the last year, and over 10 per cent never see one at all (Wadsworth, Butterfield and Blaney, 1971). There is also the problem of different doctors applying different standards of 'good' health. A similar method is to make use of clinic records, and to find out the symptoms reported by different populations (Reis *et al.*, 1984).

There is some advantage in using social-survey methods to assess health, in order to sample those who do not go to the doctor, and to find out how ill people feel. The British *General Household Survey* (1980), of about 25,000 homes, includes questions like:

Would you say your state of health in the past fourteen days
was (average of several surveys)

	%
perfect	31
good	34
fair	21
poor	10

One can ask people whether they have any of a list of possible
symptoms. They average about three for males and four and a
half for females on a particular day. The most common symptoms
experienced in a two-week period are coughs (28 per cent),
trouble with nose (27 per cent), feet (21 per cent), etc. (Hannay,
1979). Many of these symptoms are of course trivial, and are
reported by people who regard themselves as being in perfect
health. In the *General Household Survey* (1980) people were asked
'How would you describe the amount of pain or discomfort
caused by this symptom?', with the following results:

	%
none	28
slight	39
moderate	19
severe	2

They were also asked 'How much inconvenience or disability
does this symptom cause?'

	%
none	44
slight	32
moderate	9
severe	2

In other words, while males have three symptoms each on
average, and females four and a half, only 2 per cent of these
symptoms are regarded as painful or incapacitating.

Some symptoms are of short duration, while others are long-
standing or chronic. When the *General Household Survey* asked 'Do
you suffer from any long-standing illness, disability or infirmity?', 20.6 per cent said they did. And when people were asked
'Do you have chronic health problems?', 63 per cent said they
had. Obviously these people were including very minor complaints. It is only when symptoms reach a certain degree of

painfulness, cause sufficient incapacity, or are regarded as possibly dangerous that most people go to see the doctor. For 56 per
cent of symptoms people do nothing, for 10 per cent they consult
friends or relations, and for 34 per cent they see a doctor.

Another measure is reported frequency of seeing the doctor in
the last year. This is about three times a year for males, four for
females, though 40 per cent of males and 30 per cent of females
have not been at all in the past year. Six per cent have been
in-patients and 22 per cent have attended out-patient clinics at
hospitals. About 25 per cent see a doctor five times a year or more.

We can also find out how many days people's activity is
limited, or how often they are away from work. The average
number of days of limited activity per year is 17.6; the average
number of days off work is 8. Coughs and colds, 'flu, bronchitis,
arthritis and rheumatism are the most frequent causes of absence
from work.

Another measure is the amount of medicine taken. Over a
two-week period 80 per cent of people had taken some medicine,
most of it not prescribed, with an average of 2.2 doses each. The
commonest medicines are aspirin, indigestion remedies, skin
ointments, cough medicines, sleeping pills, tranquillizers, and
laxatives (Dunnell and Cartwright, 1972). People also take a lot of
'other' medicines – tonics, vitamin pills and so on.

How valid are individuals' reports on their state of health?
They do correlate, though not very highly, with doctors' opinions
of their health status. Some people complain about more pains,
etc., than doctors can find a basis for – and are sometimes given
psychotherapy or tranquillizers. Others are less concerned about
their state of health than their doctors are, as for example in the
case of those who are very unfit and overweight, and heading for
trouble in the future. And among people with the same level of
health, as assessed by their doctors, those who are unhappy or
nervous feel that they are in worse physical health (Tessler and
Mechanic, 1978). So feelings of subjective health are not only due
to bodily condition.

There are fashions and cultural differences in illness. When,
in the West, we are under a lot of stress, we may take to drink
or have a 'nervous breakdown', but we do not 'run amok' as
they do in Malaya and elsewhere. Ways of being ill, together with
names for them, are partly cultural products or inventions. The

same is true of the labels doctors give to the conditions they see. There are cultural trends and differences with regard to the level of health to which people aspire, or feel entitled.

Finally, let us put together the various measures we have described of the distribution of health. Thirty to 35 per cent of the population think they are in perfect health or have only minor and short-term health problems. About 30 per cent are in fair or poor health, see the doctor five or more times a year, go to hospital or visit out-patient clinics, and take a lot of medicine. While most people suffer from some symptoms of ill-health, most of these are very minor and many are short-term.

Another measure of health is simply staying alive. Some researchers have compared the proportion of people who have survived, among for example the employed and unemployed, or those with weak or strong social networks (Berkman and Syme, 1979), see Figure 10.1.

The numbers who die in Britain at different ages are shown in Table 10.1. It can be seen that 6 per cent of men die before they are 40 and 10 per cent before the age of 50, while 31.5 per cent do not live to collect their pensions at 65.

The most common causes of death, taking all age groups

Table 10.1 Percentages who die by different ages

age	men %	women %
10	3.1	2.4
20	3.7	2.6
30	4.7	3.2
40	6.2	4.3
50	9.9	6.9
55	14.1	9.3
60	21.1	13.0
65	31.5	18.7
70	45.2	27.5
75	61.1	40.6
80	77.1	58.1
85	91.8	76.8
90	97.0	92.2
95	99.4	98.0

Source Occupational Mortality Tables, 1971.

together, are: coronary thrombosis, cancer, stroke, etc., bronchitis, other heart diseases, pneumonia, and hypertension. However, the causes of death are quite different at different ages. The most common causes of early death are: heart disease, cancer (especially lung cancer), cirrhosis of the liver, accidents (other than car), 'flu and pneumonia, motor-vehicle accidents, suicide, and (in USA) homicide (*Social Trends*, 1983). It is obvious that several of these causes of death are largely avoidable. Suicide is due to depression and social isolation, and heart disease is strongly affected by stress, obesity, smoking and unfitness. A great deal of early death is in principle avoidable – without intervention by doctors.

Early death is certainly affected by physical ill-health, though this in turn may be brought on or exacerbated by stress, emotional states or an unwise way of life. Early death is not much affected, however, by mental ill-health. It is not yet known whether unhappiness can cause death, though it seems very likely, especially death by suicide, car accidents, cirrhosis of the liver or heart disease.

SOCIAL RELATIONSHIPS

The effects of social relationships on health and length of life are similar to the effects for mental health, though with some differences. In a famous study in California (Berkman and Syme, 1979), 7000 people were interviewed to ascertain the strength of their supportive social networks. Nine years later they were interviewed again – to see which interviewees were still alive. As Figure 10.1 shows, those with strong networks did better, even after being matched for initial health, health practices, obesity, smoking, drinking and social class; for men in their fifties, for example, 30.8 per cent of those with the weakest networks had died, compared with only 9.6 per cent of those with the strongest networks. The effects were greater for marriage than for friends and relatives, which in turn were greater than those due to belonging to churches or other organizations. These results were not because healthy people had more friends, since the results were independent of health at the time of the first interview.

Other studies have shown that social support can buffer the effects of stress on physical illness. For example, in a study of men

Figure 10.1 Social networks and mortality

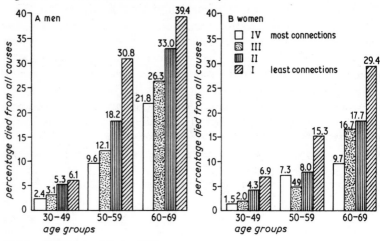

Source Berkman and Syme, 1979.

whose jobs were abolished, the rate of contracting arthritis (in two joints) was much reduced if they had strong social support. Forty-one per cent of those with weak social support had arthritis, compared with 4 per cent of those with strong support. Similar results have been obtained for a variety of medical conditions, including pregnancy complications, asthma, cholesterol level, angina, and recovery from illnesses, such as TB, heart attacks and operations (Cobb, 1976; Cohen and Hoberman, 1982).

Marriage

Again, marriage is the most potent form of social support. Ratios of married/single people show some quite large differences for a range of illnesses and conditions, as Table 10.2 shows, from a study in the USA of men and women over the age of 15. The figures show for instance that six widowed men die of TB for every married man of the same age. Other research shows that the married/single mortality ratio is greatest between the ages of 25 and 44 (Lynch, 1977).

Friends

As part of a loneliness study it was found that the frequency with which female students visited the doctor, for a wide range of

Table 10.2 The effects of marriage on health and mortality

	widowed: married		divorced or separated: married	
	men	women	men	women
TB	6.00	2.00	10.00	2.50
cirrhosis of the liver	4.36	3.25	7.18	4.42
pneumonia	4.17	1.75	7.33	2.50
breast cancer	2.50	1.02	2.50	1.13
cancer of mouth and throat	2.12	1.47	4.10	1.67
diabetes	2.00	1.57	2.83	1.14
stroke	1.92	1.63	2.42	1.47
coronary	1.56	1.52	2.06	1.41

Source Lynch, 1977.

complaints, was less if there was a better quality of contact with friends. The rate of illness was considerably less if their social contacts were rated high on pleasantness, intimacy, self-disclosure and satisfaction, especially for females (Reis, 1984).

Work relationships

As for distress and mental health, the effects of stress on physical health are buffered mainly by relationships at work. In a study of scientists and administrators at NASA it was found that social support from work-mates and subordinates reduced the effect of work stress on blood pressure (Caplan, 1971, cited by Cohen and McKay, 1984). Just one supportive relationship at work can make a difference. Other studies have found some effect on ulcers, angina, coughs, itches, rashes, and other complaints, but the effects are quite small compared with the effects on mental health (House, 1980).

Women who are employed have better health than those who are housewives, and this difference is much greater for those who are unmarried and for those who are not well educated. Those at work also engage less in illness behaviour. Further analysis showed that work both selects those in better health, and protects them against illness (Nathanson, 1980).

Other investigations confirm the effects on health of relationships at work, especially with work-mates, but also with supervisors and subordinates (Cohen and McKay, 1984).

Other relationships

The most interesting case here is children. Despite the stress which they create, they are clearly good for health. Table 10.3 shows the results of a US study, that couples with children are less likely to die, at different ages, than those without.

Table 10.3   The effects of children on mortality rate: ratio childless/those with children

	age		
	35–44	45–54	55–60
men	2.1	1.3	0.9
women	2.4	1.6	1.1

Source   Kobrin and Hendershot, 1977.

How do relationships buffer the effects of stress on health?

One way in which stress is bad for health is that it impairs the immune system, the natural defence against disease. There is a lot of experimental evidence to show that people are more likely to catch colds, 'flu or other infectious diseases if they are under stress or have recently experienced stressful life events (Jemmott and Locke, 1984). Social support could restore the immune system, by its power to replace negative emotions like anxiety and depression, and their accompanying bodily states, by positive emotions.

A second way in which relationships may affect health is through the adoption of better health practices. It is found for example that people who live alone drink and smoke more (House, 1980). Some of the illnesses to which single people are more prone than married couples reflect this – including TB, pneumonia and cirrhosis of the liver (see Table 10.2). Those who have good relationships are able to cope with stress by seeking help and social support. Those without are more likely to use other means of coping, like smoking and drinking (Badura, 1984). Unmarried people die more from car accidents, from suicide, and from heart disease – all manifestations of stress.

WORK AND UNEMPLOYMENT

Work affects health in a number of ways. Work can be stressful: research shows that the rates of heart attacks vary greatly between occupations, from 71 per cent of the national average for university teachers to 176 per cent for unskilled car workers (Sales and House, 1971). The mortality rate (i.e. the numbers dying per year in relation to the national average) varies from 76 per cent for clergymen to 317 per cent for electrical engineers, 273 per cent for labourers and 233 per cent for sailors (Fletcher, 1983).

While mortality rates are partly due to accidents it has been found that low job satisfaction is one of the best predictors of length of life among workers (Palmore, 1969). Table 10.4 shows coronary rates as ratios for each occupation to the national average for deaths from coronories, age being held constant. The 'social status' figures are from a sociological index of the status of different occupations. The table shows that death from heart disease in particular is correlated with low job satisfaction; the correlation is in the region of .6 to .7. This is partly due to the effects of social status (higher status is associated with higher job

Table 10.4 Occupational differences in job satisfaction, coronary heart disease and social status

	satisfied %	coronary rate	social status
university teachers	93	71	84
biologists	89	69	80
physicists	89	69	80
chemists	86	100	79
farmers	84	66	14
lawyers	80	124	93
managers	69	116	79
sales	52	126	50
skilled printers	52	110	49
clerical	42	103	44
paper workers	42	73	19
skilled car workers	41	68	21
skilled steelworkers	41	85	15
textile workers	31	120	3
unskilled steelworkers	21	125	4
unskilled car workers	16	176	13

Source Sales and House, 1971.

satisfaction and lower rates of heart disease). However, with status held constant there is still a strong relation between dissatisfaction and heart disease (Sales and House, 1971).

Many studies have shown that the unemployed are in worse health than the employed. During earlier economic depressions this was probably due in part to poverty and poor diet: during periods of high employment the unemployed were likely to be out of work *because* of poor health (Kelvin, 1980). We are mainly concerned here with the recent and current situation of high unemployment and fairly adequate unemployment benefits.

Various attempts have been made to discover if unemployment *causes* ill-health. A small-scale American study of workers who had lost their jobs as a result of factory closure found that they had 'anticipatory' ill-health before becoming unemployed, e.g. increased blood pressure, which fell to normal if they found another job. These workers also suffered increased cholesterol levels – which increases the danger of heart disease and strokes – and were likely to contract arthritis (Cobb and Kasl, 1977), especially if they lacked strong social support at home. (See also Table 10.2, p. 182.)

A British investigation of 2300 men who lost their jobs in 1978 found that most of them were healthy at the time, and remained so (Moylan, Millar and Davies, 1984), while other research has shown that a proportion of people lose or give up their jobs because of poor health. A careful ten-year census study of British men who lost their jobs in 1971 found that their death rate was 36 per cent greater than for the whole population of males aged between 15 and 64, and 21 per cent greater if age and class were equated. The figure for their wives was 20 per cent, and the effect was greater in the second half of the decade, both results suggesting stress rather than previous illness as the cause (Moser, Fox and Jones, 1984).

It looks as if unemployment has a modest but definite effect on health and longevity, for which there are several possible reasons. The unemployed are under stress, as we have seen (p. 34f), have a worse diet and poorer living conditions, and tend to drink and smoke more (Smith, 1985–6).

LEISURE

Is leisure good for health? Some kinds of leisure certainly are. Sport and exercise are the most important, especially aerobic activities like running and swimming, and such exercise has been found to reduce the incidence of heart disease, high blood pressure, obesity, arthritis, and various effects of ageing on the heart, lungs, and circulation (Browne and Mahoney, 1984). It has been found that former athletes live on average two to six years longer than non-athletes (*Exercise and Health*, 1984). Some forms of leisure can be bad for health (too much eating and drinking, and participating in dangerous sports, for example), while other leisure activities probably have little effect either way (for instance watching TV, watching football and fishing). Holidays are good for health, especially for minor aspects of mental health (see Table 10.5, which presents US data).

A study of people on holiday in Brampton Island, near the Australian Barrier Reef, found a marked drop in symptoms like those listed in Table 10.5 by the fourth or fifth day of the holiday (Pearce, 1982). It has long been known that relaxation is good for mental health, especially for those who are anxious, tense or under stress. It has now been found that exercise has a similar beneficial effect, and will even reduce depression (McCann and Holmes, 1984). Vigorous exercise reduces anxiety and depression, and fitter people are generally found to be in better mental health (*Exercise and Health*, 1984). Participation in sport can also lead to improved self-esteem and self-confidence (Folkins

Table 10.5   The effects of holidays on health

	holiday %	during past year %
tired	12	34
irritable	8	30
constipation, worry, anxiety	7	27
loss of interest in a sex	6	12
digestive problems	6	16
insomnia	4	11
headaches	3	21

Source   Rubenstein, 1980.

and Sime, 1981). Competitive team games are supposed to be good for training people to co-operate and to develop 'character', but they can also lead to an excessive need to win, and hostility towards other sides (Kraus, 1978).

CLASS DIFFERENCES

There is good evidence from the British *General Household Surveys* and other studies about the reported health of people of different classes (see Table 10.6 which includes data from the 1970s and 1980s). In every case the lower social classes have the highest rates of reported illness. If men and women are analysed separately, the rate of increase, moving down the social classes, is greater for men – a ratio of 2.1:1 for illness rates between classes VI to I for men, and 1.7:1 for women. For most of the indices there is quite a large gap between classes I–II, and between classes V–VI. The class differences for numbers of people with long-standing illness in 1974–76 in Britain are shown in Figure 10.2.

There is more objective evidence about length of life in different classes. This can be expressed as the expectation of life in years for men aged 15 (see Table 10.7, which uses British data collected in 1978). Exactly comparable figures for women are not available, but it has been found that the death rates of wives are very similar to those of husbands, for any given occupation of husbands. It can be seen that, while there is the expected class difference, it is

Table 10.6 Illness and social class (UK)

	Classes					
	I	II	III	IV	V	VI
long-standing illness (%)	13.0	16.8	19.2	19.2	26.5	31.7
limiting long-standing illness (%)	6.5	9.0	10.4	11.3	16.2	20.8
number of working days lost per year	3	6	6	9	11	18

	I	II	III(N)	III(M)	IV	V
number of repeated symptoms	3.4	3.7	3.6	4.0	4.0	4.6
percentage rating health fair or poor	17	28	28	36	37	43

Sources Dunnell and Cartwright, 1972; *General Household Survey*, 1980.

quite small – only 3.7 years for men. It was much greater in former times. However, class inequalities in health have *increased* since 1950 in Britain (Black, 1980).

We now turn to the illnesses which are most current in different classes. It is difficult to give any representative figures here since the pattern of health changes from time to time, and varies between countries. Most illnesses are more common in the lower classes, especially:

infectious diseases, e.g. TB;
diseases of the respiratory system, including pneumonia, bronchitis and influenza;
most forms of cancer, including lung cancer;
diseases of the digestive system, including ulcers and cirrhosis of the liver; and
accidents, at work and elsewhere. (Reid, 1982)

Class differences are very great for death at birth (2:1), and in the first year of life, and for accidents to children (4:1 comparing classes V and I) (Black, 1980).

However, some diseases are more common in classes I and II, at certain periods. Coronaries were more common when men in these classes did sedentary jobs and ate too much; now they take more exercise and diet more carefully, with the result that there is little class difference. Polio is now rare, but was once more common in classes I and II because their better sanitary conditions meant that middle-class children did not acquire immunity. The upper social classes have more leukemia, as a result of having more medical tests, and hence more X-rays (Susser and Watson, 1971).

However, the lower social classes are affected by most illnesses more often, take more days off from work, and die a little sooner because of them. This is partly due to inequalities in the conditions of life – smaller homes, less heating, larger families, less good food, and so on.

Do middle-class people receive better medical attention? The *General Household Surveys* show that working-class people in Britain visit the doctor *more* often, though a lot of this is in order to get medical certificates (to be paid for time away from work through illness). And in relation to the number of days of restricted activity, working-class people see the doctor *less* often.

Figure 10.2 Long-standing illness and social class: A men 1974–76;

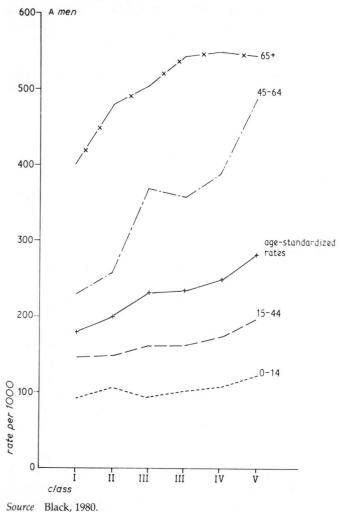

Source Black, 1980.

They make less use of preventive services – antenatal clinics, vaccination programmes, cervical screening, the dentist (Black, 1980). Doctors spend more time with middle-class patients, and there is evidence that National Health Service expenditure on middle-class people is 40 per cent higher than on those in classes IV to VI – because classes I and II know how to make better use of

B women 1974–76

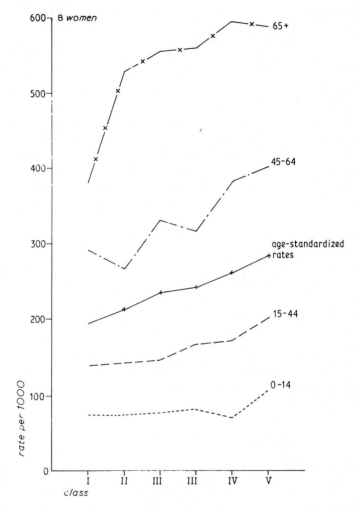

the system, and manage to get better attention (Reid, 1981).

In countries like the USA, which do not have a national health service, the class difference in access to doctors and other medical facilities is much greater. It has been found that those who are upwardly mobile retain their childhood health habits, for instance being less likely to see the doctor when ill (Kessler and

Table 10.7 Social class and expectations of life at age 15 (UK, 1978)

	class					
	I	II	III(N)	III(M)	IV	V
men	57.2	57.0	56.0	55.7	55.1	53.5

Source Reid, 1981.

Cleary, 1980). In Norway and Sweden class differences in health are less than in Britain (Black, 1980).

There is a further reason for class differences in health: middle-class people have been the first to repond to health-education propaganda, and to lead healthier lives. In particular there is clear evidence, using other classification systems, that middle-class people:

smoke less	males 2.32:1	class 6 v. 1
	females 1.58:1	class 6 v. 1
are less obese	males 1.5:1	class DE v. AB
	females 1:58:1	class DE v. AB
take more exercise	jogging 4.7:1	class AB v. E
	swimming 2.8:1	class AB v. E (Reid, 1981)

In other words, there are very large class differences in health-related behaviour, which are reflected in differences in health. A factor which works in the opposite direction is that much working-class work is healthier than middle-class work. Manual labour involves exercise; managerial and professional work does not. In addition the latter often involves a great deal of stress – which is bad for physical as well as for mental health.

The effect of changes in wealth

The British pools winners who formed the basis of the Smith and Razzell study (p. 97) were in somewhat better health than a comparison group, though they had more headaches. Studies of the effect of economic changes on health show that downward swings in the economy are followed a few months or up to a year later by an increased level of ill-health and of accidents. Economic decline leads to undesirable job and financial events for many people (loss of job, lower pay, inability to pay bills, etc.), which in turn lead to ill-health and accidents. (Catalano and Dooley, 1983)

CULTURAL DIFFERENCES

If the expectation of life is plotted against *per capita* income, it is very clear that on average people live longer in richer countries. From Figure 10.3, it can be seen that expectation of life at birth increased from about 30 years for the poorest countries to over 70 for the richest, in 1960. There was an overall increase in life expectancy after 1930, due to the world improvement in medical facilities and public health, and this has continued at a slower rate since that date. Life expectancy for women in rich countries is now 77–8 years. Other studies, of rich countries, show that there is a small improvement in length of life at the upper end of the average income scale, not shown in Figure 10.3, with the greatest expectation of life in the USA, Sweden, Norway and Japan (United Nations, 1982).

The present average length of life in different parts of the world can be summarized as follows:

35–45   most of Central Africa, Pakistan
45–55   most of the rest of Africa, India, Indonesia
55–65   N. Africa, Middle East, S. E. Asia, Mongolia, Brazil
65–70   China, Mexico, Argentina
70+   Britain, Europe, N. America, Australia, Japan, Russia.
                                   (*World Health Statistics*, 1982)

Figure 10.3   Life expectancy and national income in the 1900s, 1930s and 1960s

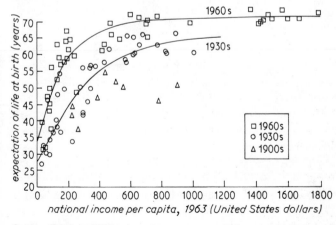

national income per capita, 1963 (United States dollars)

Source   Preston, 1975.

The length of life in developing countries increases as prosperity increases, since this affects both diet and living standards, and as a result of improved education (Pendleton and Yang, 1985).

The causes of death are very different in developed and less developed countries. The main causes of death in developed countries are heart disease (48 per cent), cancer (19 per cent) and lung complaints (15 per cent). These are relatively unimportant in developing countries, where people die from a number of causes which have been eradicated in richer countries, such as TB, enteritis, other infectious diseases and parasites.

In the USA the mortality rates of ethnic minority groups are considerably higher than for the white majority. The exceptions are Japanese- and Chinese-Americans, whose mortality rates and infant mortality rates are lower than for Caucasians (Cockerham, 1981).

PERSONALITY

Do some kinds of personality have better health? A particular form of unhappiness is related to poor health: neuroticism consists in part of somatic complaints like headaches and stomach aches; neurotic people are more upset by stress, producing anxiety, depression and feelings of tension, which in turn lead to bodily complaints (e.g. French, Caplan and van Harrinson, 1982). Neuroticism is found to be a risk factor for more serious illnesses too. A longitudinal study of 1000 men undertaken over twelve years found that indications of neuroticism predicted the probability of a wide variety of illnesses (Costa and McCrae 1980). However, this is partly because neurotics complain more, for the same level of symptoms, partly because they are more upset by stressful life events. A number of studies have found that heart disease is more common in those who have certain aspects of neuroticism (depression, impulsivity, but not anxiety), and certains aspects of psychotism (hostility, aggressiveness and cynicism) (Eysenck, 1985).

There are other personality variables which distinguish between those who are often ill and those who are not, between people who are upset by stress and those who can withstand it. Those who do *not* become ill as a result of stress have been labelled as 'hardy'. Hardiness consists of at least three aspects of personality: *commitment* – believing in the truth, importance and value of who one is and what one is doing, an overall sense of purpose; *control* (internal control again); *challenge* – believing that change rather than stability is normal, and interpreting stressful life events as an opportunity for growth (Kobasa, 1982).

Heart disease is particularly affected by psychological variables, and is related to a particular type of personality – 'type A' – which has three main components: achievement-striving, competitive, hard-driving and aggressive behaviour; speed and time urgency, for example, thinking that time is passing faster than it really is; and job involvement. There is evidence that type As like competition and time pressure, and that they actively seek them out. They are high in both extraversion and neuroticism (Furnham, 1984b). Type A personalities are twice as likely to have heart attacks, even after age, cholesterol level and smoking are held constant. More men are type As, though more women with jobs are type As than are housewives. Such people try very hard when under stress to control aspects of the environment that seem likely to harm them physically or psychologically. They are particularly concerned with self-esteem, but may lack clear ways of evaluating their behaviour (Innes, 1981; Matthews, 1982). A further aspect of type As is that they tend to have poor relationships with other people. They compete aggressively or prefer to work alone, thus weakening their social networks (Kobasa, 1982). Since individuals in positions of high responsibility tend to be type As, it is a matter of some importance to keep them in good health, and therapeutic programmes based on relaxation have been devised to do this (Suinn, 1982).

We have seen that cancers of different kinds are affected by stress, and prevented by social support, probably because of the effect of these factors on the immune system (p. 184). Is cancer also affected by personality? Is there a 'type C' personality? A considerable number of studies have come to the conclusion that there is. Cancer patients are more likely to be unable to express anger, and to be compliant, conforming, unassertive and patient. As a result they become highly aroused by stress and are less able to discharge these tensions (Greer and Watson, 1985). There is evidence that they are particularly upset when faced with interpersonal problems like envy and competition, and they become hopeless, helpless and depressed (Ormont, 1981). Depression also leads to cancer: in a seventeen-year follow-up study of 2000 industrial workers in Chicago, MMPI depression scores predicted death from cancer, even after smoking, drinking, age, occupational status and family history of cancer had been held constant (Shekelle *et al.*, 1981). However, depression equally could be due to early manifestations of cancer. What can be said is that depression and helplessness are associated with poorer changes of recovery and survival (Krantz, Grunberg and Baum, 1985). However, cancer makes an interesting contrast with heart disease: while neuroticism and psychoticism make heart disease more likely, they make cancer *less* likely (Eysenck, 1985).

Religion is good for health as well as for happiness. Perhaps rather surprisingly, religious people have a much lower rate for a number of diseases, especially heart disease, lung complaints, cirrhosis of the liver, and some kinds of cancer. Some of the findings are given in Table 10.8. There are several possible explanations for these findings. One is that many religious people drink and smoke less than others, and are less likely to engage in promiscuous sex, which could explain the lower rates of heart, chest, liver and vaginal complaints. A second possibility is that religion produces peace of mind and release of tension, which could reduce blood pressure. Third, the social support provided by the Church could buffer stress in the usual way.

American studies have found that, among students, the religious ones are more anxious, tense and lacking in self-esteem. Among the general adult population, church-goers are less neurotic, probably because the more distressed are less able to attend public events – they are more likely to pray in private. However, among the elderly, there is a clear relationship between church-going and positive mental health. In a study of 5000 people aged 60 and over, there were substantial differences in 'happiness, enjoyment, or satisfaction with or from health, friendship, employment status, religion, feelings of usefulness towards family' (see Table 10.9, which gives scores on an index of adjustment) (Moberg and Taves, 1965). Other studies have found that the clergy are particularly well adjusted in all age groups, despite their low incomes (Freedman, 1978).

Traditionally Catholics had a lower suicide rate than Protestants, but this difference has almost disappeared. However, church-goers as a whole have a much lower suicide rate than

Table 10.8 Church attendance and health

	Once or more per week	Less than once per week	Infre-quent attenders
arteriosclerotic heart disease			
females, death in 5 years per 1000	8.52	18.12	2.1*
males, deaths per year per 1000 (smoking, social status and water hardness held constant)	4.9	8.7	
lung emphysema deaths in 3 years per 1000	0.74	1.70	2.3
cirrhosis of the liver deaths in 3 years per 1000	0.21	0.82	3.9
tuberculosis new cases in 5 years per 100,000	57	84	138
trichomoniasis females incidence %	12.4		17.8
cancer of the cervix females incidence %	0.64		1.88

*Unreliable, since numbers small.

Source Comstock and Partridge, 1972.

others. In one study the rate per 1000 over six years was 0.45 for those who went to church once a week or more, 0.95 for irregular attenders, 2.1 for infrequent attenders (Comstock and Partridge, 1972).

We can now put together the ways in which personality factors affect health. The main link is via *health-related behaviour*. Smoking causes lung cancer, drinking causes alcoholism, over-eating leads to obesity and increases the likelihood of heart disease. These three are all partly reactions to stress, and are forms of coping behaviour. Exercise on the other hand makes heart disease and many other ailments less likely, reduces the effects of stress and improves mental health. Exercise is affected by propaganda and by holding beliefs about its value. *Health beliefs* are important, since they lead people to engage in better health-related behaviour, and to look after themselves. We used these

Table 10.9 Church membership and happiness in the elderly

	church leaders	other church members	non-church members
married	15	15	12
widowed	15	11	7
single	12	8	5
65–70	18	14	10
71–79	15	12	7
80+	13	8	6
fully employed	18	18	17
partly employed	16	16	13
fully retired	15	12	7
health (self-rated)			
excellent	17	14	13
good	15	14	11
fair	17	6	8
more active in religious organizations than in fifties	16	13	9
less active	14	11	7

Source Moberg and Taves, 1965.

principles to explain some of the results in previous chapters: middle-class people have better health because they take more exercise, women live longer because they look after themselves better. *Relaxation* is good for health, since it keeps blood pressure down, keeps down the incidence of heart attacks and reduces the effects of stress on health in general, including mental health. Type A personalities need to relax more; holidays are good for health because they induce relaxation. Persistent anxiety leads to ulcers and similar psychosomatic complaints. *Too much emotionality*, high neuroticism, is a risk factor for heart disease and a range of other illnesses, via the heightened effects of stress, leading to increased blood pressure and other physiological effects. *Too little emotionality*, inhibition of anger, and even low neuroticism, appears to be linked to cancer. From the point of view of bodily health there may be an optimal level of emotionality (Wood, 1985). *Social support*, partly related to having good social skills, buffers the effects of stress, reduces anxiety and anger, and restores the immune system. We have seen that type As may weaken their social networks by their competitive behaviour and preference for working alone.

CONCLUSIONS

Health is closely linked with happiness: it is often the cause of happiness and satisfaction, particularly for older people.

Relationships, particularly marriage and other close, confiding and supportive relationships, enhance health by preserving the immune system and encouraging good health habits.

Job satisfaction affects overall life satisfaction, health and mental health, whereas there are serious effects from unemployment on levels of mental ill-health, such as depression and suicide, and on health, particularly for middle-aged men and working-class people.

Leisure, as well as being a major source of life satisfaction, is often beneficial to health (particularly taking regular exercise) and mental health.

Some of the largest differences between classes are in their health: working-class people suffer at least twice as much from most forms of illness, though their length of life is not much affected. The better health of middle-class people may be due to better access to treatment and a healthier way of life.

Health, as measured by average length of life, is far better in more prosperous countries, though the effect levels off at a moderate degree of affluence.

Personality factors are strongly predictive of health. Neuroticism is a source of ill-health in general, and 'hardiness' enables people to stand up to the effects of stress. Heart disease is more common in type A personalities, and cancer is more common in type Cs – individuals who are very unassertive and cannot express aggression.

11

·ENHANCEMENT·

We have looked at the main causes of happiness, and the psychological processes that are involved. We now turn to the main practical application: can the happiness of oneself or others be increased? I shall assume that 'the pursuit of happiness' is a legitimate goal, as the American Constitution proclaims. The question is, can it be done, and if so, how? Some of the methods that will be described are aimed at happiness in the sense of a prevailing positive mood, others at life satisfaction. Some are relevant to good health or avoiding distress.

It has often been said that happiness must be a by-product of other activities and goals, and cannot be aimed for directly. However, the modification of emotional states is now widely practised: anxiety is reduced by relaxation and meditation, excitement is increased by TV thrillers and by roller-coasters. Indeed extreme unhappiness, clinical depression, is widely and successfully treated by anti-depressant drugs, electro-convulsive therapy, and various forms of behaviour therapy and psychotherapy. Some of these methods have also been used with mildly depressed students, and with normals who are not depressed at all. We shall consider them later in this chapter.

Psychiatry is concerned with relieving distress, while we are more interested in the enhancement of satisfaction with life and in positive emotions, which are somewhat independent of distress. There are also qualitatively different positive subjective states: different individuals may obtain their greatest satisfaction from friends, or music, exercise, sex, drinking, making money, work, and so on. It is not for psychologists to say which is better, or who has the better quality of life.

METHODS OF INDUCING POSITIVE MOODS

As everyone knows, there are ways of cheering people up. There has been a great deal of research into the effectiveness of different ways of doing it. A number of methods have been used in laboratory experiments to create positive moods, and have been shown to work. However there is a question about how long the effects last, and for how many people they do work. These techniques are of interest, in confirming some of the sources of joy described earlier, and suggesting the ingredients of more potent experiences, to be described later.

The best-known laboratory technique was devised by Velten (1968), and consists in asking people to read silently, then aloud, 50 or 60 statements such as 'this is great, I really do feel good, I *am* elated about things', trying to put themselves in the mood suggested. Later versions of this procedure have asked people to spend 20 seconds each on 12 statements taking about seven minutes in all, and to try to put themselves in the mood suggested (Teasdale and Russell, 1983). Some of the statements are about competence and self-worth, others about the bodily states characteristic of the mood. There is no doubt that the Velten method does produce a more positive mood for many people; however the effects are very short-lived, and disappear after 10–15 minutes (Frost and Green, 1982). Furthermore between 30 and 50 per cent of subjects are not affected at all (Clark, 1983).

Showing films has been widely used to induce positive moods in the study of emotion (e.g. Buck, 1984). The Peter Sellers films of discarded sequences when the actor lost control have sometimes been used. TV research has found that TV affects mood in a variety of ways, including the induction of cheerfulness. An experiment compared the Velten technique with five minutes' worth of funny film. Both had effects on mood immediately afterwards, but after ten minutes the Velten subjects had returned to normal, while the film subjects still rated themselves as in a more positive mood, and more amused, than controls.

	mood after 10 minutes' delay		
	Velten	film	controls
positive	2.50	1.70*	3.06
amused	3.68	2.60	3.75
refreshed, alert		no differences	

*1 is the highest positive score

Source Isen and Georgoglione, 1983.

Listening to cheerful music, again asking subjects to try to get into the mood suggested, has also been studied. It has been found to be rather more effective than Velten methods (Sutherland, Newman and Rachman, 1982), and it affects all the subjects tested, not just some of them (Clark, 1983).

Asking people to think about a very pleasant recent event has strong effects both on mood and on estimates of life satisfaction (p. 145). It is necessary for subjects to put some effort into it. In one successful version of this method subjects were asked to spend twenty minutes describing a happy event 'in as much detail as possible' (Schwarz and Clore, 1983), and the effects were greater if concrete images were called up (Strack, Schwarz and Gschneidinger, 1984). Experiments by Argyle and Crossland have found that the effects are greater if people do this in pairs, telling one another about the happy events. The effect is greater if they are friends rather than strangers, and if the pairs talk face to face than if they cannot see one another, confirming the importance of facial signals.

We saw that funny films induce good moods. The mood induced by humour is a combination of joy and excitement (p. 127), and is often combined with enjoyment of a social encounter. Two things happen when people laugh. The joke has the effect of redefining some situation as less threatening, less serious, and at the same time the incongruity of the joke induces catharsis, a discharge of tension, a pleasurable drop in anxiety or other negative emotion. To cheer someone up one of the commonest techniques is to tell them a joke.

Giving people a small present, or allowing them to 'find' a coin, puts them in a good mood, for a time. An experiment found that if householders were given a free sample of stationery at the door, and then telephoned with a request to help pass a message, they were more likely to help, but that the effect lasted only about 15 minutes (Isen, Clark and Schwartz, 1976).

Giving people success experiences, such as allowing them to succeed at an experimental task, or telling them how well they have done, also produces positive moods (Clark and Waddell, 1983).

Hypnosis has also been successfully used in a number of experiments, to induce good and other moods, though only a minority of subjects were susceptible to hypnotic treatment (Bower, 1983).

We have discussed a number of other ways of inducing good moods earlier in this book, such as giving good news, testing in an attractive room, on a sunny day, and simply getting people to smile for a few minutes. However the conclusion about these minor techniques for mood induction is that they all appear to last for a very short time, 10 to 15 minutes at the most. If rather more substantial good experiences were arranged, perhaps these effects would last longer, but this takes us into the field of 'pleasant activities', which is our next general method.

If mood induction techniques are used regularly, or become a habit, they could have more enduring effects. Some methods of therapy for depression and some happiness-enhancement courses have included Velten-type recitations for 10 minutes each morning. One such course found changes in daily mood, depression scores and satisfaction, after two weeks (p. 214).

One of the ways in which people try to bring about more positive moods is by means of drugs. As we saw earlier (p. 132f), alcohol produces positive moods in most people. Strictly speaking it is a 'depressant', that is of central nervous system activity. But it can certainly cheer people up, mainly because it is usually consumed in the company of others and inhibitions are reduced, with the result that there is more fun, perhaps more sex, sometimes more aggression. There can be terrible hangovers, and there can be addiction.

Table 11.1   Pleasant activities which affect mood for the whole day

social interaction
1 being with happy people
2 having people show interest in what you have said
3 being with friends
4 being noticed as sexually attractive
5 kissing
6 watching people
7 having a frank and open conversation
8 being told I am loved
9 expressing my love to someone
10 petting, necking
11 being with someone I love
12 complimenting or praising someone
13 having coffee, tea, a coke, and so on with friends
14 being popular at a gathering
15 having a lively talk
16 listening to the radio
17 seeing old friends
18 being asked for my help or advice
19 amusing people
20 having sexual relationships with a partner of the opposite sex
21 meeting someone new of the same sex

incompatible with depression
22 laughing
23 being relaxed
24 thinking about something good in the future
25 thinking about people I like
26 seeing beautiful scenery
27 breathing clean air
28 having peace and quiet
29 sitting in the sun
30 wearing clean clothes
31 having spare time
32 sleeping soundly at night
33 listening to music
34 smiling at people
35 seeing good things happen to my family or friends
36 feeling the presence of the Lord in my life
37 watching wild animals

self-efficacy
38 doing a project in my own way
39 reading stories, novels, poems or plays
40 planning or organizing something
41 driving skilfully
42 saying something clearly
43 planning trips or vacations
44 learning to do something new
45 being complimented or told I have done well
46 doing a job well

miscellaneous
47 eating good meals
48 going to a restaurant
49 being with animals

Source   Lewinsohn and Graf, 1973.

Other drugs are used presumably because people find them rewarding. However, as we saw earlier, they produce excitement and arousal rather than joy. And of course they can have serious side-effects and long-term consequences for health.

Tricyclic anti-depressants and lithium are quite successful with depressed patients. For those whose depression is mainly a reaction to depressing events both drugs and psychological treatment (as described later) are effective. For those with endogenous depression a combination of the two is needed (Williams, 1984). And there is no evidence that drugs do any good to individuals who are not depressed.

INCREASING THE FREQUENCY OF POSITIVE LIFE EVENTS

We have seen that positive moods are produced by pleasant activities and events such as seeing friends, eating out, taking exercise, listening to music, going to a party, sexual activity and leisure activities (p. 129f). Some of these have been found to be commonly associated with a positive mood at the end of the day, or for the day as a whole for many people, but they have not so far been found to have any carry-over effect to the next day (Rehm, 1978; Stone and Neale, 1984). Depressed and unhappy people report fewer positive events of this kind (Lewinsohn and Graf, 1973).

Despite possible doubts about the direction of causation here (p. 129), this line of research has led to a method of therapy for depression which applies equally well to the induction of greater happiness for normals. Individuals are asked to keep daily records, for a month, of pleasant events from the list, and daily mood. Computer analysis is then used to discover which activities have the greatest effect on mood for each person, and he or she is then encouraged to engage in these activities more often (Lewinsohn, Sullivan and Grosscup, 1982).

Several methods have been used to induce patients to engage in pleasant activities more often, including: (1) planning small increases between sessions; (2) reward by therapist if more activities are performed (more therapist time is given); (3) teaching patients to reward themselves (Biglan and Dow, 1981).

One follow-up study did find the expected sequence of results.

Clients were taught to increase their pleasant activities, they did so, their depression lifted (Turner, Ward and Turner 1979). In this study the clients were university students and staff who were depressed, and they were seen five times during a month. The activities to be increased were those which were found pleasant for each individual. However, other studies have found that depression can lift without any change in pleasant activities, or that there can be an increase in pleasant activities with no change in depression: this is only *one* way of relieving depression (Blaney, 1981).

An important condition is probably that the activities chosen should be pleasant for each individual. Another condition is that people should choose to engage in these activities of their own volition rather than from external pressure. Experiments have shown that pleasant activities have more effect on relieving depression if they are freely chosen, less if subjects are paid or coerced (Hammen, Rook and Harris, 1979).

Pleasant-activity training has been found to be successful when combined with goal-setting or with self-monitoring or cognitive therapy (described later, p. 212f) (Blaney, 1981; Miller and Berman, 1983). It is also common to combine pleasant-activities treatment with social skills or assertiveness training, either of which can make pleasant social events more available, or with relaxation training, to make unpleasant events more tolerable (Lewinsohn, Sullivan and Grosscup, 1982).

These methods have been found to be effective with normal people, who are not depressed. In one experiment, members of an experimental group chose 12 activities from a longer list, and members of another group chose two activities, which they regarded as highly pleasurable and had not done for two weeks. These included sporting, academic, cultural and social activities. Forty-eight subjects agreed to perform them during the next two weeks. After a month it was found that the two experimental groups had higher scores for quality of life and for pleasantness, compared with a control group. It made no difference whether they did two or 12 activities (Reich and Zautra, 1983).

Some happiness-enhancement courses for normal people have included daily positive activities, and in one such course this was one of the most important ingredients. Subjects developed individual lists of 10 pleasant activities which they could do every day, in addition to increased social activity in general and greater activity overall (Fordyce, 1977).

This all sounds a bit like unrestrained hedonism, the selfish pursuit of pleasure. In fact many of these pleasant activities are quite harmless, and if they make people happier they can be engaged in without causing problems: seeing friends, sport or exercise, going to church, listening to music, spending more time with the children, getting enough sleep, to give some examples. But there are some other pleasant activities which would have to be undertaken cautiously, or not at all. Some are illegal or unethical, some cost too much, take up too much time, cause trouble for other people, or are bad for health. The pleasant activities chosen would have to fit into the daily or weekly timetable of oneself and the family. For example, gardening is good for health, and saves money, but may reduce time spent with the family. Dancing is cheap and good for health, but the spouse should do it too.

IMPROVEMENT OF THE MATERIAL CONDITIONS OF LIFE

A widely shared, commonsense theory about the cause of happiness runs something like this: in order to be happier one should earn more money, which is in itself a disagreeable task, spend it on houses, or better houses, cars, furniture, holidays, food and drink, and these things will make one happy. As we have seen, the evidence does not give much support to this theory. Richer people are a little happier than poorer people in the same country, but not much happier. If economic conditions improve for everyone there is sometimes a reduction in general satisfaction. And there is little relationship between happiness and prosperity when different countries are compared.

Satisfaction with income depends more on comparisons with the incomes of others than on actual income – what people really want is to have more than other people (p. 148f). An individual is also 'more satisfied' if things are better for him or her than they were in the past (p. 147). On the other hand if the change is too great the effects can be less positive, as has been found for the winners of large football pool pay-outs, who usually give up their jobs and lose most of their social network (p. 97).

The greater life satisfaction of richer people may not be due to the spending of money; it could be because they have more satisfying jobs, spend their leisure more actively, or have better social networks. There are class differences in each of these areas. Here is an analogy: to keep warm one can saw logs for the fire, but sawing them may be more warming than burning them.

However, I do not want to suggest that the things which money can buy have no effect on happiness. It is nice for young couples to have a home of their own, we have seen that holidays are good for us, warmth and food are good for health and comfort, having a car removes a lot of frustrations with transport and makes more activities possible. Above all most of the world's population do not have these things, and many in our own society do not, so there is no question of complacency, or suggesting that the material things of life can be forgotten about.

When such 'necessities' have been provided, further expenditure probably does not add very much to happiness. It is nice to have a larger or newer car, but it does not make much difference. The satisfaction derived from, say jewellery, is mainly symbolic – it signals that the wearer is rich, and may therefore contribute to his or her self-esteem. Wealth for some people is one index of success, though for many kinds of activity there is little connection between success and wealth, indeed this is the case with some of the most satisfying occupations, like the church, science and university teaching.

I believe that the conditions of life which really make a difference to happiness are those covered by our 'three sources' – social relations, work and leisure. And the establishment of a satisfying state of affairs in these spheres does not depend much on wealth, either absolute or relative, or on the material conditions of life.

THE COMPANY OF OTHER PEOPLE

The first of our three sources of happiness was other people, and in Chapter 2 we showed that marriage, family, friendship and other social relationships are major sources of happiness. Many of the positive activities of the last section were in fact social activities. To enhance happiness, one should get married, stay married, have children, keep up with relatives, have plenty of friends, and keep on good terms with the neighbours. In order to do these things some social-skills training may be needed. For example, people who have difficulty in making friends may need to acquire skills of rewardingness, sending positive non-verbal signals, and to learn the rules of friendship (Argyle, 1983; Argyle and Henderson, 1985). Such training is included as part of the Lewinsohn positive life-events therapy for depression. The important thing about social relationships is that, once established, they promise regular rewarding social experiences in the future. The people with greatest vulnerability for depression are those who lack a close confidant (Williams, 1984).

In addition to starting new relationships, it is important to sustain and strengthen existing ones. Marriage is not a great source of happiness if the couple never see one another, or are cool or hostile when they do. Marital therapy or marital-enrichment training can introduce couples to more rewarding forms of interaction, better negotiation skills, and to the rules which are found to make marriages work (Argyle and Henderson, 1985). Individuals who have friends but still feel lonely need to be taught how to produce more self-disclosure, to talk about more intimate topics (p. 28f).

Some people are very rewarding, able to generate positive moods in others. Experiments have found that euphoric moods are soon passed on to other people (Marks and Hammen, 1982). For students, other young people are the most rewarding, especially responsive and attractive members of the opposite sex (Davis, Rainey and Brock, 1976), followed by children, dogs, old people and birds, in that order (Cautela and Kastenbaum, 1967). The most rewarding people are those who are cheerful, attractive, interesting, interested and helpful (Argyle, 1983).

In addition to skills like rewardingness, self-disclosure, and keeping to the rules, assertiveness may be important here. It has been found that assertiveness on one day predicts positive mood on the next day better than mood predicts assertiveness (Sanchez, 1978). Several forms of social-skills training have been used with depressed patients, including assertiveness training, problem-solving and marital skills, with generally successful results (Blaney, 1981). Social skills for lonely people are often taught in groups, which provide ready-made companions; the same applies to training heterosexual skills.

INVOLVEMENT IN WORK AND LEISURE

These are the other two of our 'three sources'. Can we make use of the findings which were reported in earlier chapters to suggest ways of enhancing happiness?

Work

We can consider how to enhance each of our happiness components.

Satisfaction

Is affected most by work which is intrinsically satisfying. This is not necessarily the most highly paid work, though this tends to be more satisfying than less well paid work. It is work that gives intrinsic satisfaction, because it is interesting, seems valuable and worthwhile, requires the use of skills, is sufficiently demanding, allows some freedom and autonomy, and is not too repetitive. Many individuals do not appreciate the hidden benefits of work until they lose their jobs – filling and structuring time, giving status and identity, social contacts outside the family, and linking to broader goals and purposes. Unemployed people are happiest when they can find alternative activities which provide similar benefits.

Positive affect

There is a lot of fun to be had at work, mainly with co-workers, in the jokes and gossip at break periods, much of it based on the work (as in the cases of medical jokes and elaborate practical jokes by technical people).

Avoiding distress and ill-health

Work is a major source of stress too. This can be buffered by good relationships with work-mates and supervisors, who can provide social support and tangible help in dealing with problems.

Leisure

Satisfaction

As with work, there is a lot of intrinsic satisfaction from leisure for those who become seriously involved in projects of various kinds, alone or with others. These include serious hobbies, music and art, further education, social work, sport, amateur activities of many kinds. Such projects can become more important and more satisfying than work, and are very important for the unemployed and retired. And leisure, like work, provides status and identity, fills and structures time, and provides social contacts.

Positive affect

A great deal of leisure is spent with friends, family and members of clubs. It is on the whole less serious than work, and has a strong 'fun' component. Meals with friends, drinks in the pub, dancing, parties, all provide a lot of positive affect. And these are events which may happen every night, or once or twice a week, so can be relied upon to continue to induce good moods. Those who just sit at home every night are missing a major source of positive feelings. Exercise has a definite effect on positive mood, as many studies have shown (Wood, 1985). The effect appears to be partly physiological, through nor-adrenaline or the endorphins stimulating the pleasure centres. In addition there is usually social activity, and there may be satisfaction in achievement, or self-image gratification through dressing up in impressive sporting gear.

Avoiding stress and ill-health

Leisure is very good for relieving stress and promoting health. Exercise is very beneficial for both physical and mental health: it reduces depression as well as the incidence of heart attacks. Relaxation, in front of the TV, or on holiday, can help to relieve stresses from work or elsewhere.

LOOKING AT THINGS DIFFERENTLY

Psychotherapy has been criticized by Marxists as 'band-aid' for real social problems, and it is true that many depressed people have much to be depressed about. Nevertheless a psychologist may be able to help an individual, even though his or her problems were caused by wider social problems. Psychotherapy has also been the object of cartoons in which the characters try to tackle vast material problems 'by talking about it'. On the other hand there are plenty of unhappy people who are simply 'depressed', and who are in much the same objective situation as others who are perfectly happy.

We saw in Chapter 6 on personality that happy and unhappy people look at the world in different ways. Unhappy people see more bad things, make negative interpretations of events, evaluate themselves unfavourably, generalize from single instances of failure and hold a number of debilitating false beliefs Another way of describing the thought processes of depressed people is to say that they make different attributions for the causes of events. They think that failures and other bad things are caused by themselves, and that nothing can be done about them (p. 121f).

We saw earlier that the emotional impact of events depends partly on how they are interpreted (p. 136). It will help people to have pleasant experiences if they can interpret events positively. Forms of 'cognitive therapy' have been devised intended to change these ways of thinking; and have been found to be quite successful (Miller and Berman, 1983). Some training courses for normals have also been successful in increasing their reported happiness. On the other hand, there is not much evidence that faulty thinking habits are an important factor in causing depression in the first place; they are probably more a result of depressing experiences (Coyne and Gotlib, 1983).

'Rational–emotive therapy' tries to help people by argument and debate, a series of tutorials intended to show the patient that his or her beliefs are wrong (Ellis, 1962). The most popular system now is that due to Beck (1976), which has the following components:

(a) monitor negative automatic thoughts, such as 'I am a worse mother than my mother was';
(b) examine the evidence for and against such ideas;
(c) substitute more reality-based interpretations, for example

realizing this was a bad day, and not generalizing from it,
(d) recognizing the connection between mood, beliefs and behaviour – seeing that distorted beliefs can cause depression,
or that certain situations or behaviours lead to depression;
(e) identify and alter the beliefs that lead the patient to distort
and interpret experiences wrongly: these are like the false
beliefs sought by the RET method, e.g. 'to be happy I must be
liked by everyone', 'I must be successful in all I undertake', 'if
someone disagrees with me, it means he doesn't like me';
patients learn to attach less importance to such desirable but
unattainable goals.

Therapy aimed at changing attributions, to increase the perceived controllability of events, takes a similar form. Patients are
asked to keep a diary of positive and negative events. These
events are discussed during therapy, and the patient is asked to
examine negative events to look for possible external causes, and
to examine positive events to look for internal causes. Patients are
reinforced by the therapist for these kinds of attribution, and
encouraged to get into the habit of looking at events in this way. A
number of follow-up studies, though not all, have shown positive
results (Layden, 1982; Brewin, 1985).

A related form of treatment consists of getting people to read
positive self-statements, as described earlier, at a number of
points during the day. The trick is to do it immediately before
some frequent rewarding activity, like a meal or drinking tea
(Rehm and Kornblith, 1979).

These kinds of treatment have been administered to depressed
patients in several ways. Simply instructing them in the
principles involved has not been very successful. Group therapy
has been less successful than intensive individual treatment.
Courses of individual therapy, with patients and depressed
volunteers, have been found to be more successful than alternative forms of treatment, including drug therapy and insight
therapy. The most successful treatments have also included
behavioural methods like pleasant-events and social-skills training (Blaney, 1981; Hollon, 1981).

A happiness training course in New Zealand for normal people
was mainly based on improving insight and understanding, and
correcting irrational beliefs, in eight two-hour sessions over four

weeks. This was very successful: see Figure 11.1, which shows standardized scores over the period of the course and its follow-up.

The American course described earlier (Fordyce, 1977) include the following components:

1 instruction aimed at giving insight into the causes of happiness;
2 lowering aspirations;
3 developing positive, optimistic thinking; and
4 becoming more present-oriented.

Figure 11.1   Effects of a happiness training course

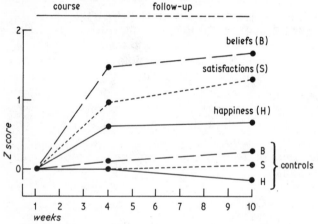

Source   Lichter, Haye and Kammann, 1980.

Goal-setting and self-reward

A central feature of depression is low self-esteem, low self-evaluation, a feeling of failure. Depressed people feel that they have failed to attain their goals, that it is their own fault, and they cannot do anything about it. We have seen that people feel happier if they compare themselves with others who are *less* successful or fortunate, rather than the reverse (p. 150), and it has been suggested that depressives set themselves standards or goals which are too high.

A form of treatment for depressed patients has been devised to increase self-control of moods. This therapy starts by getting clients to keep a record of their mood and positive activities each day. They then select minor, realistic goals, which are made more difficult in later sessions.

The next step is to teach clients to reward themselves. The client divides up a task, e.g. housework, into smaller parts, and is trained to reward him- or herself when one of these modest goals is reached, for example by complimenting themselves, feeling contented, or doing something they like such as telephoning a friend or watching TV (Williams, 1984). A course of six two-hour sessions along these lines was found to be more successful in alleviating depression than other forms of therapy (Fuchs and Rehm, 1977). A similar procedure was used with non-depressed students, who were trained in goal-setting and self-reinforcement. It was found that they rewarded themselves more and were happier after this training (Heiby, Ozaki and Campos, 1984).

ACHIEVING AN INTEGRATED PERSONALITY

We have seen that those people are happier who do not have inner conflicts, for example, large discrepancies between their achievements and their aspirations (p. 147). Aristotle's dictum that one must be virtuous in order to be happy probably has some truth in it – non-virtuous people often have stronger feelings of guilt and shame. We have seen that individuals are happier if they are involved in goal-directed projects, though the goals should not be too distant, and should be co-operative (p. 116f).

Those who have religious beliefs are somewhat happier than those who do not, especially among the elderly (p. 122). Feeling that one's life has some meaning and purpose is clearly associated with happiness (p. 123f). How is such a sense of meaning and purpose arrived at? It can be done through work for those who feel that what they are doing is worthwhile, that they are achieving something, that it will benefit others. It can be done through leisure if something is achieved, or through long-term and continuing projects like gardening, or regular activities like sport. It can be done through other people, through support for a spouse, bringing up children, long-term involvement with friends and relatives. Having some degree of self-esteem, believing that they have the ability and resources to cope with events, and to influence what happens, makes people less vulnerable to depression, more likely to be happy. This confidence is enhanced by good relationships with other people, and the successful and enjoyable use of skills at work and leisure.

CONCLUSIONS

Clearly it *is* possible to increase the happiness of oneself or others, by going about it the right way.

1 Short-term increases in positive mood can be induced by thinking about recent pleasant events, watching funny films or TV, listening to cheerful music, and to some extent by reciting positive self-statements, by smiles, jokes, small presents and hypnosis. The effects tend to be rather brief, but these activities can be engaged in regularly. The only drug which seems to be successful is alcohol, but in doses which are not too large.

2 The frequency of more potent pleasant activities can be increased. This is most effective if individuals find out by keeping a log which events are most pleasant for them, making a definite decision to increase the frequency of these events, and keeping a record of how often they are done.

3 Becoming richer, having a better house, car, etc., has a rather small effect on well-being, and this is mainly due to making comparisons with other people, or own past life.

4 Good relationships with others are a major source of happiness – being happily married, having friends, being on good terms with family and relatives, work-mates and neighbours. To achieve such relationships may require social-skills training.

5 Satisfying work and leisure are the other two major sources of happiness. They provide intrinsic satisfaction from the successful use of skills and the accomplishment of tasks, the company of other people, a sense of identity and belonging, and the structuring of time. Sport improves health and mental health, as do holidays and other forms of relaxation.

6 Depression can be relieved by various forms of treatment designed to make people look at things more positively, evaluate themselves more favourably, set themselves more attainable goals, and give up false beliefs which make for unhappiness. These methods have also been found to be beneficial for normal people. Achieving an integrated perso-

nality and a sense that life has meaning and purpose can be done either by therapy, or by successful involvement with work, leisure and other people.

7 The most successful forms of treatment for depressed patients have consisted of combinations of several of the methods listed above, such as increased pleasant activities *and* social-skills training *and* cognitive therapy. A number of successful happiness-induction courses for normals have combined several approaches in the same way. However these courses have all missed what I believe are two of the most important ingredients – the quality of work and leisure.

·REFERENCES·

Abbott, D. A. and Brody, G. H. (1985) The relation of child age, gender, and number of children to the marital adjustment of wives. *Journal of Marriage and the Family* **47**: 77–84.

Abrams, M. (1973) Subjective social indicators. *Social Trends* **4**: 35–50.

Abramson, L. Y., Seligman, M. E. P. and Teasdale, J. D. (1978) Learned helplessness in humans: critique and reformulation. *Journal of Abnormal Psychology* **87**: 49–74.

Adams, B. N. (1968) *Kinship in an Urban Setting.* Chicago: Markham.

Altman, I. and Wohlwill, J. F. (1983) (eds) *Behavior and the Natural Environment.* New York and London: Plenum.

Anderson, D. B. and Pennebaker, J. W. (1980) Pain and pleasure: alternative interpretations for identical stimuli. *European Journal of Social Psychology* **10**: 207–12.

Andrews, F. M. and McKennell, A. C. (1980) Measures of self-reported well-being: their affective, cognitive and other components. *Social Indicators Research* **8**: 127–55.

Andrews, F. M. and Withey, S. B. (1976) *Social Indicators of Well-Being.* New York and London: Plenum.

Apter, M. J. (1982) *The Experience of Motivation.* London: Academic Press.

—— (1984) Reversal theory and personality: a review. *Journal of Research in Personality* **18**: 265–88.

Argyle, M. (1972) *The Social Psychology of Work*. Harmondsworth: Penguin.

—— (1983) *The Psychology of Interpersonal Behaviour* (4th edn). Harmondsworth: Penguin.

Argyle, M. and Beit-Hallahmi, B. (1975) *The Social Psychology of Religion*. London and Boston: Routledge & Kegan Paul.

Argyle, M. and Crossland, J. (In press) The dimensions of positive emotions. *British Journal of Social Psychology*.

Argyle, M. and Furnham, A. (1982) The ecology of relationships: choice of situation as a function of relationship. *British Journal of Social Psychology* 21: 259–62.

—— (1983) Sources of satisfaction and conflict in long-term relationships. *Journal of Marriage and the Family* 45: 481–93.

Argyle, M., Furnham, A. and Graham, J. A. (1981) *Social Situations*. Cambridge: Cambridge University Press.

Argyle, M. and Henderson, M. (1984) The rules of friendship. *Journal of Social and Personal Relationships* 1: 211–37.

—— (1985) *The Anatomy of Relationships*. London: Heinemann; Harmondsworth: Penguin.

Ax, A. F. (1953) The physiological differentiation of fear and anger in humans. *Psychosomatic Medicine* 15: 433–42.

Badura, B. (1984) Life-style and health: some remarks on different view points. *Social Science and Medicine* 19: 341–7.

Bammel, G. and Bammel, L. L. B. (1982) *Leisure and Human Behavior*. New York: W. C. Brown.

Banks, M. H. and Jackson, P. R. (1982) Unemployment and risk of minor psychiatric disorder in young people: cross sectional and longitudinal evidence. *Psychological Medicine* 12: 789–98.

Barrow, R. (1980) *Happiness*. Oxford: Martin Robertson.

Barschak, E. (1951) A study of happiness and unhappiness in the childhood and adolescence of girls in different cultures. *Journal of Psychology* 32: 173–215.

Bateman, T. S. and Strassen, S. (1983) A cross-lagged regression test of the relationships between job tension and employee satisfaction. *Journal of Applied Psychology* 68: 439–45.

Batson, D., Coke, J. S., Chard, F., Smith, D. and Taliaferro, A. (1979) Generality of the 'Glow of Goodwill': effects of mood on helping and information acquisition. *Social Psychology Quarterly* 42: 176–9.

Beck, A. T. (1976) *Cognitive Therapy and the Emotional Disorders*. New York: International Universities Press.

Beisser, A. R. (1967) *The Madness in Sports*. New York: Appleton.

Benin, M. H. and Nienstedt, B. C. (1985) Happiness in single- and dual-earner families: the effects of marital happiness, job satisfaction, and life cycle. *Journal of Marriage and the Family* 47: 975–84.

Berkman, L. F. and Syme, S. L. (1979) Social networks, host resistance, and mortality: a nine year follow-up study of Alameda county residents. *American Journal of Epidemiology* **109**: 186–204.

Berscheid, E. and Walster, E. (1974) Physical attractiveness. *Advances in Experimental Social Psychology* **7**: 158–216.

Bhagat, R. S. (1982) Conditions under which stronger job performance – job satisfaction relationships may be observed: a closer look at two situational contingencies. *Academy of Management Journal* **25**: 772–89.

Biglan, A. and Dow, M. G. (1981) Toward a second-generation model: a problem-specific approach. In L. P. Rehm (ed.) *Behavior Therapy for Depression*. New York: Academic Press.

Binitie, A. (1975) A factor analytical study of depression across cultures (African and European). *British Journal of Psychiatry* **127**: 559–63.

Birch, F. (1979) Leisure patterns 1973 and 1977. *Population Trends* **17**: 2–8.

Birnbaum, J. A. (1975) Life patterns and self-esteem in gifted family-oriented and career-committed women. In M. T. S. Mednick *et al.* (eds) *Women and Achievement*. New York: Wiley.

Black, D. (1980) *Inequalities in Health*. London: DHSS.

Blaney, P. H. (1981) The effectiveness of cognitive and behavioral therapies. In L. P. Rehm (ed) *Behavior Therapy for Depression*. New York: Academic Press.

Blauner, R. (1960) Work satisfaction and industrial trends in modern society. In W. Galenson and S. M. Lipset (eds) *Labor and Trade Unions*. New York: Wiley.

Bower, G. H. (1981) Mood and memory. *American Psychologist* **36**: 129–48.

—— (1983) Affect and cognition. *Philosophical Transactions of the Royal Society*, *B302*, 387–402.

Bower, R. T. (1973) *Television and the Public*. New York: Holt, Rinehart & Winston.

Bradburn, N. M. (1969) *The Structure of Psychological Well-Being*. Chicago: Aldine.

Braiker, H. B. and Kelley, H. H. (1979) Conflict in the development of close relationships. In R. L. Burgess and T. L. Huston (eds) *Social Exchange in Developing Relationships*. New York: Academic Press.

Brandt, R. B. (1972) Happiness. *Encyclopedia of Philosophy* **3**: 413–14.

Brayfield, A. H. and Crockett, W. H. (1955) Employee attitudes and employee performance. *Psychological Bulletin* **52**: 396–424.

Breakwell, G. (1984) Knowing your place: finding your place. *ESRC Newsletter*, June, p. 29.

Brewin, C. R. (1985) Depression and causal attributions: what is their relationship? *Psychological Bulletin* **98**: 297–309.

Brickman, P. and Campbell, D. T. (1971) Hedonic relativism and planning the good society. In M. H. Appley (ed.) *Adaptation Level Theory*. New York: Academic Press.

Brickman, P., Coates, D. and Janoff-Bulman, R. (1978) Lottery winners and accident victims: is happiness relative? *Journal of Personality and Social Psychology* **36**: 917–27.

Briere, J., Downes, A. and Spensley, J. (1983) Summer in the city: urban weather conditions and psychiatric emergency-room visits. *Journal of Abnormal Psychology* **92**: 77–80.

Brim, J. A. (1974) Social network correlates of avowed happiness. *Journal of Nervous and Mental Disease* **158**: 432–9.

Brown, G. W. and Harris, T. (1978) *Social Origins of Depression*. London: Tavistock.

Browne, M. A. and Mahoney, M. J. (1984) Sport psychology. *Annual Review of Psychology* **35**: 605–25.

Bryant, F. B. and Veroff, J. (1982) The structure of psychological well-being: a sociohistorical analysis. *Journal of Personality and Social Psychology* **43**: 653–73.

Bryant, J. and Zillman, D. (1984) Using television to alleviate boredom and stress: selective exposure as a function of induced excitational states. *Journal of Broadcasting* **28**: 1–20.

Buck, R. (1984) *The Communication of Emotion*. New York: Guilford.

Buck, C. N. and Aucoin, J. B. (1975) Voluntary association participation and life satisfaction: a replication note. *Journal of Gerontology*, **30**, 73–6.

Burchfield, S. R., Holmes, T. H. and Harrington, R. L. (1981) Personality differences between sick and rarely sick individuals. *Social Science and Medicine, 15E*: 145–8.

Burton, T. L. (1971) *Experiments in Recreation Research*. London: Allen & Unwin.

Campbell, A. (1981) *The Sense of Well-Being in America*. New York: McGraw-Hill.

Campbell, A., Converse, P. E. and Rodgers, W. L. (1976) *The Quality of American Life*. New York: Sage.

Cantril, H. (1965) *The Pattern of Human Concerns*. New Brunswick, NJ: Rutgers University Press.

Caplan, R. D., Cobb, S., French, J. R. P., Harrison R. V., and Pinnean, S. R. (1975) *Job Demands and Worker Health*. US Department of Health, Education and Welfare.

Caplow, T. (1954) *The Sociology of Work*. Minneapolis: University of Minnesota Press.

Carp, F. M. and Carp, A. (1982) Test of a model of domain satisfaction and well-being. *Research on Aging* **4**: 503–22.

Catalano, R. and Dooley, D. (1983) Health effects of economic instability:

a test of economic stress hypothesis. *Journal of Health and Social Behavior* **24**: 46–60.

Catalano, R., Dooley, D. and Jackson, R. (1981) Economic predictions of admissions to mental health facilities in a nonmetropolitan community. *Journal of Health and Social Behavior* **22**: 284–97.

Cautela, J. R. and Kastenbaum, R. (1967) A reinforcement survey schedule for use in therapy, training and research. *Psychological Reports* **20**: 1115–30.

Chalip, L., Csikszentmihalyi, M., Kleiber, D. and Larson, R. (1984) Variations of experience in formal and informal sport. *Research Quarterly for Exercise and Sport* **55**: 109–16.

Cheek, N. H. and Burch, W. R. (1976) *The Social Organization of Leisure in Human Society*. New York: Harper & Row.

Chesser, E. (1956) *The Sexual, Marital and Family Relationships of the English Woman*. London: Hutchinson.

Clark, D. M. (1983) On the induction of depressed mood in the laboratory: evaluation and comparison of the Velten and musical procedures. *Advances in Behavior Research and Therapy* **5**: 24–49.

Clark, D. M. and Teasdale, J. D. (1982) Diurnal variation in clinical depression and accessibility to memories of positive and negative experiences. *Journal of Abnormal Psychology* **91**: 87–95.

Clark, M. S. and Isen, A. M. (1982) Toward understanding the relationship between feeling states and social behavior. In A. Hastorf and A. M. Isen (eds) *Cognitive Social Psychology*. New York: Elsevier.

Clark, M. S. and Waddell, B. A. (1983) Effects of moods on thoughts about helping, attraction and information acquisition. *Social Psychology Quarterly* **46**: 31–5.

Cleary, P. D. and Mechanic, D. (1983) Sex differences in psychological distress among married people. *Journal of Health and Social Behavior* **24**: 111–21.

Clegg, C. W. (1983) Psychology of employee lateness, absence, and turnover: a methodological critique and an empirical study. *Journal of Applied Psychology* **68**: 88–101.

Cobb, S. (1976) Social support as a moderator of life stress. *Psychosomatic Medicine* **38**: 300–14.

Cobb, S. and Kasl, S. V. (1977) *Termination: the Consequences of Job Loss*. Cincinatti: US Dept of Health, Education and Welfare.

Cochrane, R. (1983) *The Social Creation of Mental Illness*. London: Longman.

Cockerham, W. C. (1981) *Sociology of Mental Disorder*. Englewood Cliffs, NJ: Prentice-Hall.

Cohen, S. and Hoberman, H. M. (1982) Positive events and life events as buffers of life change stress. *Journal of Applied Social Psychology* **13**: 99–125.

Cohen, S. and McKay, G. (1984) Social support, stress and the buffering hypothesis: an empirical and theoretical analysis. In A. Baum, J. E. Singer and S. E. Taylor (eds) *Handbook of Psychology and Health*, Vol. 4. Hillsdale, NJ: Erlbaum.

Cohen, S. and Wills, T. A. (1985) Stress, social support, and the buffering hypothesis. *Psychological Bulletin* **98**: 310–57.

Collett, P. (1986) Video-recording the viewers in their natural habitat; In *New Developments in Media Research*. Amsterdam: Esdmar.

Comstock, G. (1980) *Television in America*. Beverly Hills: Sage.

Comstock, G., Chaffee, S., Katzman, N., McCombs, M. and Roberts, D. (1978) *Television and Human Behavior*. New York: Columbia University Press.

Comstock, G. W. and Partridge, K. B. (1972) Church attendance and health. *Journal of Chronic Diseases* **25**: 665–72.

Cook, J. D., Hepworth, S. J., Wall, T. D. and Warr, P. B. (1981) *The Experience of Work*. London: Academic Press.

Cooper, C. (1985) Your place in the stress league. *The Sunday Times*, 24 February.

Cooper, C. L. and Marshall, J. (1976) Occupational sources of stress: a review of the literature relating to coronary heart disease and mental ill-health. *Journal of Occupational Psychology* **49**: 11–28.

Costa, P. T. and McRae, R. R. (1980) Somatic complaints in males as a function of age and neuroticism: a longitudinal analysis. *Journal of Behavioral Medicine* **3**: 245–57.

Costa, P. T., McRae, R. R. and Norris, A. H. (1981) Personal adjustment to aging: longitudinal prediction from neuroticism and extraversion. *Journal of Gerontology* **36**: 78–85.

Coyne, J. C. and Gotlib, I. H. (1983) The role of cognition in depression: a critical appraisal. *Psychological Bulletin* **94**: 472–505.

Crandall, J. E. (1984) Social interest as a moderator of life stress. *Journal of Personality and Social Psychology* **47**: 164–74.

Crandall, R., Nolan, M. and Morgan, L. (1980) Leisure and social interaction. In S. E. Iso-Ahola (ed.) *Social Psychological Perspectives on Leisure and Recreation*. Springfield, Ill.: Thomas.

Crown, S. and Crisp, A. H. (1979) *Manual of the Crown-Crisp Experiential Index*. London: Hodder & Stoughton.

Csikszentmihalyi, M. (1975) *Beyond Boredom and Anxiety*. San Francisco: Jossey-Bass.

—— (1981) Leisure and socialization. *Social Forces* **60**: 332–40.

—— (1982) Toward a psychology of optimal experience. *Review of Personality and Social Psychology* **3**: 13–36.

Csikszentmihalyi, M. and Kubey R. (1981) Television and the rest of life: a systematic comparison of subjective experiences. *Public Opinion Quarterly* **45**: 317–28.

Cunningham, M. R. (1979) Weather, mood, and helping behavior: quasi experiments with the sunshine Samaritans. *Journal of Personality and Social Psychology* **37**: 1947–56.

Daly, E. M., Lancee, W. J. and Polivy, J. (1983) A conical model for the taxonomy of emotional expression. *Journal of Personality and Social Psychology* **45**: 443–57.

Davies, R., Hamill, L., Moylan, S. and Smee, C. H. (1982) Incomes in and out of work. *Department of Employment Gazette*, June, 237–43.

Davis, D., Rainey, H. G. and Brock, T. C. (1976) Interpersonal physical pleasuring: effects of sex combinations, recipient attitudes, and antici- pated future interaction. *Journal of Personality and Social Psychology* **33**: 89–106.

Deci, E. L. and Ryan, R. M. (1980) The empirical exploration of intrinsic motivational processes. *Advances in Experimental Social Psychology* **13**: 39–80.

Dermer, M., Cohen, S. J., Jacobson, E. and Anderson, E. A. (1979) Evaluative judgments of aspects of life as a function of vicarious exposure to hedonic extremes. *Journal of Personality and Social Psy- chology* **37**: 247–60.

Diener, E. (1984) Subjective well-being. *Psychological Bulletin* **95**: 542–75.

Diener, E., Horowitz, J. and Emmons, R. A. (1985) Happiness of the very wealthy. *Social Indicators Research*, **16**: 263–74.

Diener, E. and Larsen, R. J. (1984) Temporal stability and cross- situational consistency of positive and negative affect. *Journal of Per- sonality and Social Psychology* **47**: 871–83.

Diener, E., Larsen, R. J. and Emmons, R. A. (1984) Person × situation interactions: choice of situations and congruence response models. *Journal of Personality and Social Psychology* **47**: 580–92.

Diener, E., Larsen, S., Levine, S. and Emmons, R. A. (1985) Intensity and frequency: dimensions underlying positive and negative affect. *Journal of Personality and Social Psychology* **48**: 1253–65.

Diener, E., Sandvik, E. and Larsen, R. J. (1985) Age and sex effects for emotional intensity. *Developmental Psychology* **21**: 542–6.

Dohrenwend, B. P. (1975) Sociocultural and socio-psychological factors in the genesis of mental disorders. *Journal of Health and Social Behavior* **16**: 365–92.

Dooley, R. D. and Catalano, R. (1980) Economic change as a cause of behavioral disorder. *Psychological Bulletin* **87**: 450–68.

Dovidio, J. F. (1984) Helping behaviour and altruism: an empirical and conceptual overview. *Advances in Experimental Social Psychology* **17**: 362–427.

Dunnell, K. and Cartwright, A. (1972) *Medicine Takers, Prescribers and Hoarders*. London: Routledge & Kegan Paul.

Easterlin, R. A. (1974) Does economic growth improve the human lot? Some empirical evidence. In P. A. David and M. Abramovitz (eds) *Nations and Households in Economic Growth*. New York: Academic Press.

Eaton, W. W. (1978) Life events, social support, and psychiatric symptoms: a re-analysis of the New Haven data. *Journal of Health and Social Behavior* **19**: 230–7.

Edwards, J. N. and Klemmack, D. L. (1973) Correlations of life satisfaction: a re-examination. *Journal of Gerontology* **28**: 497–502.

Ekman, P. (1982) *Emotion in the Human Face* (2nd edn). Cambridge: Cambridge University Press.

Elder, G. H. (1974) *Children of the Great Depression*. Chicago: Chicago University Press.

Ellis, A. (1962) *Reason and Emotion in Psychotherapy*. New York: Lyle Stuart Press.

Ellison, D. L. (1969) Alienation and the will to live. *Journal of Gerontology* **24**: 361–7.

Emmons, R. A. and Diener, E. (1985) Personality correlates of subjective well-being. *Personality and Social Psychology Bulletin* **11**: 89–97.

Emmons, R. A., Diener, E. and Larsen, R. J. (1986) Choice and avoidance of everyday situations and affect congruence: two models of reciprocal interactionism. *Journal of Personality and Social Psychology*, in press.

Euro-Barometre (1983) No. 20, p. 1–38. The mood of Europeans.

Exercise and Health (1984) American Academy of Physical Education, Champaign, Ill.: Human Kinetics Inc.

Eysenck, H. J. (1976) *The Measurement of Personality*. Lancaster: MTP Press.

—— (1985) Personality, cancer and cardiovascular disease: a causal analysis. *Personality and Individual Differences* **6**: 535–56.

Eysenck, H. J. and Eysenck, S. B. G. (1975) *Manual of the Eysenck Personality Questionnaire*. London: Hodder & Stoughton.

Farrell, D. (1983) Exit, voice, loyalty and neglect as responses to job satisfaction: a multidimensional scaling study. *Academy of Management Journal* **26**: 596–607.

Feather, N. T. (1982) Unemployment and its psychological correlates: a study of depressive symptoms, self-esteem, Protestant Ethic values, attributional style and apathy. *Australian Journal of Psychology* **34**: 309–23.

Feather, N. T. and Bond, M. J. (1983) Time structure and purposeful activity among employed and unemployed university graduates. *Journal of Occupational Psychology* **56**: 241–54.

Feather, N. T. and Davenport, P. R. (1983) Unemployment and depressive affect: a motivational and attributional analysis. *Journal of Personality and Social Psychology* **41**: 422–36.

Festinger, L., Schachter, S. and Back, K. (1950) *Social Pressures in Informal Groups*. New York: Harper & Row.

Finlay-Jones, B. and Eckhardt, B. (1981) Psychiatric disorder among the young unemployed. *Australian and New Zealand Journal of Psychiatry* **15**: 265–70.

Finlay-Jones, R. A. and Burrill, P. W. (1977) The prevalence of minor psychiatric morbidity in the community. *British Journal of Psychiatry* **7**: 475–89.

Fletcher, B. (1983) Marital relationships as a cause of death: an analysis of occupational mortality and the hidden consequences of marriage – some U.K. data. *Human Relations* **36**: 123–34.

Folkins, C. H. and Sime, W. E. (1981) Physical fitness training and mental health. *American Psychologist* **36**: 373–89.

Fordyce, M. W. (1977) Development of a program to increase personal happiness. *Journal of Counseling Psychology* **24**: 511–21.

Forgas, J. P., Bower, G. H. and Krantz, S. E. (1984) The influence of mood on perceptions of social interaction. *Journal of Experimental Social Psychology* **20**: 497–513.

Fox, J. W. (1980) Gove's sex-role theory of mental illness: a research note. *Journal of Health and Social Behavior* **21**: 260–7.

Franzoi, S. L., Davis, M. H. and Young, R. D. (1985) The effects of private self-consciousness and perspective taking on satisfaction in close relationships. *Journal of Personality and Social Psychology* **48**: 1584–94.

Fraser, C. (1984) Pay comparisons and pay satisfaction. Paper to conference of European Association for Experimental Social Psychology, Tilburg.

Freedman, J. L. (1978) *Happy People*. New York: Harcourt Brace Jovanovich.

French, J. R. P., Caplan, R. D. and Harrison, R. van (1982) *The Mechanisms of Job Stress and Strain*. Chichester: Wiley.

Frost, R. O. and Green, M. L. (1982) Duration and post-experimental removal of Velten mood induction procedure effects. *Personality and Social Psychology Bulletin* **8**: 341–7.

Fryer, D. and Payne, R. (1984) Proactive behaviour in unemployment: findings and implications. *Leisure Studies* **3**: 273–95.

Fuchs, C. Z. and Rehm, L. P. (1977) A self-control behavior therapy program for depression. *Journal of Consulting and Clinical Psychology* **45**: 206–15.

Fuchs, E. and Havighurst, R. (1973) *To Live on this Earth: American Indian Education*. Garden City, NY: Doubleday, Anchor Books.

Furnham, A. (1981) Personality and activity preference. *British Journal of Social Psychology* **20**: 57–68.

—— (1982a) The Protestant work ethic and attitudes towards unemployment. *Journal of Occupational Psychology* **55**: 277–81.

—— (1982b) Explanations of unemployment in Britain. *European Journal of Social Psychology* **12**: 335–52.

—— (1984a) Many sides of the coin: the psychology of money usage. *Personality and Individual Differences* **5**: 501–9.

—— (1984b) Extraversion, sensation-seeking, stimulus screening and type 'A' behaviour pattern: the relationships between various levels of arousal. *Personality and Individual Differences* **5**: 133–40.

—— (1984c) Work values and beliefs in Britain. *Journal of Occupational Psychology* **5**: 281–91.

—— (1984d) The Protestant Work Ethic: a review of the psychological literature. *European Journal of Social Psychology* **14**: 87–104.

Furnham, A. and Lewis, A. (1986) *The Economic Mind: The Social Psychology of Economic Behaviour*. Brighton: Wheatsheaf.

Furnham, A. and Schaeffer, R. (1984) Person-environment fit, job satisfaction and mental health. *Journal of Occupational Psychology* **57**: 295–307.

Gallup, G. H. (1976) Human needs and satisfaction: a global survey. *Public Opinion Quarterly* **40**: 459–67.

General Household Survey (1980, 1983) Nos. 11 and 12. London: HMSO.

Gentry, J. W. and Doering, M. (1979) Sex role orientation and leisure. *Journal of Leisure Research* **11**: 102–11.

Gerstel, N., Riessman, C. K. and Rosenfield, S. (1985) Explaining the symptomatology of divorced women and men; the role of material conditions and social networks. *Social Forces* **64**: 84–101.

Ginandes, C. (1977) Life satisfaction and self-esteem values in men of four different socio-economic groups. Ph.D. Boston University.

Glenn, N.D. and McLanahan, S. (1981) The effects of offspring on the psychological well-being of older adults. *Journal of Marriage and the Family* **43**: 409–21.

Glenn, N. D. and Weaver, C. N. (1978) A multivariate, multisurvey study of marital happiness. *Journal of Marriage and the Family* **40**: 269–82.

Goldberg, D. (1972) *The Detection of Psychiatric Illness by Questionnaire*. Oxford: Oxford University Press.

—— (1978) *Manual of the General Health Questionnaire*. Windsor: NFER.

Goldman, W. and Lewis, P. (1977) Beautiful is good: evidence that the physically attractive are more socially skilled. *Journal of Experimental Social Psychology* **13**: 125–30.

Goldthorpe, J., Lockwood, D., Bechofer, F. and Platt, J. (1968) *The Affluent Worker*. Cambridge: Cambridge University Press.

Gomberg, E. S. and Franks, V. (eds) (1979) *Gender and Disordered Behavior: Sex Differences in Psychopathology*. New York: Brunner/Mazel.

Gouaux, C. (1971) Induced states and interpersonal attraction. *Journal of Personality and Social Psychology* **20**: 37–43.

Gove, W. R. (1972) The relationship between sex roles, marital status, and mental illness. *Social Forces* **51**: 34–44.

—— (1984) Gender differences in mental and physical illness: the effects of fixed roles and nurturant roles. *Social Science and Medicine* **19**: 77–91.

Gove, W. R. and Tudor, J. (1973) Adult sex roles and mental illness. *American Journal of Sociology* **77**: 812–35.

Graef, R., Csikszentmihalyi, M. and Gianinno, S. M. (1983) Measuring intrinsic motivation in everyday life. *Leisure Studies* **2**: 155–68.

Greer, S. and Watson, M. (1985) Towards a psychobiological model of cancer: psychological considerations. *Social Science and Medicine* **20**: 773–7.

Griffit, W. and Veitch, R. (1971) Hot and crowded: influences of population density on interpersonal affective behavior. *Journal of Personality and Social Psychology* **17**: 92–8.

Gruneberg, M. M. (1979) *Understanding Job Satisfaction*. New York: Wiley.

Gurin, G., Veroff, J. and Feld, S. (1960) *Americans View their Mental Health*. New York: Basic Books.

Gurney, R. M. (1980) The effects of unemployment on the psycho-social development of school-leavers. *Journal of Occupational Psychology* **53**: 205–13.

Guttentag, M., Salasin, S. and Belle, D. (1980) *The Mental Health of Women*. New York: Academic Press.

Hackett, R. D. and Guion, R. M. (1985) A re-evaluation of the absenteeism – job satisfaction relationship. *Organizational Behavior and Human Decision Processes* **35**: 340–87.

Hackman, J. R. (1977) Work design. In J. R. Hackman and J. L. Suttle (eds) *Improving Life at Work*. Santa Monica: Goodyear.

Hall, J. A. (1984) *Nonverbal Sex Differences*. Baltimore and London: Johns Hopkins University Press.

Hammen, C. L. and Peters, S. D. (1978) Interpersonal consequences of depression: responses to men and women enacting a depressed role. *Journal of Abnormal Psychology* **87**: 322–32.

Hammen, C. L., Rook, K. S. and Harris, G. (1979) 'Effect of activities and attributions on depressed mood.' Unpublished ms, University of California, Los Angeles. Cited by Blaney (1981).

Hannay, D. R. (1979) *The Symptom Iceberg*. London and Boston: Routledge & Kegan Paul.

Harackiewicz, J. M., Sansome, C. and Manderlink, G. (1985) Competence, achievement orientation, and intrinsic motivation: a process analysis. *Journal of Personality and Social Psychology* **48**: 493–508.

Harding, S. D. (1982) Psychological well-being in Great Britain: an evaluation of the Bradburn affect balance scale. *Personality and Individual Differences* **3**: 167–75.

Haring-Hidore, M., Stock, W. A., Okun, M. A. and Witter, R. A. (1985)

Marital status and subjective well-being: a research synthesis. *Journal of Marriage and the Family*, **47**, 947–53.

Harré, R., Clarke, D. D. and De Carlo, N. (1985) *Motives and Mechanisms*. London: Methuen.

Havighurst, R. J. (1961) The nature and values of meaningful free-time activity. In R. W. Kleemeier (ed.) *Aging and Leisure*. New York: Oxford University Press.

Haw, A. H. (1982) Women, work and stress: a review and agenda for the future. *Journal of Health and Social Behavior* **23**: 132–44.

Headey, B., Holmstrom, E. and Wearing, A. (1984) Well-being and ill-being: different dimensions? *Social Indicators Research* **14**: 115–39.

Headey, B, and Wearing, A. (1986) Chains of well-being, chains of ill-being, International Sociological Association conference, New Delhi.

Heath, A. (1981) *Social Mobility*. London: Fontana.

Heiby, E. M. (1983) Assessment of frequency of self-reinforcement. *Journal of Personality and Social Psychology* **44**: 1304–7.

Heiby, E. M., Ozaki, M. and Campos, P. E. (1984) The effects of training in self-reinforcement and reward: implications for depression. *Behavior Therapy* **15**: 544–9.

Henderson, M. and Argyle, M. (1985) Social support by four categories of work colleagues: relationship between activities, stress and satisfaction. *Journal of Occupational Behaviour* **6**: 229–39.

Henderson, M., Argyle, M. and Furnham, A. (1984) 'The assessment of positive life events.' Unpublished.

Henderson, S., Byrne, D. G., Duncan-Jones, P., Scott, R. and Adcock, S. (1980) Social relationships, adversity and neurosis: a study of associations in a general population sample. *British Journal of Psychiatry* **136**: 574–83.

Henderson, S. and Duncan-Jones, P. (1981) *Neurosis and the Social Environment*. Sydney: Academic Press.

Henry, A. F. and Short, J. F. (1959) *Suicide and Homicide*. Glencoe, Ill.: Free Press.

Herzberg, F., Mausner, B. and Snyderman, B. (1959) *The Motivation to Work*. New York: Wiley.

Hobbs, J. E. (1980) *Applied Climatology*. Folkestone: Dawson.

Hoffman, L. W. and Manis, J. D. (1982) The value of children in the United States. In F. I. Nye (ed.) *Family Relationships*. Beverly Hills: Sage.

Hofstede, G. (1980) *Culture's Consequences: International Differences in Work and Related Values*. Beverly Hills: Sage.

Holahan, C. and Moos, R. (1981) Social support and psychological distress: a longitudinal analysis. *Journal of Abnormal Psychology* **90**: 365–70.

Hollon, S. D. (1981) Comparisons and combinations with alternative approaches. In L. P. Rehm (ed.) *Behavior Therapy for Depression*. New York: Academic Press.

Hoppock, R. (1935) *Job Satisfaction*. New York: Harper.

Horowitz, L. M., French, de S. and Anderson, C. A. (1982) The prototype of a lonely person. In L. Peplau and D. Perlman (eds) *Loneliness*. New York: Wiley.

House, J. S. (1980) *Occupational Stress and the Mental and Physical Health of Factory Workers*. Ann Arbor: University of Michigan Survey Research Center.

Howard, M. and Dawes, R. M. (1976) Linear prediction of marital happiness. *Personality and Social Psychology Bulletin* 2: 478–80.

Hughes, M. and Gove, W. R. (1981) Living alone, social integration, and mental health. *American Journal of Sociology* 87: 48–74.

Hulin, C. L. and Blood, M. R. (1968) Job enlargement, individual differences, and worker responses. *Psychological Bulletin* 69: 41–55.

Hulin, C. L. and Smith, P. C. (1964) Sex differences in job satisfaction. *Journal of Applied Psychology* 48: 88–92.

Iaffaldano, M. T. and Muchinsky, P. M. (1985) Job satisfaction and job performance: a meta analysis. *Psychological Bulletin* 97: 251–73.

Innes, J. M. (1981) Social psychological approaches to the study of the induction and alleviation of stress: influences upon health and illness. In G. M. Stephenson and J. H. Davis (eds) *Progress in Applied Social Psychology*, 1. Chichester: Wiley.

Isen, A. M., Clark, M. and Schwartz, M. F. (1976) Duration of the effect of good mood on helping: 'footprints on the sands of time'. *Journal of Personality and Social Psychology* 34: 383–93.

Isen, A. M. and Daubman, K. A. (1984) The influence of affect on categorisation. *Journal of Personality and Social Psychology* 47: 1206–17.

Isen, A. M. and Georgoglione, J. M. (1983) Some specific effects of four affect-induction procedures. *Personality and Social Psychology Bulletin* 9: 136–43.

Isen, A. M., Johnson, M. M. S., Mertz, E. and Robinson, G. F. (1985) The influence of positive affect on the unusualness of word association. *Journal of Personality and Social Psychology* 48: 1413–26.

Isen, A. M. and Means, B. (1983) The influence of positive affect on decision-making strategy. *Social Cognition* 2: 18–31.

Isen, A. M., Schalker, T. E., Clark, M. and Karp, L. (1978) Affect, accessibility of material in memory, and behavior: a cognitive loop? *Journal of Personality and Social Psychology* 36: 1–12.

Iversen, S. D. and Iversen, L. L. (1981) *Behavioral Pharmacology*. New York: Oxford University Press.

Izard, C. E. (1977) *Human Emotions*. New York and London: Plenum.

Jackson, P. (1984) Efficacy, self-esteem and unemployment. Paper at BPS Social Section Conference, Oxford.

Jackson, P. and Warr, P. B. (1984) Unemployment and psychological ill-health: the moderating role of duration and age. *Psychological Medicine* **14**: 605–14.

Jahoda, M. (1981) Work, employment, and unemployment. *American Psychologist* **36**: 184–91.

Jemmott, J. B. and Locke, S. E. (1984) Psychosocial factors, immunology mediation, and human susceptibility to infectious diseases: how much do we know? *Psychological Bulletin* **95**: 78–108.

Jenkins, D. (1981) QWL – current trends and directions. *Issues in the Quality of Working Life*. No. 3. Toronto: Ontario Ministry of Labour.

Johnson, A. (1977) Sex differentials in coronary heart disease: the explanatory role of primary risk factors. *Journal of Health and Social Behavior* **18**: 46–54.

Kabanoff, B. (1980) Work and nonwork: a review of models, methods and findings. *Psychological Bulletin* **88**: 60–77.

—— (1982) Occupational and sex differences in leisure needs and leisure satisfaction. *Journal of Occupational Behaviour* **3**: 233–45.

Kahn, R. L. (1981) *Work and Health*. New York: Wiley.

Kalleberg, A. L. and Loscocco, K. A. (1983) Aging, values and rewards: explaining age differences in job satisfaction. *American Sociological Review* **48**: 78–90.

Kammann, R. and Flett, R. (1983) Affectometer 2: a scale to measure current level of general happiness. *Australian Journal of Psychology* **35**, 259–65.

Kammann, R., Smith, R., Martin, C. and McQueen, M. (1984) Low accuracy in judgments of others' psychological well-being as seen from a phenomenological perspective. *Journal of Personality* **52**: 107–23.

Kandel, D. B., Davies, M. and Raveis, V. H. (1985) The stressfulness of daily social roles for women: marital, occupational and household roles. *Journal of Health and Social Behavior* **26**: 64–78.

Kanner, A. D., Coyne, J. C., Schaefer, C. and Lazarus, R. S. (1981) Comparison of two methods of stress measurement: daily hassles and uplifts versus major life events. *Journal of Behavioral Medicine* **4**: 1–39.

Kaplan, E. M. and Cowen, E. L. (1981) Interpersonal helping behavior of industrial foremen. *Journal of Applied Psychology* **66**: 633–8.

Kasl, S. V. (1973) Mental health and the work environment: an examination of the evidence. *Journal of Occupational Medicine* **15**: 509–18.

Kearl, M. C. (1981–2) An inquiry into the positive personal and social effects of old age stereotypes among the elderly. *International Journal of Aging and Human Development* **14**: 277–90.

Kelly, J. R. (1983) *Leisure Identities and Interactions*. London: Allen & Unwin.

Kelvin, P. (1980) The social psychological bases and implications of structural unemployment. In R. Gilmour and S. Duck (eds) *The Development of Social Psychology*. London: Academic Press.

—— (1981) Work as a source of identity. *British Journal of Counselling and Guidance* 9: 2–11.

Kelvin, P. and Jarrett, J. (1985) *The Social Psychological Effects of Unemployment*. Cambridge: Cambridge University Press.

Kessler, R. C. (1982) A disaggregation of the relationship between socioeconomic status and psychological distress. *American Sociological Review* 47: 752–64.

Kessler, R. C., Brown, R. L. and Broman, C. L. (1981) Sex differences in psychiatric help-seeking: evidence from four large-scale surveys. *Journal of Health and Social Behavior* 22: 49–64.

Kessler, R. C. and Cleary, P. D. (1980) Social class and psychological distress. *American Sociological Review*, 45: 463–78.

Kessler, R. C. and Essex, M. (1982) Marital status and depression: the importance of coping resources. *Social Forces* 61: 484–507.

Kessler, R. C. and McRae, J. A. (1981) Trends in the relationship between sex and psychological distress: 1957–76. *American Sociological Review* 46: 443–52.

—— (1983) Trends in the relationship between sex and attempted suicide. *Journal of Health and Social Behavior* 24: 98–110.

Kessler, R. C., Price, R. H. and Wortman, C. B. (1985) Social factors in psychopathology: stress, social support and coping processes. *Annual Review of Psychology* 36: 531–72.

Klemmack, D. L. and Roff, L. L. (1984) Fear of personal aging and subjective well-being in later life. *Journal of Gerontology* 39: 356–58.

Kobasa, S. C. (1982) The hardy personality: toward a social psychology of stress and health. In G. S. Sanders and J. Suls (eds) *Social Psychology of Health and Illness*. Hillsdale, NJ: Erlbaum.

Kobasa, S. C. and Puccetti, M. C. (1983) Personality and social resources in stress resistance. *Journal of Personality and Social Psychology* 45: 839–50.

Kobrin, F. E. and Hendershot, G. E. (1977) Do family ties reduce mortality? Evidence from the United States 1966–68. *Journal of Marriage and the Family* 39: 737–45.

Kohn, M. L. (1972) Class, family and schizophrenia: a reformulation. *Social Forces* 50: 295–304.

Krantz, D. S., Gruneberg, N. E. and Baum, A. (1985) Health psychology. *Annual Review of Psychology* 36: 349–83.

Kraus, R. (1978) *Recreation and Leisure in Modern Society*. Santa Monica: Goodyear.

Kraut, R. E. and Johnston, R. E. (1979) Social and emotional messages of smiling: an ethological approach. *Journal of Personality and Social Psychology* **37**: 1539–53.

Laird, J. D. (1984) The real role of facial response in the experience of emotion: a reply to Tourangeau and Ellsworth, and others. *Journal of Personality and Social Psychology* **47**: 909–17.

Lane, R. E. (1983) Money and the varieties of happiness. Paper at International Society of Political Psychology, Oxford.

Langner, T. S. (1962) A twenty-two item screening score of psychiatric symptoms indicating impairment. *Journal of Health and Social Behavior* **3**: 269–79.

Langner, T. S. and Michael, S. T. (1963) *Life Stress and Mental Health.* Glencoe: Free Press.

Lanzetta, J. T., Cartwright-Smith, J. and Kleck, R. E. (1976) Effects of nonverbal dissimulation on emotional experience and autonomic arousal. *Journal of Personality and Social Psychology* **33**: 354–70.

LaRocco, J. M., House, J. S. and French, J. R. P. (1980) Social support, occupational stress and health. *Journal of Health and Social Behavior* **21**: 202–18.

Larson, R. (1978) Thirty years of research on the subjective well-being of older Americans. *Journal of Gerontology* **33**: 109–25.

Larson, R. W. (1984) States of consciousness in personal relationships: a life span perspective. Paper at International Conference on Personal Relationships, Madison.

Larson, R., Csikszentmihalyi, M. and Freeman, M. (1984) Alcohol and marihuana use in adolescents' daily lives: a random sample of experiences. *International Journal of the Addictions* **19**: 367–81.

Lawler, E. E. (1971) *Pay and Organizational Effectiveness.* New York: McGraw-Hill.

Lawler, E. E. and Porter, L. W. (1967) The effect of performance on job satisfaction. *Industrial Relations* **8**: 20–8.

Layden, M. A. (1982) Attributional style therapy. In C. Antaki and C. Brewin (eds) *Attributions and Psychological Change.* London: Academic Press.

Lazarus, R. S., Averill, J. R. and Opton, E. M. (1970) Towards a cognitive theory of emotion. In M. B. Arnold (ed.) *Feeling and Emotion.* New York: Academic Press.

Lester, D. (1984) The association between the quality of life and suicide and homicide rates. *Journal of Social Psychology* **124**: 247–8.

Levenson, R. and Gottman, J. (1985) Physiological and affective predictors of change in relationship satisfaction. *Journal of Personality and Social Psychology* **49**: 85–94.

Levinthal, C. F. (1983) *Introduction to Physiological Psychology* (2nd edn). Englewood Cliffs, NJ: Prentice-Hall.

Lewinsohn, P. M. and Graf, M. (1973) Pleasant activities and depression. *Journal of Consulting and Clinical Psychology* **41**: 261–8.

Lewinsohn, P. M. and MacPhillamy, D. J. (1974) The relationship between age and engagement in pleasant activities. *Journal of Gerontology* **29**: 290–4.

Lewinsohn, P. M., Mischel, W., Chaplin, W. and Barton, R. (1980) Social competence and depression: the role of illusory self-perceptions. *Journal of Abnormal Psychology* **89**: 203–12.

Lewinsohn, P. M., Steinmetz, J. L., Larson, D. W. and Franklin, J. (1981) Depression-related cognitions: antecedents or consequence? *Journal of Abnormal Psychology* **90**: 213–19.

Lewinsohn, P. M., Sullivan, J. M. and Grosscup, S. J. (1982) Behavioral therapy: clinical applications. In A. J. Rush (ed.) *Short-term Therapies for Depression*. New York: Guilford.

Liang, J. and Fairchild, T. J. (1979) Relative deprivation and perception of financial adequacy among the aged. *Journal of Gerontology* **34**: 746–59.

Lichter, S., Haye, K. and Kammann, R. (1980) Increasing happiness through cognitive training. *New Zealand Psychologist* **9**: 57–64.

Liem, R. and Liem, J. (1978) Social class and mental illness reconsidered: the role of economic stress and social support. *Journal of Health and Social Behavior* **19**: 139–56.

Littlewood, R. and Lipsedge, M. (1982) *Aliens and Alienists*. Harmondsworth: Penguin.

Lloyd, G. G. and Lishman, W. A. (1975) Effect of depression on the speed of recall of pleasant and unpleasant experiences. *Psychological Medicine* **5**: 173–80.

Locke, E. A. (1976) The nature and causes of job satisfaction. In M. D. Dunnette (ed.) *Handbook of Industrial and Organizational Psychology*. Chicago: Rand McNally.

Loher, B. T., Noe, R. A., Moeller, N. L. and Fitzgerald, M. P. (1985) A meta analysis of the relation of job characteristics to job satisfaction. *Journal of Applied Psychology* **70**: 280–9.

Lynch, J. J. (1977) *The Broken Heart*. New York: Basic Books.

Lynn, R. (1981) Cross-cultural differences in neuroticism, extraversion and psychoticism. In R. Lynn (ed.) *Dimensions of Personality*. Oxford: Pergamon.

Lynn, R. (1982) National differences in anxiety and extraversion. *Progress in Experimental Personality Research* **11**: 213–58.

McCann, I. L. and Holmes, D. S. (1984) Influence of aerobic exercise on depression. *Journal of Personality and Social Psychology* **46**: 1142–7.

McEvoy, G. M. and Cascio, W. F. (1985) Strategies for reducing employee turnover: a meta analysis. *Journal of Applied Psychology* **70**: 342–53.

McKennell, A. C. and Andrews, F. M. (1980) Models of cognition and affect in perception of well-being. *Social Indicators Research* 8: 257–98.

MacPhillamy, D. J. and Lewinsohn, P. M. (1976) Manual for the *Pleasant Events Schedule*. University of Oregon.

Malatesta, C. Z. (1985) *The Development of Expressive Behavior*. Orlando: Academic Press.

Mangoine, T. W. and Quinn, R. P. (1975) Job satisfaction, counter productive behavior and drug use at work. *Journal of Applied Psychology* 60: 114–16.

Mann, F. C. and Baumgartel, H. J. (1953) *Absences and Employee Attitudes in an Electric Power Company*. Ann Arbor, Michigan: Institute for Social Research.

Manucia, G. K., Baumann, D. J. and Cialdini, R. B. (1984) Mood influences on helping: direct effects or side effects? *Journal of Personality and Social Psychology* 46: 357–64.

Marcus, A. C. and Siegel, J. M. (1982) Sex differences in the use of physician services: a preliminary test of the fixed role hypothesis. *Journal of Health and Social Behavior* 23: 186–97.

Marks, T. and Hammen, C. L. (1982) Interpersonal mood induction: situational and individual determinants. *Motivation and Emotion* 6: 387–99.

Marsella, A. J. (1980) Depressive experience and disorder across cultures. In H. Triandis and J. Draguns (eds) *Handbook of Cross-Cultural Psychology, Vol. 6*, Boston: Allyn & Bacon.

Marsh, P. and Harré, R. (1978) The world of football hooligans. *Human Nature* 1: 62–9.

Marsh, P., Rosser, E. and Harré, R. (1978) *The Rules of Disorder*. London: Routledge & Kegan Paul.

Martin, M., Ward, J. C. and Clark, D. M. (1983) Neuroticism and the recall of positive and negative personality information. *Behaviour Research and Therapy* 21: 495–503.

Maslow, A. H. (1968) *Toward a Psychology of Being*. Princeton: Van Nostrand.

Masters, W. H. and Johnson, V. E. (1970) *Human Sexual Inadequacy*. London: Churchill.

Matheson, D. W. and Davison, M. A. (1972) (eds) *The Behavioral Effects of Drugs*. New York: Holt, Rinehart & Winston.

Matlin, M. W. and Gawron, V. J. (1979) Individual differences in Pollyannaism. *Journal of Personality Assessment* 43: 411–12.

Matthews, K. A. (1982) Psychological perspectives on the Type A behavior pattern. *Psychological Bulletin* 91: 293–323.

Mednick, M. T. S., Tangri, S. S. and Hoffman, L. W. (eds) (1975) *Women and Achievement*. New York: Wiley.

Metzner, H. and Mann, F. (1953) Employee attitudes and absences. *Personnel Psychology* 6: 467–85.

Michaelos, A. C. (1980) Satisfaction and happiness. *Social Indicators Research* **8**: 385–422.

—— (1985) Multiple discrepancies theory (MDT). *Social Indicators Research* **16**: 347–413.

Miller, R. C. and Berman, J. S. (1983) The efficacy of cognitive behavior therapies: a quantitative review of the research evidence. *Psychological Bulletin* **94**: 39–53.

Mintz, N. (1956) Effects of esthetic surroundings. *Journal of Psychology* **41**: 459–66.

Moberg, D. O. and Taves, M. J. (1965) Church participation and adjustment in old age. In A. M. Rose and W. A. Peterson (eds) *Older People and their Social World*. Philadelphia: F. A. Davis.

Mobley, W. H. (1977) Intermediate linkages in the relationship between job satisfaction and employee turnover. *Journal of Applied Psychology* **62**: 237–40.

MORI (1983) *Loneliness*. London: Market and Opinion Research International.

Moser, K. A., Fox, A. J. and Jones D. R. (1984) Unemployment and mortality in the OPCS longitudinal study. *Lancet* **2**: 1324–9.

Motowidlo, S. J. (1984) Does job satisfaction lead to consideration and personal sensitivity? *Academy of Management Journal* **27**: 910–15.

Moylan, S., Millar, J. and Davies, R. (1984) *For Richer for Poorer: DHSS Study of Unemployed Men*. London: HMSO.

Murray, J. P. and Kippax, S. (1979) From the early window to the late night show: international trends in the study of television's impact on children and adults. *Advances in Experimental Social Psychology* **12**: 253–320.

Nathanson, C. A. (1980) Social roles and health status among women. *Social Science and Medicine* **14A**: 463–71.

Near, J. P., Rice, R. W. and Hunt, R. G. (1980) The relationships between work and nonwork domains. *Academy of Management Review* **5**: 415–29.

Oakley, A. (1974) *The Sociology of Housework*. London: Routledge & Kegan Paul.

O'Connor, P. and Brown, G. (1984) Supportive relationships: fact or fancy? *Journal of Social and Personal Relationships* **1**: 159–75.

Office of Population and Censuses and Surveys (OPCS) (1978) *Life Tables*. The Registrar General's decennial supplement for England and Wales 1970–72. London: HMSO.

Okun, M. A., Stock, W. A., Haring, M. J. and Witten, R. A. (1984) Health and subjective well-being: a meta-analysis. *International Journal of Aging and Human Development* **19**, 111–32.

Olds, J. and Milner, O. (1954) Positive reinforcement produced by electrical stimulation of septal areas and other regions of the rat brain. *Journal of Comparative and Physiological Psychology* **47**: 419–27.

O'Malley, M. N. and Andrews, L. (1983) The effects of mood and incentives on helping: are there some things money can't buy? *Motivation and Emotion* **7**: 179–89.

Ormont, L. R. (1981) Aggression and cancer in group treatment. In J. G. Goldberg (ed.) *Psychotherapeutic Treatment of Cancer Patients.* New York: Free Press.

Pahl, R. E. (1984) *Divisions of Labour.* Oxford: Basil Blackwell.

Pahnke, W. H. (1966) Drugs and mysticism. *International Journal of Parapsychology* **8**: 295–314.

Palmore, E. (1969) Predicting longevity: a follow-up controlling for age. *The Gerontologist* **9**: 247–50.

Palmore, E. B., Fillenbaum, G. G. and George, L. K. (1984) Consequences of retirement. *Journal of Gerontology* **39**: 109–16.

Paloutzian, R. F. and Ellison, C. W. (1982) Loneliness, spiritual well-being and the quality of life. In L. A. Peplau and D. Perlman (eds) *Loneliness.* New York: Wiley.

Palys, T. S. and Little, B. R. (1983) Perceived life satisfaction and the organization of personal project systems. *Journal of Personality and Social Psychology* **44**: 1221–30.

Parker, S. (1983) *Leisure and Work.* London: Allen & Unwin.

Parkes, K. R. (1980) Social desirability, defensiveness and self-report psychiatric inventory scores. *Psychological Medicine* **10**: 735–42.

—— (1982) Occupational stress among student nurses: a natural experiment. *Journal of Applied Psychology* **67**: 784–96.

—— (1984) Locus of control, cognitive appraisal, and coping in stressful episodes. *Journal of Personality and Social Psychology* **46**: 655–68.

Paykel, E. S., Emms, E. M., Fletcher, J. and Rassaby, E. S. (1980) Life events and social support in puerperal depression. *British Journal of Psychiatry* **136**: 339–46.

Payne, R. (1980) Organizational stress and social support. In C. L. Cooper and R. Payne (eds) *Current Concerns in Occupational Stress.* Chichester: Wiley.

Payne, R., Warr, P. and Hartley, J. (1984) Social class and psychological ill-health during unemployment. *Sociology of Health and Illness* **6**: 152–74.

Pearce, P. L. (1982) *The Social Psychology of Tourist Behaviour.* Oxford: Pergamon.

Pearlin, L. I., Liebermann, M. A., Menaghan, E. G., and Mullan, J. T. (1981) The stress process. *Journal of Health and Social Behavior* **22**: 337–56.

Pendleton, B. F. and Yang, S-O, W. (1985) Socioeconomic and health effects on mortality declines in developing countries. *Social Science and Medicine* **20**: 453–60.

Peplau, L. A. and Perlman, D. (eds) (1982) *Loneliness.* New York: Wiley.

Persons, J. B. and Rao, P. A. (1980) Longitudinal study of cognitions, life events, and depression in psychiatric inpatients. *Journal of Abnormal Psychology* **94**: 51–63.

Platt, S. (1984) Unemployment and suicidal behaviour: a review of the literature. *Social Science and Medicine* **19** (2): 93–115.

Preston, S. H. (1975) The changing relation between mortality and level of economic development. *Population Studies* **29**: 231–48.

Privette, G. (1983) Peak experience, peak performance, and peak flow: a comparative analysis of positive human experiences. *Journal of Personality and Social Psychology* **45**: 1361–8.

Privette, G. and Landsman, T. (1983) Factor analysis of peak performance: the full use of potential. *Journal of Personality and Social Psychology* **44**: 195–200.

Public Opinion (1981) Oct/Nov issue.

Radloff, L. S. (1980) Risk factors for depression. In M. Guttentag (ed) *The Mental Health of Women.* New York: Academic Press.

Rapoport, R. and Rapoport, R. N. (1975) *Leisure and the Family Life Cycle.* London: Routledge & Kegan Paul.

Rehm, L. P. (1978) Mood, pleasant events, and unpleasant events: two pilot studies. *Journal of Consulting and Clinical Psychology* **46**: 854–9.

Rehm, L. P. and Kornblith, S. J. (1979) Behavior therapy for depression: a review of recent developments. *Progress in Behavior Modification* **7**: 277–318.

Reich, A. and Zautra, J. (1980) Positive life events and reports of well-being: some useful distinctions. *American Journal of Community Psychology* **8**: 657–70.

—— (1981) Life events and personal causation. *Journal of Personality and Social Psychology* **41**: 1002–12.

—— (1983) Demands and designs in daily life: some influences on well-being. *American Journal of Community Psychology* **11**: 41–58.

Reid, I. (1981) *Social Class Differences in Britain.* London: Grant McIntyre.

Reid, I. and Wormald, E. (1982) *Sex Differences in Britain.* London: Grant McIntyre.

Reis, H. T. (1984) Social interaction and well-being. In S. Duck (ed.) *Personal Relationships, 5: Repairing Personality Relationships.* London: Academic Press.

Reis, H. T., Nezlek, J., Kernis, M. H. and Spiegel, N. (1984) On specificity in the impact of social participation on physical and mental health. *Journal of Personality and Social Psychology* **48**: 456–71.

Reskin, B. F. and Coverman, S. (1985) Sex and race in the determinants of psychophysical distress: a reappraisal of the sex-role hypothesis. *Social Forces* **63**: 1038–59.

Rhodes, S. R. (1983) Age-related differences in work attitudes and behavior: a review and conceptual analysis. *Psychological Bulletin* **93**: 328–67.

Rimland, B. (1982) The altruism paradox. *Psychological Reports* **51**: 521–2.

Roberts, K. (1981) *Leisure* (2nd edn). London: Longman.

Robinson, J. P. (1977) *How Americans Use Time*. New York and London: Praeger.

Rodgers, W. L. and Converse, P. E. (1975) Measures of the perceived overall quality of life. *Social Indicators Research* **2**: 127–52.

Rohrbaugh, J. (1981) *Women: Psychology's Puzzle*. London: Sphere Books.

Rolls, E. T. (1979) Effects of electrical stimulation of the brain on behaviour. *Psychology Surveys* **2**: 151–69. London: Allen & Unwin.

Rosenhan, D. L., Salovey, P. and Hargis, K. (1981) The joys of helping: focus of attention mediates the impact of positive affect on altruism. *Journal of Personality and Social Psychology* **40**: 899–905.

Ross, C. E., Mirowsky, J. and Ulbrich, P. (1983) Distress and the traditional female role: a comparison of Mexicans and Anglos. *American Journal of Sociology*: 670–82.

Ross, H. G. and Milgram, J. L. (1982) Important variables in adult sibling relationships: a quantitative study. In M. E. Lamb and B. Sutton-Smith (eds) *Sibling Relationships*. Hillsdale, NJ: Erlbaum.

Roy, D. F. (1959) Banana time: job satisfaction and informal interaction. *Human Organization* **18**: 158–68.

Rubenstein, C. (1980) Vacations. *Psychology Today* **13**, May: 62–76.

Runciman, W. G. (1966) *Relative Deprivation and Social Justice*. London: Routledge & Kegan Paul.

Rusbult, C. E. and Farrell, D. (1983) A longitudinal test of the investment model: the impact on job satisfaction, job commitment, and turnover of variations in rewards and costs, alternatives and outcome. *Journal of Applied Psychology* **68**: 429–38.

Russell, D., Cutrona, C. E., Rose, J. and Yurko, K. (1984) Social and emotional loneliness: an examination of Weiss's typology of loneliness. *Journal of Personality and Social Psychology* **46**: 1313–21.

Russell, J. A. (1980) A circumplex model of affect. *Journal of Personality and Social Psychology* **39**: 1161–78.

—— (1983) Pancultural aspects of the human conceptual organization. *Journal of Personality and Social Psychology* **45**: 1281–8.

Sales, S. M. and House, J. (1971) Job dissatisfaction as a possible risk factor in coronary heart disease. *Journal of Chronic Diseases* **23**: 861–73.

Sanchez, V. C. (1978) Assertion training: effectiveness in the treatment of depression. PhD thesis, University of Oregon. Cited by Blaney (1981).

Sarason, B. R., Sarason, I. G., Hacker, T. A. and Basham, R. B. (1985) Concomitants of social support: social skills, physical attractiveness and gender. *Journal of Personality and Social Psychology* **49**: 469–80.

Schachter, F. F. (1982) Sibling deidentification and split-parent identification: a family tetrad. In M. E. Lamb and B. Sutton-Smith (eds) *Sibling Relationships*. Hillsdale, NJ: Erlbaum.

Schachter, S. and Singer, J. (1962) Cognitive, social and physiological determinants of emotional state. *Psychological Review* **69**: 379–99.

Scherer, K. R., Summerfield, A. B. and Wallbott, H. G. (1983) Cross-national research on antecedents and components of emotion: a progress report. *Social Science Information* **22**: 355–85.

Schmitt, N. and Bedian, A. G. (1982) A comparison of LISREL and two-stage least squares analysis of a hypothesised life – job satisfaction, reciprocal relationship. *Journal of Applied Psychology* **67**: 806–17.

Schulz, R. and Decker, S. (1985) Long-term adjustment to physical disability: the role of social support, perceived control, and self-blame. *Journal of Personality and Social Psychology* **48**: 1162–72.

Schwab, D. P. and Wallace, M. J. (1974) Correlates of employee satisfaction with pay. *Industrial Relations* **13**: 78–89.

Schwab, J. J. and Schwab, M. E. (1978) *Sociocultural Roots of Mental Illness.* New York: Plenum.

Schwartz, J. C. and O'Connor, C. J. (1984) The social ecology of memorable emotional experiences. Paper at Second International Conference on Personal Relationships, Madison.

Schwarz, N. and Clore, G. L. (1983) Mood, misattribution and judgments of well-being: information and directive functions of affective states. *Journal of Personality and Social Psychology* **45**: 513–23.

Schwarz, N., Strack, F., Kommer, D. and Wagner, D. (1984) Success, rooms and the quality of your life: further evidence on the informative function of affective states. Conference of European Association of Experimental Social Psychology, Tilburg.

Sennett, R. and Cobb, J. (1972) *The Hidden Injuries of Class.* New York: Random House.

Shaver, P. and Buhrmeister, D. (1983) Loneliness, sex-role orientation and group life: a social needs perspective. In P. B. Paulus (ed.) *Basic Group Processes.* New York: Springer.

Shekelle, R. B. *et al.* (1981) Psychological depression and 17-year risk of death from cancer. *Psychosomatic Medicine* **43**: 117–25.

Shikiar, R. and Freudenberg, R. (1982) Unemployment rates as a moderator of the job dissatisfaction – turnover relation. *Human Relations* **10**: 845–56.

Simmons, R. G. (1978) Blacks and high self-esteem: a puzzle. *Social Psychology Quarterly* **41**: 54–7.

Singer, E., Garfinkel, R., Cohen, S. M. and Srole, L. (1976) Mortality and mental health: evidence from the Midtown Manhattan restudy. *Social Science and Medicine* **10**: 517–25.

Singer, K. (1984) Depressive disorders from a transcultural perspective.

In J. E. Mazzich and C. E. Berganza (eds) *Culture and Psychopathology*. New York: Columbia University Press.

Smith, P. C., Kendall, L. M. and Hulin, C. L. (1969) *The Measurement of Satisfaction in Work and Retirement*. Chicago: Rand McNally.

Smith, R. (1985–6) Occupationless health. *British Medical Journal* (11 articles) 12 October – 25 January.

Smith, S. and Razzell, P. (1975) *The Pools Winners*. London: Caliban Books.

Smith, T. W. (1979) Happiness: time trends, seasonal variations, inter-survey differences and other mysteries. *Social Psychology Quarterly* **42**: 18–30.

Social Trends (1982–6) London: HMSO, vols 12–16.

Spector, P. E. (1985) Higher order need strength as a moderator of the job scope – employee outcome relationship: a meta analysis. *Journal of Occupational Psychology* **58**: 119–27.

Spreitzer, E. and Snyder, E. E. (1974) Correlates of life satisfaction among the aged. *Journal of Gerontology* **29**: 454–8.

Stafford, E. M., Jackson, P. R. and Banks, M. H. (1980) Employment, work involvement and mental health in less qualified young people. *Journal of Occupational Psychology* **53**: 291–304.

Stebbins, R. A. (1979) *Amateurs*. Beverly Hills: Sage.

Steers, R. M. (1975) Effect of need achievement on the job perform-ance – job attitude relationship. *Journal of Applied Psychology* **60**: 678–82.

Stengel, E. (1964) *Suicide and Attempted Suicide*. London: MacGibbon and Kee.

Stokes, G. and Cochrane, R. (1984) A study of the psychological effects of redundancy and unemployment. *Journal of Occupational Psychology* **57**: 309–22.

Stokes, J. P. (1985) The relation of social networks and individual difference variables to loneliness. *Journal of Personality and Social Psychology* **48**: 981–90.

Stone, A. A. and Neale, J. M. (1984) Effects of severe daily events on mood. *Journal of Personality and Social Psychology* **46**: 137–44.

Strack, F., Schwarz, N. and Gschneidinger, E. (1985) Happiness and reminiscing: the role of time perspective, affect, and mode of thinking. *Journal of Personality and Social Psychology* **49**.

Suinn, R. M. (1982) Intervention with type A behavior. *Journal of Consulting and Clinical Psychology* **50**: 797–803.

Surtees, P. G. (1980) Social support, residual adversity and depressive outcome. *Social Psychiatry* **15**: 71–80.

Susser, M. W. and Watson, W. (1971) *Sex Differences in Britain*. London: Grant McIntyre.

Sutherland, G., Newman, B. and Rachman, S. (1982) Experimental investigation of the relation between mood and intrusive unwanted cognitions. *British Journal of Medical Psychology* **55**: 127–38.

Szalai, A. (1980) The meaning of comparative research on the quality of life. In A. Szalai and F. M. Andrews (eds) *The Quality of Life*. Beverly Hills: Sage.

Szalai, A., Converse, P., Feldheim, P., Schench, E. and Stone, P. (1972) *The Use of Time*. The Hague: Mouton.

Tavris, C. and Offir, C. (1977) *The Longest War*. New York: Harcourt Brace Jovanovich.

Taylor, M. C. (1982) Improved conditions, rising expectations, and dissatisfaction: a test of the past/present relative deprivation hypothesis. *Social Psychology Quarterly* **45**: 24–33.

Teasdale, J. D. and Russell, M. L. (1983) Differential effect of induced mood on the recall of positive, negative, and neutral words. *British Journal of Clinical Psychology* **22**: 163–71.

Tessler, R. and Mechanic, D. (1978) Psychological distress and perceived health status. *Journal of Health and Social Behavior* **19**: 254–62.

Thoits, P. A. (1982) Conceptual, methodological and theoretical problems in studying social support as a buffer against stress. *Journal of Health and Social Behavior* **23**: 145–59.

Thomas, K. (1964) Work and leisure in pre-industrial society. *Past and Present* **29**: 50–62.

Tiggemann, M. and Winefield, A. H. (1984) The effects of unemployment on the mood, self-esteem, locus of control, and depressive affect of school leavers. *Journal of Occupational Psychology* **57**: 33–42.

Tokarski, W. (1985) Some social psychological notes on the meaning of work and leisure. *Leisure Studies* **4**: 227–31.

Tolor, A. (1978) Personality correlates of the joy of life. *Journal of Clinical Psychology* **34**: 671–6.

Tomkins, S. S. (1962) *Affect, Imagery, Consciousness. Vol. 1. The Positive Affects*. New York: Springer.

Trist, E. L., Higgin, G. W., Murray, H. and Pollack, A. B. (1963) *Organizational Choice*. London: Tavistock.

Tunstall, J. (1983) *The Media in Britain*. London: Constable.

Turner, J. and Giles, H. (eds) (1981) *Intergroup Behaviour*. Oxford: Blackwell.

Turner, R. J. and Noh, S. (1983) Class and psychological vulnerability among women: the significance of social support and personal control. *Journal of Health and Social Behavior* **24**: 2–15.

Turner, R. W., Ward, M. F. and Turner, D. J. (1979) Behavioral treatment for depression: an evaluation of therapeutic components. *Journal of Clinical Psychology* **35**: 166–75.

Tyrer, S. and Shopsin, B. (1982) Symptoms and assessment of mania. In

E. S. Paykel (ed.) *Handbook of Affective Disorders*. Edinburgh: Churchill Livingstone.

United Kingdom Census (1979) *Decennial Life Tables 1970–72*. London: OPCS.

Valentine, C. W. (1962) *The Experimental Psychology of Beauty*. London: Methuen.

Vanfossen, B. E. (1981) Sex differences in the mental health effects of spouse support and equity. *Journal of Health and Social Behavior* **22**: 130–43.

Van Zelst, R. H. (1951) Worker popularity and job satisfaction. *Personnel Psychology* **4**: 405–12.

—— (1952) Validation of a sociometric regrouping procedure. *Journal of Abnormal and Social Psychology* **47**: 299–301.

Veblen, T. (1899) *The Theory of the Leisure Class*. New York: American Library.

Vecchio, R. P. and Keon, T. L. (1981) Predicting employee satisfaction from congruency among individual need, job design, and system structure. Journal of Occupational Behaviour **2**: 283–92.

Velten, E. (1968) A laboratory task for induction of mood states. *Behaviour Research and Therapy* **6**: 473–82.

Verbrugge, L. M. (1976) Sex differentials in morbidity and mortality in the United States. *Social Biology* **23**: 275–96.

—— (1985) Gender and health: an update on hypotheses and evidence. *Journal of Health and Social Behavior* **26**: 156–82.

Veroff, J., Douvan, E. and Kulka, R. A. (1981) *The Inner American*. New York: Basic Books.

Wadsworth, M. E. J., Butterfield, W. J. H. and Blaney, R. (1971) *Health and Sickness: The Choice of Treatment*. London: Tavistock.

Waldron, I. (1976) Why do women live longer than men? *Journal of Human Stress* **2**: 2–13.

Waldron, I. and Johnston, S. (1976) Why do women live longer than men? *Journal of Human Stress* **2**: 19–30.

Walker, C. (1977) Some variations in marital satisfaction. In R. Chester and J. Peel (eds) *Equalities and Inequalities in Family Life*. London: Academic Press.

Wall, T. D., Clegg, C. W. and Jackson, P. R. (1978) An evaluation of the job characteristics model. *Journal of Occupational Psychology* **51**: 183–96.

Warheit, G. J. (1979) Life events, coping, stress, and depressive symptomatology. *American Journal of Psychiatry* **136**: 502–7.

Warr, P. (1978) A study of psychological well-being. *British Journal of Psychology* **69**: 111–21.

—— (1982) A national study of non-financial employment commitment. *Journal of Occupational Psychology* **55**: 297–312.

—— (1983) Job loss, unemployment and psychological well-being. In E. van de Vliert and V. Allen (eds) *Role Transitions*. New York: Plenum.

—— (1984) Reported behaviour changes after job loss. *British Journal of Social Psychology* **23**: 271–5.

Warr, P., Barter, J. and Brownbridge, G. (1983) On the independence of positive and negative affect. *Journal of Personality and Social Psychology* **44**: 644–51.

Warr, P., Cook, J. and Wall, T. D. (1979) Scales for the measurement of some work attitudes and aspects of psychological well-being. *Journal of Occupational Psychology* **52**: 129–48.

Warr, P. and Jackson, P. (1984) Men without jobs: some correlations of age and length of employment. *Journal of Occupational Psychology* **57**: 77–85.

Warr, P. and Parry, G. (1982) Paid employment and women's psychological well-being. *Psychological Bulletin* **91**: 498–516.

Warr, P. and Payne, R. (1982) Experience of strain and pleasure among British adults. *Social Science and Medicine* **16**: 1691–7.

—— (1983) Social class and reported changes in behaviour after job loss. *Journal of Applied Social Psychology* **13**: 206–22.

Warr, P. and Routledge, T. (1969) An opinion scale for the study of managers' job satisfaction. *Occupational Psychology* **43**: 95–109.

Warr, P. B. and Wall, T. D. (1975) *Work and Well-Being*. Harmondsworth: Penguin.

Wasserman, I. M. and Chua, L. A. (1980) Objective and subjective social indicators of the quality of life in American SMSAs: a reanalysis. *Social Indicators Research* **8**: 365–81.

Watson, D. and Tellegen, A. (1985) Toward a consensual structure of mood. *Psychological Bulletin* **98**: 219–35.

Weaver, C. N. (1980) Job satisfaction in the United States in the 1970s. *Journal of Applied Psychology* **65**: 364–7.

Webster, M. and Driskell, J. E. (1983) Beauty as status. *American Journal of Sociology* **89**: 140–65.

Weeks, D. G., Michela, J. L., Peplau, L. A. and Bragg, M. E. (1980) Relation between loneliness and depression: a structural equation analysis. *Journal of Personality and Social Psychology* **39**: 1238–44.

Weissman, M. M. and Klerman, G. L. (1979) Sex differences and the epidemiology of depression. In E. S. Gomberg and Franks (eds) *Gender and Disordered Behavior*. New York: Brunner/Mazel.

Wessman, A. E. and Ricks, D. F. (1966) *Mood and Personality*. New York: Holt, Rinehart & Winston.

Weyant, J. M. (1978) Effects of mood states, costs and benefits on helping. *Journal of Personality and Social Psychology* **36**: 1169–76.

Wheaton, B. (1978) The sociogenesis of psychological disorder: re-examining the causal issues with longitudinal data. *American Sociological Review* **43**: 383–403.

—— (1980) The sociogenesis of psychological disorder: an attributional theory. *Journal of Health and Social Behavior* **21**: 100–23.

Wheeler, L., Reis, H. and Nezlek, J. (1983) Loneliness, social interaction and social roles. *Journal of Personality and Social Psychology* **45**: 943–53.

Whitehorn, C. (1984) Whistle while you work. *Observer Colour Supplement.* 21 October, pp. 91–2.

Wilcox, B. L. (1981) Social support, life stress, and psychological adjustment: a test of the buffering hypothesis. *American Journal of Community Psychology* **9**: 371–86.

Williams, J. G. and Solano, C. H. (1983) The social reality of feeling lonely. *Personality and Social Psychology Bulletin* **9**: 237–42.

Williams, J. M. G. (1984) *The Psychological Treatment of Depression.* London: Croom Helm.

Wills, T. A. (1981) Downward comparison principles in social psychology. *Psychological Bulletin* **90**: 245–71.

Wilson, J. (1980) Sociology of leisure. *Annual Review of Sociology* **6**: 21–40.

Wilson, W. (1967) Correlates of avowed happiness. *Psychological Bulletin* **67**: 294–306.

Wing, J. K. (1976) A technique for studying psychiatric morbidity in inpatient and outpatient series and in general population samples. *Psychological Medicine* **6**: 665–72.

Wingerson, L. (1981) Executive women – healthier than thou? *New Scientist*, 17 September, pp. 718–21.

Witt, D. W., Lowe, C. D., Peek, C. W. and Curry, G. W. (1980) The changing association between age and happiness: emerging trend or methodological artefact? *Social Forces* **58**: 1302–7.

Wood, C. (1985) The healthy neurotic. *New Scientist*, February, pp. 12–15.

WHO (1982) *World Health Statistics: Vital Statistics and Causes of Death.* Geneva: WHO.

Young, M. and Wilmott, P. (1973) *The Symmetrical Family.* London: Routledge & Kegan Paul.

Zajonc, R. B. (1985) Emotion and facial efference: a theory reclaimed. *Science* **228**: 15–21.

Zuckerman, M. (1979) *Sensation Seeking: Beyond the Optimal Level of Arousal.* Hillsdale, NJ: Halsted.

·NAME INDEX·

Page numbers in italics refer to figures and tables.

SUBJECT INDEX